CALLING THE SHOTS

DIRECTING THE NEW SERIES OF DOCTOR WHO

CALLING THE SHOTS

DIRECTING THE NEW SERIES OF DOCTOR WHO

GRAEME HARPER

WITH ADRIAN RIGELSFORD

REYNOLDS & HEARN LTD
LONDON

Dedicated to
Douglas Camfield, Moira Armstrong, John Davies and Martin Campbell

First published in 2007 by
Reynolds & Hearn Ltd
61a Priory Road
Kew Gardens
Richmond
Surrey TW9 3DH

A CIP catalogue record for this book is available from the British Library.

ISBN 978 1 905287 41 3

Printed and bound in Great Britain by Biddles Ltd, King's Lynn, Norfolk.

ACKNOWLEDGEMENTS

We would both like to thank: Bernadette, Jamie and Emilie for putting up with so many hours of waffling in the kitchen; Helen Solomon for such diligent help researching and transcribing; Clive Banks, Marnie and Thomas for always being there with advice, facts and friendship; John Henderson, Gordon Anderson and Gary for advice from afar; Chris Fitzgerald, for monsters from the past; Peter Thomas, for enthusiasm and helpful ideas; and Marcus Hearn and Richard Reynolds for having faith in the idea, and for giving us a chance.

CONTENTS

INTRODUCTION: OPENING TITLES

Darkness…

Midnight's just a memory. It must be, what? Two, maybe three o'clock in the morning. The coffee's kicking in.

21st November 2005. Or is it the 22nd now?

The Cybermen are about to invade the Tyler family's luxurious mansion, targeting the great and the good at the party inside for upgrading… Well, that's the theory.

The headlights of the Pantechnicon we've hired blaze into life. Their strips of illumination merge into four bright spheres. Two above, two directly below. There's a light dusting of frost on the grass verge that we've positioned it in front of. The setting looks harsh, clinical and sinister.

"Stand bye… Ready… And action!"

There's a noise just out of range of the camera that can only be described as sounding like armfuls of loose buckets rattling together.

"And left, right, left, right, left, right…"

The lower lights blur slightly as a line of ten figures march into shot, silhouetted against them. It's like *Close Encounters of the Third Kind*. You know the bit I mean? Where the mother ship's landed, the aliens are slowly coming out of the hatchway and down the gangplank, and all we initially see are strange ethereal shapes floodlit from behind.

So far so good.

"And turn… Left, right, left, right…"

Not so good… The perfect military precision of the unstoppable killing machines… Well it's not exactly there yet… The lead Cyberman is beginning to veer right, and the others are losing all sense of the symmetrical line-up they're meant to be in. Now the ones flanking to the left are crashing into each other. One has actually turned round and started to head back the way he came.Nope. There's no sense of menace here. It's sort of scarpered. Someone's laughing. Now more than one. The crew are in hysterics. Benefit of the doubt… It's just first take nerves.

Reset and Take Two.

There's minimal visibility in those masks anyway. I've already heard that one's got a cold and has to have his faceplate taken off now and again to wipe out the inside. No, their only hope of moving in sync is to shout out their marching orders.

Now they're all veering to the right in a large metallic cluster. Rethink and retake.

"And action!"

The first assistant, Clare Nicholson, is somewhere out there in the dark. She's wrapped in thermal layers like everyone else. It feels like tonight redefines the meaning of the word 'cold'. How much of the sound that the Cybermen are making is marching, and how much of it comes from shivering?

"From the top! Left, right, left, right…"

A new strategy. Now each Cyberman is touching the sleeve of the actor's costume directly in front of him. Slowly they emerge from the glare of the lights… And now it looks as though they're holding hands. If they were skipping, the image would be complete.

Let's scrap that and rethink. We're moving on.

It's going to be a long night.

EPISODE ONE: HOW IT ALL WORKS

Page One. Scene One.

Entrances and exits are made, dialogue rattles off the plot points as the story unfolds and stage directions tell you where it's being said.

Inside the TARDIS, outside the Queen Vic, walking across the surface of the moon... It doesn't really matter where, because at the moment it only exists on the printed page. The script's been written, so what happens next?

My job, as a television director in drama, is to tell that story both visually and dramatically, and in a way that I would love to see it as a viewer. On behalf of the writer, the producer and whoever the production company behind it is, I have to bring energy, pace, colour and, most important of all, a sense of reality and imagination to translating it to the screen.

No matter how big or small the reaction, the look, the smile, the frown, the explosion, the chase or even the kiss, the director has to channel the dreams that the script initially conjured up in his mind and recreate them for sound and vision.

There are many different ways to do that.

Each director's different, although they're all the same in the sense that they're storytellers and all have their own unique style. Visual tricks they like to use again and again, which can sometimes become a kind of signature. They all follow their own geography – how to physically make a programme – but they also bring their own voice to it, their own ideas on how to share their interpretation with the actors, the special effects team, the production designer, etc.

I think it was Terry Gilliam who said that, when he first directed a film, he was very precise about the whole process of sticking to the storyboards he'd drawn up and desperately tried to communicate every aspect of every frame, but now he doesn't do that. He likes to think that he can get whatever is going on in his head onto the screen because, basically, he knows how to do that now.

To be honest, he's absolutely right, but making television shows is a very different beast to making movies.

I've always been in television. I started directing in soaps with a show called

Angels. In order to get through *Angels*, you had to do a five-day rehearsal period for two half-hour episodes. I had to plan out every shot and, with a vision mixer, cut and assemble the studio scenes as they evolved.

Fine-tuning of performances was done through the rehearsals and finally put down on tape when we reached the sets. Everything had to be thought through and meticulously organised. There was never the luxury of being able to do what Terry Gilliam does and just go in with an idea, like framing a two shot and a couple of singles.

But, multi-camera studios? Surely you can just walk in and do anything you like with them? Well, no… You can't just do that. You actually have to plan what each camera does, everything it'll see throughout the recording of whatever the piece is you're directing. The trick is to be able to negotiate with the actors and technicians to get the shots you've planned.

It still applies today. Negotiation, negotiation, negotiation, on so many levels. It makes the mechanisms tick, the engine run smoothly, like a juggernaut. Anything you watch, any production you see, it always starts with planning.

Right, you're making *Doctor Who*. What's the order of events? You've got the job, so now what? You've got to sit down and direct it. But how?

Well, as I said, you've got to move forward in very specific stages. There's an unwavering set process, and it's there because it works.

PRE-PRODUCTION

The first phase of anything being made for TV is pre-production. The director, the producer, the script editor… The core members of the creative team… The designer, the location manager… They've been brought together, and they've got to start planning a kind of strategic shape for how they're going to tackle the scripts we've been assigned.

Now, with *Doctor Who*, specifically the series which began filming in 2005 (Season Two), I'm in a position where I've got to embark on scheduling a massive filming block for two stories, all to create enough material for four episodes in total.

Both of them involve the Cybermen and, unbeknownst to me until a little later during pre-production, the Daleks are going to be there for the second story as well. So we're not only talking iconic monsters, but ultimately one hell of a battle between them as well.

Time for some basic number crunching. That's a lot of screen time we're talking about. *Doctor Who* takes roughly 11, maybe 12 or 13 days to complete each episode. That means I'm looking at roughly ten weeks' solid filming to get anywhere near the amount of footage that's required.

No choice other than to face it head on. There are clearly going to be some alarm bells ringing, immediate concerns that I've got to start talking about right away. No time for sitting and mulling it over, we're already running out of time.

First things first. Boil it down to basics. What about the design of the Cybermen? What's the style and feel of the first story going to be like? The second story's modern and real, lots of it's easy to relate to and simple to achieve, but how are we going to make a parallel world look distinct and different?

Let's just pause for a moment and rewind.

Picture this – it's 1976. Tom Baker's in full flight, at the height of his powers as the Doctor, and I'm part of the crew making *The Seeds of Doom*.

I'll always remember Douglas Camfield, that story's director, saying, "We are planning a military campaign." There were alien Krynoids attempting to invade and trips to the Arctic to complete. Well, sort of. Dougie was the director, the commanding officer, and I was his regimental sergeant major, in other words his first assistant. Between us, we planned out how we were going to feed that information down to the crew, the troops, mainly with me and the production secretary organising what was required in order to give Douglas the time to create the dreams he wanted to put on screen.

Now it's me, I'm the commanding officer, I have my own regimental sergeant major. It really does start to feel like a military campaign, and it's up to me to lead it. I've got to rally the troops. But how have I wound up in this position?

Fast forward to 2005 again.

Generally speaking, a show starts to come to life when it's initiated by the producer. Phil Collinson offered me the job on *Doctor Who*, so he's the one who's employed me as a director. He's the Boss, the Head Honcho, the Governor... If there's money to be spent or major decisions to be made, you've got to get it past Phil first. But he's not the only voice of power.

THE POWERS THAT BE

The mechanics behind driving the physical realisation of the story, that's certainly Phil's domain, but creatively there are three distinct voices to be heard. Alongside Phil is executive producer Julie Gardner. Russell T Davies is also an executive producer, and in American TV terminology he could also be referred to as *Doctor Who*'s 'showrunner'. His concepts develop the story arcs that run through the seasons, and he oversees everything on a creative level. But more about that later.

As soon as I've read the scripts, Phil wants a meeting to gauge my reactions, talk through how I see it all and hear the wish list of changes I've come up with – basic suggestions to try and help improve the story.

Phil might turn round and say, "I don't agree… I already like the way that aspect works, I'd rather keep it as it is. But the other notes, I'll take them on board and we'll add those to the list of rewrites…" Equally, he might have his own agenda and say, "I can see a problem here, here and here, what d'you think we should do about it?"

We've reached this far because the script editor, Helen Raynor, will have guided the writer through the whole development of their story, which has run right from the point they were commissioned at to where it's been agreed that it's nearly ready to shoot. Taking in what I've said, there'll now be another draft, maybe after I've had a chance to meet them, but that's a luxury. The clock's ticking, and there's rarely time.

However, I'll always be kept appraised of how it's going, and I'm there on the end of the phone if there are any questions about character development or plot points. You're looking at two, maybe five days maximum for all that to be done and dusted.

SO, WHAT'S IT GOING TO LOOK LIKE?

Now I can talk to Ed Thomas, the production designer. Ideas are thrown around. Do we want to use a distinctive colour scheme for the look of the story? What are the major props that have to be built? What sets need to be in the studio?

We're trying to define a feeling, an overall atmosphere of what we want the thing to look like. In this situation, the big point of contention that's right at the front of our minds is the opening two Cyberman episodes. You tend to talk using bullet-points. Phrases that sum up your instincts over what you should see, like Art Deco, pre-Second World War austerity in England and Europe, the Nuremberg rallies, the bleakness of concrete gun turrets on the sand banks at Calais, specifically their octagonal shape.

What about the second story? What about the Torchwood HQ? More key thoughts… Modern building designs, sparse interiors and hi-tech equipment, but slightly minimalist all round.

This will evolve into talking about broader stylistic concepts, which will have to be agreed by Phil, Russell and Julie. Once that's green-lit, once those boxes have been ticked, then you can talk to the rest of the team, passing on that feeling you've hit upon, building up your thoughts on the atmosphere you want to evoke.

OKAY THEN, WHERE ARE WE GOING TO FILM IT?

Next in line? The location manager. *Doctor Who* has one basic free-standing set. It's immovable, because nearly every director will need it at some point, so I guess the TARDIS really is a fixed point in time. No problem there, then. What about everything else?

From talking to Ed Thomas, you'll have a rough idea what's got to be sourced on location, and sometimes that can be tricky. That's why you need to bring in people like location managers Gareth Skelding and Lowri Thomas as soon as you can. Their knowledge of every nook and cranny around Wales is pretty encyclopaedic but, if you ask for something that throws them slightly, take it from me, it doesn't take them long to offer a solution that'll really open up the possibilities for what you're planning to shoot.

Sometimes, these guys have to box clever. Look at the Season Two stories *Rise of the Cybermen* and *The Age of Steel*. No two ways about it, Battersea Power Station's right in the thick of the plot, and somehow you've got to show it on screen without doing night shoots in London.

Now, sure, the easy way out is to hire stock shots or footage you can incorporate from other shows, and the fact of the matter was that Battersea was an unsafe environment to film in at that time. So, they've got to find substitutes where we can visually offer aspects of it, and still maintain the illusion that we're really there. But, that's not the only way they have to work.

What about Pete and Jackie's house? The now well-heeled Tyler abode? Gareth and Lowri will go through logical steps to narrow down what we need.

Pete's one of the villain's right-hand men, a propaganda officer, so that means big dividends salary-wise, right? The alternate Jackie's no stranger to displaying her ego, she'll want to demonstrate her wealth loud and clear, so the house hasn't just got to be big. We're talking faux landed gentry, acres of land, Georgian architecture, antiques she really doesn't understand the value of.

But that's not all.

The Cybermen storm the house in the finale of Episode Five. So they've got to look for access points, plenty of space to cover the Cybermen moving around. And then there are facilities to think about. Is there going to be plenty of space for the crew? The generators? Catering, costume, wardrobe? So many different considerations, and so little time to find the answers.

ANY IDEA WHO'S GOING TO BE IN IT?

Forget David Tennant and Billie Piper for the moment, they're there for the long haul and have a far broader story arc to keep them busy. We're talking about the additional characters. What do you look for? How do they develop? How key are they to the plot?

Phil, Julie and Russell will all have thoughts on where they see the characterisations going, what their specific journeys are and how they'd like to see them being played, so there's a round-table debate that hammers it down to a set of notes you're all happy with.

You go to talk to Andy Pryor, the casting director. Probably a couple of times on the phone initially, and it's time to sit down and plough through different permutations he's come up with. What about *him*? Is *she* available? Do you think they'd be right? Would they accept that kind of role? I've not seen them play anything like that before, what do you think they'd bring to it?

Actors are lined up, meetings are set, readings and auditions rattle past like lightning, all to a tight schedule. Face after face after face. Does that voice sound right? Do they move like I think this character should, or are they even the right shape for the way I see that one in my head? Pleasantries pour thick and fast, and the list of possibilities rapidly starts to take shape.

Casting sessions work like this. The actors come in, read through some scenes, working to my direction, and then we record the results on video. We'll try playing the material in various ways, emphasising different meanings, different levels of emotion, and that gives Julie, Russell and Phil the chance to judge whether the actors can take direction. Versatility is the key. If they can show different ways of playing the role, still convey whatever instructions I'm throwing at them and add elements that make it their own, then that's brilliant, but that's not the only point to consider.

Do they look right? Do we think they've got the range the part needs? Will they listen to and take on board my decisions? If we cast them, how do they compare with people we already have? Are they too imposing, too meek or too slight?

Andy goes away with a hit list of our favourites that's been whittled down. Actors whom we'd ideally like as first, second and third choices for roles, and, with that template, he starts to pull the cast together, trying to secure everyone against the filming schedules that are beginning to take shape.

Don't get me wrong, though, it's not always that easy. Most of the time, the producer and executives will go with the choices you've brought them, but now and again, well... They say you're heading in entirely the wrong direction and you have to start again. You can grumble, but that wastes time. You have to be prepared to take that on board and just get on with it.

Moving on, moving on, always watching the clock. So where are we at?

Sketches of monsters, buildings, guns, cars and chairs arrive. Plenty of options. Some of that, a hint of this, none of that ... but that one, I'll have some of that. Polaroid and camcorder footage, ground plans and maps, the wheres, whys and how to's of locations are starting to be solved.

WHAT ARE THEY GOING TO WEAR?
AND WHAT ABOUT THE MONSTERS?

Onto the next layer: costume and make-up.

What to do with the Cybermen? How much is costume, how much is make-up, and how much is special effects? Should the 'build' be split between Louise Page's wardrobe team and Neill Gorton's Millennium Effects? How do you define the boundaries in this situation?

It's a physical, mechanical build. Over to Neill. Each one will look like a machine-shopped, burnished suit of steel, and that's probably a relief for Louise – she has more than 50 characters to dress already!

Then there has to be a fitting, with the main Cyber actor, Paul Kasey, working with Neill to ensure that the costume is manoeuvrable as it's developed, testing out its flexibility and fixing any problems way, way before they ever get on set.

THE TONE MEETINGS

All this time, there'll be a variety of tone meetings, drawing the heads of department and some of the crew together. The big one, which kick-starts everything and puts names to faces from the production unit's list, usually happens during your first week on the programme.

Russell usually presides over things and chairs the meeting, while Julie and Phil offer comments, advice and admonition, all in equal doses and depending entirely on how outlandish your ideas get. If you push hard for something, you're bound to find a happy medium somewhere along the line. If one of them is missing, you'll get a combination drawn from those three so answers can always be given directly from head office, if you see what I mean.

Decisions can be made and put into action there and then, no matter what the problem, because somebody will be there who can deal with it. Solutions are found, ideas are energised and a thick dose of good-natured humour, sometimes self-deprecating and sometimes incredibly black, carries it all through.

One thing is crystal clear. Julie Gardner is absolutely emphatic that there should be deadlines, strict cut-off points, when the discussions stop about whatever's needed, so it starts being made, hired or found. That way, we know it'll be ready in time. No more talk, sign it off and make it real, then everyone has time to say, "That's perfect, but what about if we just did this, or adjusted that ever so slightly?"

Then at least there's a chance to fix it, and not face an eleventh hour nightmare panic. The Cybermen are a case in point. We'll need to know how many will be ready and by what date. Even if there's just one working costume to begin with, it's still going to be something we can work around.

Tone meetings hammer all this down, and always act as a combined step forward for everybody, driving things closer to being the point of focus for a camera lens.

WHAT'S ANOTHER REWRITE OR MORE TONE MEETINGS GOING TO ACHIEVE?

There's been a rewrite, but elements of the script still have to be fine-tuned. Everything's got to be tailored to fit the direction you can see the episodes heading in.

That bit's not quite right… That bit has an impact later on, so we need to emphasise the point being made… We've not managed to find a location for that sequence, so it'll have to be merged with another setting… That character needs to be stronger – punch up the dialogue and put them through hell…

If some of the principal guest cast have been locked down, their strengths as actors might give you another reason to work on the lines. Look at the character Yvonne Hartman in *Army of Ghosts* and *Doomsday*. You get Tracy-Ann Oberman signed up, and you know from her work precisely what kind of sparks she can bring to the role, and you'd be mad not to draw on that.

This is maybe the third pass at the script the writer's made since I've been on board, so Russell will certainly be making his presence felt to help lock it down. Julie's deadlines will be hovering, and the lock-down point's approaching fast.

While that's going on, contracts have got to be signed and all manner of permissions granted for where we're going to shoot. When I get to see a location on a recce, I can start visualising how we're going to use it, building where scenes move to in your mind's eye, framing different angles and checking to see if they can be achieved.

Gareth and Lowri will be trying to ensure that it can all be realised practically and efficiently. It's a waste of time to look in a cave, say "Yes, please" and start mentally blocking it out, if there's no way to get generators there to power the lights.

Tone meetings also start to close in on finite details – special hand-held props, futuristic and old-fashioned technology, graphics on computer screens, mobile phone caller displays. It's all looked at, frowned upon or quickly approved. Everything, absolutely everything is discussed and signed off before it's painted, moulded, nailed or welded together.

It's a fail-safe mechanism. Nothing can turn up looking completely wrong, no one can plead, "But you didn't ask for that!" Because this way it's monitored and approved every step of the way.

THE CAMERA SCRIPT

These days, a lot of TV programmes are made with multi-camera studio set-ups. Say you're making *EastEnders* or *Coronation Street* – even though they both have location filming, the same rule applies for both of them. For indoor scenes, you utilise three or four cameras moving around the set, calling which shots to use from each one, so a vision mixer can cut the material together in a control gallery, right there and then.

Now a camera script's exactly the same as the one that's been issued to every department, but I've inserted lines showing where the cutting points are and what the various shots are going to be – close ups, mid-shots, wide close ups, long shots and very wide shots.

It details how I want to cover every aspect of each scene, and how it should cut be together by the vision mixer. Or at least it would if *Doctor Who* was still being made like that. Now it's shot on a single camera, although sometimes you might have two, laboriously building up the different visual bites, varying angles and detail with each take, just like you'd have to on a feature film.

It's a template to show how I want the action to flow. I might want a shot favouring one character, gradually revealing their reactions to what's being said, or I might home in on the Doctor, who's busy laying in the plot or trying to figure out what's happening around him.

Basically, the camera script clarifies my intentions for the story, showing all the jigsaw pieces I want to piece it together with, at the same time laying down my working style, highlighting the way I like to use the lenses to get certain tricks, or specific technical effects, etc.

If it's done properly and succinctly, then it defines quite clearly what every shot has to achieve.

While all this is happening, there's something you've got to remember. Just keep it there at the back of your mind: as soon as you start to press certain buttons in the production, and the juggernaut starts to roll, it doesn't stop until we get to the end.

The fundamental rule to remember? If you're slow you'll be left behind. The whole thing will keep on rolling and you'll be left trying to catch up, and if it's not already too late there are very few ways you can do that.

What you've all got to do is hit the road running, you don't stop until it's over. You've got to be on time, no matter what level of the production you're working at. Sometimes you're ahead of the game, everything's ready; even if it's it at the last minute, just the fact that's it's done keeps everything on schedule.

The whole unit can then leave one location, or a set, and move onto the next with no mishaps. However, if there is a delay, there has to be a Plan B; some other scene, or a set of locations that's ready. Don't forget that the story's being shot completely out of sequence. Have we got all the people we need? Are all the actors available, or on stand-by? You have to plan for A, B and even C, just in case things go wrong.

If you've got everything covered, while problems are being sorted, you can move into this secondary area. The juggernaut keeps running, just going down a side road until you get back on the main route. But we're getting ahead of ourselves. Back to the camera script.

Once I've got it written, it's photocopied and given to the script supervisor, Non Eleri Hughes, who'll check that the plot's not got lost along the way. The sound operator also needs one, so he can see where the dialogue cuts will be and work out how to cover what's being said on screen.

It used to be the case that everyone on the studio floor or location would work from it. It's more 'tell' than 'show' now, however.

Take the first assistant director. He's not got time to continually go through what I've written. I have to discuss what shots we're going to do with him, because, you see, it changes, thanks to what happens when we start to rehearse.

You begin to map out the angles, the close ups and wide shots, everything I've dreamt up. Well, suddenly you can find that it's not enough, it's not going to cover it all. Working with the actors, the drama's evolved and maybe gone off at different tangents, creating a better way to play the scene, so I've got to continually adapt how I'm going to frame it.

I've got to think on my feet to get it shot, always finding a way through with the director of photography, the camera operator and the lighting supervisor, but even then, I'll always keep my notes in my back pocket.

I'll photocopy the relevant pages, fold them up and always have them to hand. So the camera script is basically for me to check the dialogue, remind myself of what I'd originally thought and give me a framework to work with day by day. It'll also give me an idea of how many set ups we've got to achieve.

What's a set up? Well, imagine you've got the Doctor and his companions Rose and Mickey arguing in a large room. While this is going on, one of them – let's say the Doctor – gets up from the chair he's sitting on, walks round and leans against the back of it.

The camera has to be positioned so we can get the maximum amount of visual information on him. A medium shot when he's just sitting, a wide shot when he gets up and a close up behind the chair as he makes a point. That's a set up.

From the footage we get, when we're editing I can cut into it ten, maybe 20 times as we build up the drive of what's happening. Equally, there'll be a set up favouring Rose, Mickey and maybe one for the whole room. So we're looking at four in total, with a similar number of cutting shots for each – which is what we call them on the camera script.

Lensing up so everything's in view on the set or location, and all of the action is being covered – that's the master shot. It could be a high angle, a tracking shot, in fact anything you like. But once that's done, the detail you mop up working around it, that's what energises the scene.

While that's under way, one of the cardinal rules for the crew is to never cross 'The Line'. This is the 180-degree rule, which is basically the boundary line you work behind – and don't cross – while a scene is being shot. It's dictated by the direction the camera is facing, even if it moves or swings round, because as long as you're behind it, you're not in shot. Even if the set up is pretty elaborate, I'll consult with Roger Pearce, the camera operator, who'll help define how to work round it, but he won't have a clue for certain sites until he's been to see them.

WHEN DO THE CREW GET TO SEE THE LOCATIONS?

If you're going to film for six weeks, chances are you'll have six weeks of pre-production, and the camera recce usually falls somewhere around the start of the fifth week. Decisions will have been made, major locations selected, and Gareth and Lowri will have got clearances signed for the various sites we want. Everything, bar maybe two or three places, will be in place.

At least a dozen of the heads of department, except for make-up and wardrobe, pile into a mini-bus and do the grand tour, spending a couple of days methodically working their way from the Cyber factory to the Tylers' mansion, then onto the Preachers' base, then the Torchwood Hangar. You get the picture?

Part of the location manager's brief is to figure out journey times, and the most efficient route to take. So, let's take it as read that you've got there. You're actually on one the sites. It's time to articulate exactly what you want to do, how you see the rooms or landscape being utilised, and make sure that any issues these ideas may present get solved way before even an inch of tape unspools. Out come the camcorders, tape measures, notebooks and light meters as everyone checks for potential department-specific problems. Is the ground even enough to lay camera track? Is there any natural light? Where can scaffolding be rigged, light towers stabilised and power cables laid?

Basic points are clarified. Which direction will you be filming in or around, so unit vehicles can be kept well out of the way? How far will make-up, wardrobe and the props team be from where the action's being staged?

I've got to make it perfectly clear what I want to visually accomplish, so everyone's working towards making that happen. For example, if I want a big crane shot on one of the locations as the TARDIS lands, that might need an extra hundred feet of camera track on top of what's normally being carried. So it's all got to be thrown into the open, then no one will be caught out by anything unexpected.

Health and safety also has to be covered. You're drilled over where danger areas are, what evacuation procedures are in place, even told how many people can realistically be in one area at the same time, if it's hazardous. We're not always within a comfort zone when the cameras start to roll.

The actual filming schedule is a still a basic plan at the moment, so it can be changed depending on any problems the recce throws up. As soon as we're back, the first assistant director is going to have an evening of trying to hammer it into shape. He's got to take a lot into consideration.

Ed Thomas might ask to change two locations, swapping them around, so while you work on the one that was meant to come second, he's now got time to do a proper set build on the first. Equally, we might not be able to get onto a site, say an abandoned factory, until the morning we arrive with the crew. The first area we're due to shoot in might need cleaning up, so you swap it round with the second to allow time for that to happen.

It's all a case of juggling logistics.

SO, IS EVERYTHING NOW FINALISED?

Far from it.

As soon as the revised schedules are handed out, a major production meeting is called. Twenty to thirty people, all key members of the crew, spaced out round a vast table lined with coffee and croissants. There's Red Bull and Lucozade on stand-by, because this is going to be a long haul.

Day by day, we inch through it, flicking script pages backwards and forwards, checking we're all hitting the same beats of the song, on key and in sync. This was agreed on the recce, that was checked out, the camera crane won't arrive until four in the afternoon. So many things to take into consideration. And it goes on, and on, and on.

The end always seems just out of reach. There are enough reams of scribbled notes and post-it stickers to kill a rainforest. It all works fine up to Day 27. Hang on, Day 28 could affect Day 30, so if we swap it round with Day 18? And so on it goes. Seemingly simple decisions like that have huge knock-on effects. Costumes might not be ready if you do that. We'll only have two Cybermen when there's meant to be ten...

From all of this, the schedule is refined and rubber-stamped, but only when there's absolute agreement that each department can hit their targets, so there won't be any time lost once the cameras start to roll.

As soon as the final version is issued, it becomes the production bible. Everything revolves around it and it affects all of the crew in some way. It also forms the basis of what the daily call sheets are drawn up from, which is the second assistant director's responsibility.

You're not always going to complete every scene you're scheduled to wrap on any given day. Some carry over to the next morning, others maybe even a week. Nevertheless, call sheets stick pretty rigidly to the final schedule and, even though the running order of what you're shooting can move about a bit, and the cast can change at the last minute, they basically ensure that everybody knows what the intent is for that day.

It keeps everyone up to speed on where actors have to be, who's taking them there, when they're going to be in costume or made-up and, critically, when they're going to be in front of the camera so I can get on with my job!

NOW YOU'RE READY FOR THE CAST
TO BREATHE LIFE INTO THE SCRIPT

It's another large table, more coffee and croissants, but a lot of new faces. Maybe 15 to 20 actors, all with speaking parts to play.

Phil, Russell and Julie will all be there, wanting to hear the dialogue come to life, anxiously waiting to see if it works. Scenes have been added, cut, rewritten and restructured, right up to the point the previous day when the final drafts were issued.

Is there enough drama in it? Are the story highs and lows working? Has that character got enough to say? Do they get a satisfactory resolution? As the director, I'm handcuffed, I can't tell them to do much other than to find their way through it with plenty of energy. This is just a straight read-through.

It's all a bit raw, the first time the script's actively been performed, and it's not only nerve-wracking for the actors. I've got to remember everyone's name and introduce them, and there's probably 35 people here who I've never seen before in my life! Stress factor ten, but I'm still desperate to hear it read.

"Listen everybody, lift your voices, let's make sure everybody in the room can hear you and just give it your best shot verbally."

It's all I can say. Russell acts as the stage directions, reading them out and gently cueing in scene after scene. Non's there with her stopwatch, timing each one, trying to get a feel for the episode's length. There's no action or movement, so if it comes in at 30 minutes she'll allow for that and mark it between 35 to

37, so my first worry is going to be, "Will we over run when it's cut together?" *Doctor Who* is usually about 43 minutes per episode, so that's pretty tight.

Afterwards, Phil might ask for one particular actor to really beef up what they're doing, play heavy on the weeping, or hold back more and play it quiet but deadly. If the moment's right there can be nothing more frightening than sudden silence and calm.

Any worries he has are all taken in, as are any similar notes from Russell and Julie, because that's pretty much the last time they'll see any aspect of the story being played out, unless they come to the set or maybe until the rushes start landing in their DVD players. But the read-through only gives a hint of what's coming.

It's all pretty tentative. The actors are trying to find the shape of what they'll do, and the script's got to be re-read, lines memorised and the tone of the performance thought through. All Phil can honestly expect is a fairly good reading and a chance to judge whether the flow of the scenes is working.

One scene might suddenly seem quite shallow dialogue-wise, now it's no longer just on paper, or the whole story might come across as soggy and slightly limp for the middle act. Well, Phil, and particularly Russell will be onto that like a shot, saying we really need to look at tightening it all up, or whatever.

It's also the last chance for make-up and wardrobe to grab one or two of the actors, who just haven't been available up till now, for costume fittings or prosthetic or wig tests. Mainly, everyone kind of acclimatises to the fact they're going to be working together for the next couple of weeks.

"Look, that was a great read-through, when we do this what I am after is energy, pace and a real kick up the backside to make the story come alive… Let's really, really hit it running."

It's a chance to say what your instincts are and what your feel for it is. If the read-through is on a Saturday, then the first take could be as close as Monday.

Time to lead the troops in – battle's about to commence.

This is going to be a long story. How we brought the Cybermen back, set them at war with the Daleks, and reached the day that Rose Tyler died.

And then it begins all over again.

Season Three. Forty-two minutes before we crash into the sun, and how do you resurrect the Doctor's greatest enemy of all?

For the moment, the juggernaut just won't stop…

EPISODE TWO: BACK IN ACTION

Let's briefly recap the basics. Nobody thought *Doctor Who* would come back, but then BBC One Controller Lorraine Heggessey suddenly announces she's given Russell T Davies the task of doing just that. Anticipation is just as high as the cynicism in the run-up to broadcast, then bang! The BBC has the biggest hit of the year on its hands, the ratings and awards start coming in, and before anyone's even had time to catch their breath, there's a new Doctor in town – David Tennant… And his first full series kicks off on Easter Saturday 2006.

Twenty-one years since I last called "Action" with the TARDIS in shot, I got asked back to do some more. This chapter is the story of what happened next – a day-to-day account of trying to bring the scripts to life and make sure that these particular episodes of *Doctor Who* were visually exciting enough to keep people hooked for 40-odd minutes. You've no way of knowing that's going to be the case, but it's certainly the plan!

I'm going to kick off right from the point where I got the job of directing for Season Two, and it will end… Well, read it and you'll see. In the months running up to the first day of filming, any key events or facts are included and, on each shooting day, there's a sub-heading that describes where and what was being done for each entry.

Quite a few of the people I've been working with – Russell, Phil, Julie, etc – have been introduced already in the first section of the book. As for anyone who's not been mentioned before and suddenly appears, I've explained what they're up to and what their job is in the text as well.

So, what about the plot? Well, for the first two-parter, *Rise of the Cybermen* and *The Age of Steel*, there's several distinct plot strands to deal with. First, you've got Rose's story – the TARDIS crashes on the parallel earth, and seconds later, she finds out her dad, Pete… Well, he's alive, wealthy and living it large with Jackie. She wants him as part of her life, but the Doctor's got to steer her away from that thought.

The second plot strand concerns one John Lumic, a billionaire industrialist whose days are numbered. Lumic gets his henchman, Mr Crane, to start preparing an army of upgraded humans to instigate his ultimate plan. His plan is basically that everyone gets turned into a Cyberman.

Third, that's Mickey. He gets to reconcile with his gran, who's also still alive on this world, and then finds he's got a parallel version of himself to contend with. The parallel Mickey – who's called Rickey – runs the Preachers, a guerrilla gang of three. Alongside Jake and Mrs Moore Ricky is trying to overthrow Lumic's Cybus Industries and everything they stand for.

All three strands have got to weave together, and the characters that survive all turn up in *Army of Ghosts* and *Doomsday*, which are a direct sequel to the Cyberman story. The Doctor, Rose and Jackie get ensnared by the Torchwood Institute. Torchwood's Yvonne Hartman and her head scientist, Dr Singh, show the Doctor a Void Ship, which quickly sets alarm bells ringing. It shouldn't exist, and the fact that it does has opened up a breach to the parallel earth, which allows Cybermen to invade. Things get even worse when the Daleks emerge from the Void Ship, armed with something called the Genesis Ark – a Time Lord device that's imprisoned millions them. Soon war is being waged in the skies above London…

As this book is being written, it's close to two years since this all began, and a hell of a lot's happened in between… as you're about to find out.

SEASON TWO
RECORDING BLOCK THREE

FEBRUARY 2005

Several weeks prior to the start of Season One being broadcast, even prior to actually being commissioned, plans are being drawn up for the shape and tone of Season Two.

During meetings between senior BBC Drama figures – including Jane Tranter and Sarah Brandist, along with producer Phil Collinson and executive producers Julie Gardner and Russell T Davies – it's clear that the Cybermen are ideal as the next 'old' Doctor Who monster to be revised, reworked and reintroduced.

MARCH 2005

Russell T Davies has by now formulated the structure for Season Two. As with the Daleks in Season One, the Cybermen will be introduced midway through and then return for the finale.

Writer Tom MacCrae is now working on the initial story with a working title of Parallel World, *dealing with their genesis. The inspiration for the themes it will address came from* Spare Parts, *an audio* Doctor Who *play released by the independent production company Big Finish, written by Marc Platt and directed by Gary Russell. It featured Peter Davison reprising his role as the Fifth Doctor. Platt received an on-screen credit on the broadcast versions of Episodes Five and Six to acknowledge his part in reviving the Cybermen.*

Davies is working on Episodes 12 and 13, which are both untitled at that point, although Army of Ghosts *is later revealed as having been a story title for the former at a very early stage. He also considered using* Torchwood Rises *and* Torchwood Falls *as titles, but these were soon dropped.*

Both Shaun Dingwall and Noel Clarke are approached about working on Season Two, returning as Pete Tyler and Mickey Smith respectively. As part of the incentive, Clarke is promised he'll get to use a proper sci-fi gun (ie, in Doomsday*).*

APRIL 2005

"We wanted you for Season One, but the dates didn't match, you were busy on something else. But you're here now, so hooray!"

Russell's not changed. It's years since I've seen him. Still ebullient, full of laughter, smiles and hoorays. I've rarely known him be any different.

It must have been, what? 1994? We didn't so much work together on as mutually survive a sitcom called *The House of Windsor*. If nothing else, I remember the laughter in a tiny office on Brewer Street, trying to come up with topical gags against impossible deadlines for a show that was more 'dead donkey' than *Drop the Dead Donkey*.

Then there was *On the Waterfront* three or four years before that. Six weeks of nerve-fuelled live Saturday morning children's TV, where Russell was rewriting the dubs for *The Flashing Blade*, an old Spanish Musketeeresque kind of romp which took on a whole new meaning once he'd finished with it.

On my front room wall at home, there's a large A3 framed cartoon of me, looming over a battlefield and still managing to look enthusiastic while facing the carnage. It's pretty much an open secret that Russell's also a brilliant cartoonist, and he gave me that as a memento when time was called to close the *Waterfront* set on Liverpool docks for the last time.

Now he's here with Phil Collinson, buying me dinner and asking whether I'd like to do four episodes of *Doctor Who* for them, starting in August. What's there to say no to? "And by the way…" Russell's eyes glint mischievously. He's been saving this one up. "You've got the Cybermen."

They talk broad strokes, making it clear this is going to be epic 'end of the world' stuff. I'm sold, it sounds brilliant. Where do I sign?

26TH MAY 2005

Doctor Who Magazine *breaks the news that the Cybermen are going to return. In fact, this wasn't the first time their return had been planned since the original* Doctor Who *came to an end...*

THE LOST WAR

The year is 2025AD.

A devastated wasteland, scorched and decaying through years of war. Several soldiers are holding the Cyber Commander prisoner. Peter Davison's Doctor is there, busily trying to question it, but he's hitting a kind of metallic brick wall of logic every time it answers him. Then bang! Cyber troops turn up to rescue their boss, and seconds later the Daleks arrive…

No, it's not what was eventually seen in *Doomsday*, but something that nearly happened 13 years earlier in the summer of 1993.

This was *The Dark Dimension* – the 30th Anniversary special that bit the dust. Now it's surrounded by hazy memories of press speculation debating what went wrong, or the thoughts of internet nay-sayers who claim that it never really existed at all.

It did exist. I was there, and pre-production was very much under way. And there certainly had to be some quick thinking to get around the fact that *Doctor*

Who had been off the air for a few years.

I wanted to try and make the confrontation spectacular, but there was a problem. We only had four Cybermen. As for the Daleks? There was one black one, two white ones and the special weapons Dalek. That was it. All that the BBC props department had left and, as it was, most of them were going to be recalled from the exhibitions that were running at the time. Parts had been cannibalised and basic electronics jerry-rigged inside to make eyestalks look from side to side and exterminators twitch.

Some photographs were produced at a production meeting to illustrate the height and scale of the props, with measurements drawn out on the walls behind them. Side views, front views… It looked like they'd been arrested and were on a police ID parade.

We also wanted the Doctor's old yellow car, Bessie. The script featured several scenes of Tom Baker's Doctor with her, with one gag involving the fact that he kept a spare set of clothes – his original costume – hidden in a compartment under the driving seat. However, any thoughts of the story's chase scenes had to be put on hold. We were warned that if she went above 20 miles an hour the wheel trims were liable to fly off. Push her past 30 and the back seat would fall out.

When it also became clear that the Ice Warrior costumes we thought we'd be able to get were in a far worse state – basically, only the main shell and helmet from one costume was left – it was obvious that some serious monster-making was required.

Time to visit Jim Henson's Creature Shop and discuss the problem with one of their freelance animatronic designers, Chris Fitzgerald. He was immediately in tune with where I wanted to go with the whole thing, and stressed that the situation was not impossible to break down and get something workable from, bearing in mind both economics and the tight pre-production time we were facing.

The plan was to shoot as much as possible at night. The campsite where the Cyber Commander was being held could be lit mainly by a bonfire. Dark orange against midnight blues. Drench it in some mist, and you can hide a lot of sins.

"We've got the normal Cybermen," I told Chris, "but I'd like to make this something else. Something that you'll really get a sense of panic from when it breaks free."

The script was reworked slightly. I wanted something towering, elegant, strangely thin and agile, very swift and precise when it moved. Maybe someone seven feet plus in height. We talked about ways to distort the physical shape of the actor inside, lengthening the legs with small raised stilts and the arms with appliances that were limb extensions, working the taloned fingers with clutch cables linked to a control like a knuckle-duster.

Then there was the big effects moment during these scenes. The showstopper. If you're going to set icons against each other, you have to give the audience a pay-off. A visual kick that makes that kind of crowd-pleasing story conceit worthwhile.

Chris stressed this could easily be done with a simple costume appliance. When the Cyber Commander breaks free of his restraints – we were going to use a raised dais, harshly lit from beneath the circular area he was standing on to show the force field surrounding him and holding him captive – the first thing to stop him reaching the Doctor is a Dalek.

Not a problem. One clenched cyber fist and a metre-long blade slides out of the tube running down the back of its forearm. An elegant arc of an arm movement later and the Dalek is history, cut clean in two.

One of the shots I'd previously planned for the 1985 story *Revelation of the Daleks*, a Dalek flying through the air as it gets shots down, was going to be done with a giant catapult. Snow stopped play on that one, but this was the same principle, different application – the Cyber Commander could smash another Dalek with real pneumatic force and send it spinning into the air.

Another simple idea: vac-formed hollow Dalek casings, made out of lightweight gel, easy to throw like that and even easier to blow up mid-air with some light explosives.

Just try to imagine it. This was a dream shot. The Cyber Commander smashing its way towards the Doctor, slicing and slinging aside anything that tried to stop it. Unstoppable, deadly; once it's moving nothing can stop it.

Kevan Van Thompson and Stan Fus, the first assistant director and location manager, then had to find somewhere to do this. Stan knew of a vast common in Surrey, somewhere near Egham. They'd used it as a First World War no man's land for Paul McCartney's 'Pipes of Peace' music video about ten years before, and the trenches they'd dug were still there, now overgrown and, in a word, ideal. Closer to London, there was Battersea Power Station.

The shell of the building was fine, but the interior was gutted. All bare timber and metal gantries. Right in the centre, an overgrown courtyard and several burnt-out, vandalised sheds. Perfect as a base to retreat to and use as a holding area for prisoners. Even on the recce, the photographs came back with two scrawny stray dogs wandering around in the background scavenging for food. That only heightened the effect.

The finale of the story had Tom Baker being chased by a creature which I guess visually had some qualities like a spider – two spider legs flanking either side of its chest, which allowed it to climb and run across walls. As the Doctor tried to get out of a mansion house, it was just centimetres behind him but, rather than running, it was leaping from floor to ceiling, springing off the walls and propelling itself forward.

By building a cantilevered set, mounting the camera at the end of the corridor so the resulting footage would always remain level, even though it was being tilted wildly, the creature could be harnessed and thereby allow the stuntman inside to take a pretty wild route. Intercut this and mix it with shots of Tom seriously legging it, and the chase is on.

Now, what if the Cyber Commander did the same kind of thing? Leaping up onto the bare metal fire escapes, swinging around and easily jumping out of range from any bullets trying to stop him. Hire a gymnast, make sure the suit's lightweight and the stunts are rehearsed till they're crystal clear. Nothing careful editing can't help to complete if you film it tight and fast.

Well, that was the idea, anyway.

The schedule was fraught, the post-production time a nightmare, but the crew were willing it to succeed.

Fast forward to 6th July 1993. Freaky Friday, we called it. The day the plug was pulled. Everyone was told to clear their desks and go home. It seemed as though a showdown between the Daleks and Cybermen would forever remain no more than a few pages of script, some sketches and a few storyboards. That was the last time I'd be asked to do anything like that.

Well, that's what I thought…

JUNE 2005

Doctor Who Magazine *announces Graeme Harper's return to direct* Doctor Who *for the third recording block of Season Two. This will consist of Episodes Five, Six, 12 and 13.*

JULY 2005

During a major script conference, Russell T Davies and Tom MacRae effectively break the story down on the scripts for Episode Five and Six as they stand, and start heavily reworking the plot.

AUGUST 2005

Two days to go before I leave for Cardiff.

Saturday: Homework. Nearly a dozen Cyberman stories across 40 years, time to dip in and see what made them tick.

The Tenth Planet. These mid-60s Cybermen are creepy; they almost look as though they've been mummified. The trick of the mouth staying open once they start to speak, and the electronic voice echoing out. Very effective.

The Tomb of the Cybermen, Earthshock… The problem I have with the Cybermen throughout, apart from *The Invasion*, is that they don't seem very powerful. It's almost as though not that much care has gone into making them the kind of imposing force they so clearly are. They seem to become watered-down versions of that threat as the stories progress.

First thoughts. We've got to make them powerful, militaristic, with a kind of symbiotic co-ordination so that, when they march, it should be unified and terrifying. There should be a noise, a distinctive sound of metal boots that should be heard before they arrive. The threat has to be clear, so that, when they turn round the corner in absolute unison, you're running for your life.

Monday.

I've reached Cardiff, it's about 11 o'clock.

I'm the new boy here. Got to find my feet, got to settle down. Don't know where anything is, or any of the faces I've got to memorise.

Tye Oldfield. Big building directly opposite BBC Broadcasting House, just a short drive from the centre of Cardiff. There's a handful of offices there that the *Doctor Who* production team use while they're in town, but they're mainly out at the studios in Newport in a place called Unit Q2.

That's the scripts read, then. I know how the Cybermen rise for the age of steel, but what I really want to do is take a look round the TARDIS. Twelve miles to Newport. Won't take long to drive there.

I find Ed Thomas, the overall production designer. He's tied up with pre-production of another recording block, and trying to orchestrate all the set requirements for the one that's shooting right now. The set's nearly ready and the crew return to base from location tomorrow, so his time's more than tight. He still manages to find time for me.

"Great, nice to meet you Graeme! What d'you want to see?"

"I just really would love to see the TARDIS and have a quick chat."

The route to the set goes right underneath the design department, through some doors and there it is.

I just couldn't believe it!

There was an architect called Hector Guimard, and there's very little left of what he designed for the Paris Metro now, maybe just the station at Porte Dauphine. But that flavour, that kind of organic growth of metallic stems, reaching up and twirling into the designs. I could kind of see it here. Fabulous!

Coral buttresses stretching up and arcing towards the tip of the time rotor, which seems to have grown up like a bio-mechanical root. There's an operatic sense of scale, kind of like entering a cathedral, with so much space around the control console.

Ed explains all of the access points for cameras, how certain areas can be lit, which bits of the walls can be moved for equipment to be moved in. The scripts are still fresh in my head, so I have to ask.

"Have you read episodes five and six?"

"I read a version of them very quickly…" (How the hell did he find the time?) "I kind of got the gist of the storyline."

I rattle out the feeling I have about the look we need, what instantly hit me.

"Ed, could you please think Art Deco?"

Other questions tumble out.

"The designs of the Cybermen? Have they been locked off yet? Have they been set up without me? Do I have to go with the designs Russell T, Phil and Julie have green-lit with you?"

"No, no, don't worry. Nothing has been finalised yet. We've set people in motion to come up with creative designs for the Cybermen. Hopefully, at the first tone meeting, there should be 20 to 30 for you to look at. Maybe some that can be amalgamated together."

Ed has to go. A couple of final thoughts.

"Just think Art Deco, like the Zeppelins. I want to go down the route of 1930s, maybe 1920s Germany. The Bauhaus movement, that kind of thing. That's what I'm after."

That was my first conversation with him. Little did I know that they had all been thinking along these lines already, but Ed graciously allowed me to feel I had initiated these ideas! At least we were all on the same wavelength.

28TH SEPTEMBER 2005

The Cybermen design phase is now well under way at Millenium Effects, under Neill Gorton's supervision.

1ST OCTOBER 2005

Time for a more detailed conversation with Ed Thomas. You go into his office, and the first thing you notice is a wall *full* of ideas. Literally dozens of different photographs, cuttings, rough sketches, images referencing architectural styles or themes, it's all there, blu-tacked and sellotaped up in front of you. Loads of thoughts and ideas already triggered just from reading the script. Art Deco!

What we do is discuss the overall shape and feel, the tone and atmosphere of what we want to create on screen. Ideas are thrown back and forth. What should the sets look like? What are the practical requirements I need that he can then work into the set designs? I might already have an idea of the shape and general geography of the caves or tunnels, etc, in order to get the best visual impact out of them, but he also has to work out what he can afford to build on his budget and what has to be found on location.

In that first couple of hours we mark out a mental sketch, which we both agree on, and over the coming weeks of pre-production it's honed down and adjusted all the time until a deadline is reached and everyone has to commit to what's been planned. Once that's signed off, it's going to be built and that's what you'll be working with.

Occasionally, in terms of shooting on location, there comes a point when it becomes impossible to find somewhere that'll accommodate what we want to shoot. The shape might be too restricted, or it might just be too complicated to stage away from the studio. Whatever the case, there comes a point when final decisions have to be made, and it's either built in studio (which will require extra funds) or Russell has to rewrite scenes so it can be broken down into sets we already have, or come up with something that's easier to achieve.

3ʀᴅ OCTOBER 2005

It's D-Day.

It's the tone meeting for the biggest recording block that's been mounted for the programme so far. Everybody seems to be full of confidence, but the reality is we're shooting the equivalent of two movies in the time it would normally take to do one.

I've been here officially now for two days and, although faces are familiar, informal introductions have been made and people know who I am, this is the first time that all of the heads of department have come together to try and break the back of planning this out.

I asked Julie to define a tone meeting in a *Doctor Who* sense, ie, what structure do you follow? What exactly are we going to be talking about today?

My worry was that I'd only had time to read the scripts for the first two episodes. Some ideas were there; what I wanted to see, certain shots, etc. But I'm far from ready to talk over anything other than a handful of concepts. She's fine about this and calms me, saying she'll get the meeting up and running, effectively chair it and drive it through.

The room is packed. Thirty or more people at a guess. One key thought is probably riding high on the mental agendas they've all got in their heads. How are we going to do the Cybermen? What does he want to see? But at the moment, it's coffee and cakes all round.

Phil's not here. There are big special effects sequences being shot today by director Euros Lynn, so he has to be on set. Everyone sits down and, moving clockwise round the table, Julie asks everyone to introduce themselves, so name after name is called out, ending with me.

I'm under the impression that Julie's going to run the meeting. All eyes look to her, but she turns to me.

"So, Graeme, over to you."

"How d'you mean?" I nervously laugh.

"Would you like to give us your take on the first two episodes?"

I'm stunned. Straight in the spotlight, not what I thought was going to happen, so time to start winging it. The words tumble out. This is what I see, this is how I dream of it, this is what I expect to initiate. Fortunately, I have got a handful of notes.

Think Art Deco, think the Bauhaus movement, 'Big Brother Is Watching You', 1920 and 30s Berlin, George Orwell's dystopian images… Exactly what I've been saying to Ed Thomas.

"Right, here we go – the Cybermen. For the last 30 to 40 years there have always been Cybermen. Some great, some not so great. What we need to do is bring them into the 21st century and show the most terrifying, unique, semi-robotic beings. They should look stylish with all metal bodies, but in some way resemble what we know historically.

"We should not lose that feel, but we should bring them right up to date. I want them to be powerful, frightening, killing machines. How many should we have? If it's say 30, then I want a body of 30 Cybermen who should be manned by the army, so we have a precision march. Uniformity. Relentless. Unflinching. They have to be seen as unstoppable. Once you see them heading towards you, bang! It's like a tank. You're running, because if they reach you, you're dead."

As I start talking about how I see them, it opens up a whole can of worms. Out come the sketch pads, the laptops, the print-outs. Thirty, maybe forty different photographs of designs already done. Skin stretched and held over a face by an exo-skeleton, with gaping eye sockets; bulky metal figures with pistons and illuminated eyes; lithe, almost balletic versions clearly capable of great speed. The choice is whittled down to six or seven.

Initially I say that I want them to be gleaming, but it's clear that the reflections on their armour would be a nightmare for lighting and filming in close-up. Russell wants the colour to be gun metal, like the radiator of an Austin Seven. He's dead right. Art Deco, gun metal and the curves of an old car. Smashing!

There's still so many key areas of what we're going to shoot, which still have to be opened up for debate. This is going to be a long, long day.

24TH OCTOBER 2005

The Girl in the Fireplace *crew, working with director Euros Lynn, splits up into two teams. One of them heads off to recce* Rise of the Cybermen *and* The Age of Steel.

The shooting scripts for the as yet untitled Army of Ghosts *and* Doomsday *are issued.*

25TH OCTOBER 2005

The shooting script for Rise of the Cybermen *is finalised and issued.*

26TH OCTOBER 2005

The Daily Mirror *breaks the news that Roger Lloyd Pack will be playing the villain, John Lumic, comparing his character to Davros, in the sense that he creates the Cybermen.*

27TH OCTOBER 2005

The shooting script for The Age of Steel *is issued.*

28TH OCTOBER 2005

CBBC presenter Andrew Hayden-Smith announces on air that he'll be away for a few weeks shooting a guest role on Doctor Who.

31st OCTOBER 2005

The cast and crew are arriving in London through the day, with any meetings prior to filming taking place that afternoon and evening.

Everyone's here. The cast, the crew, even the TARDIS Police Box has arrived in London. No escape now.

There's a last-minute pre-production meeting at special effects house The Mill. We're agreeing on what the final details are for any on-set preparation that the green-screen special effects might need.

All this time, all this prep and I've not had a serious chance to sit down and talk with Russell T Davies about any of the characters, the major scenes or what their pace and energy should be. I've marked out where the key points are, the highs and lows in each scene, what their pinnacles are. But I guess I still need a private tone meeting with the Governor. Just to make sure.

He's no absentee landlord; don't think that for a minute. While I was prepping, Euros had been filming and gearing up for another block at the same time, while other directors Dan Zeff and James Strong were waiting to begin pre-production on their episodes. Russell has to be omnipresent over all this, fine-tuning words and ensuring that no tick, twist or turn in the plots are lost.

There's simply been no time. I put the word through the grapevine, asking for a one-to-one just to get the beats right for the mammoth filming schedule that's lying in front of us, like some daunting trek.

Word comes back. No, not a problem at all. I've got him for two, maybe two and a half hours after the meeting, just before his train home to Manchester.

The guys at The Mill have given us coffee, sandwiches, a free office to talk in. *Doctor Who* has become like part of the furniture there. They seem to eat, breathe and sleep it 24/7, but no one's complaining. A vast percentage of their computer-generated imagery (CGI) output is for the show.

I talk about key scenes, the general shape and feel of the two stories I've got to try and tell. What was the subtext that Russell saw in this particular scene? Should I be aware of an underlying theme behind that scene?

"Tell me about the family, what's going on between Pete and Jackie? What's the difference between them and the parallel versions? What do you want to see? What do I need to know about the actors?"

He's calmness personified.

"You're going to have five main actors through all of this, they'll be putty in your hands and hang on every word you say, because they want to see what you've got in mind, and they'll all have something they'd like to offer you. The process'll thrill them. They're all director-friendly and you'll find it'll all be marvellous. A real great joy. Hooray!"

When Russell uses 'hooray' as punctuation, it feels like a kind of deep-rooted seal of approval from him. If there's a 'hooray' or a 'hurrah' involved, then that's good enough for me.

He explains to me how he sees all of the guest characters. I go over my initial thoughts that merged John Lumic and George Orwell into a strange hybrid, an idea that's stuck so firmly that it'll be on tape in a few days' time.

Russell agrees completely. Go for it, no complaints about that one.

Once I've got the broad strokes of his thoughts and suggestions, we discuss my take on them and quickly meet on common ground, hammering down the hows, whys, whats and wheres that'll make the words, and whatever moves the actors bring, sync up with the story and spark it into life.

Some points I make are about the attitude the characters have as soon as we meet them on screen. The Doctor and Rose are a running through-line on that score, pretty much set in stone for the viewers, because they're really the only 'constant' they have to relate to. The Doctor's reaction to a situation will always be to counteract something. He arrives and bang! You know whatever's about to happen won't go anywhere near according to plan.

It's the events that unfold around him and Rose that trigger different reactions and develop their story arcs. But it's the villains, the one-shot heroes, the amoral assistants who add the colour around them. They're only there for one story and have to hit the nail on the head pretty quickly to show which side they're coming from – or not, as the case may be.

Think of Yvonne Hartman, Torchwood's head honcho. I'd like to make her more aggressive when we eventually reach her scenes, but Russell doesn't want her to alienate the audience. Yes, she's got power and a ruthless edge, but her charm and assurance, that's got to be done just right. He wants her strength of character and personality to fight through, even when she's become a Cyberman. Mickey, Jake, Mr Crane, Adeola… We go through each and every character, making sure the pitch it's played at will be just right.

Now, although I'd come through the 1960s, 70s and 80s working on various *Doctor Who* stories in various production roles, I'd never heard anyone say what Russell said when he shared his take on this new Doctor.

"What makes the Time Lord tick?"

I've seen the episode *The Christmas Invasion*, maybe a week ago, that's done and dusted and ready to be broadcast. It's the only real hint I've had of what the new Doctor is like. Russell says that David Tennant is quickly forming his own interpretation, and as each episode's shot he's getting deeper and deeper into the character, becoming more confident of what he wants to create.

There seems to be a specific nuance to the Doctor's character, something so tangible that if you look for it you can see it underlines nearly every action he takes.

"The most important thing for me about the Doctor, is that he is an enabler. Our Doctor goes around the universe, this version of earth or wherever, then he arrives and finds a problem, which inevitably there is, and he solves it, but he doesn't do it alone. More often than not, he enables the 'little man', the innocent who's the victim or is affected by what happens in the story, to help himself. With the Doctor as back-up, using his fast brain and abstract ideas, he enables him to become heroic. The Doctor presses the right buttons to enable the little man to become marvellous and save the day."

Russell's right. It's all part of the alchemy he brings to *Doctor Who*.

When you look at the performances of David Tennant and his predecessor Christopher Eccleston, that's exactly what they do. In the episodes we're about to shoot… Ricky, Pete, Jake and ultimately even Rose are all enable to achieve great heroic deeds.

I'll find a moment, somewhere in the first couple of days on set, to discuss this with David. Mental note made, got to make sure that I'll watch for this throughout my episodes – they must all get their chance to shine.

1st NOVEMBER 2005

Episodes Five and Six – The TARDIS materialises opposite Lambeth Palace along the Thames Embankment and Rose discovers her father is still alive on the parallel world. Scenes surrounding Mickey's decision to stay behind during Episode Six's closing moments are also shot.

Day one of the shoot.

I absolutely hate planning. Loathe it with a passion. It's mind-numbingly frustrating. When I'm on the initial location recce, I basically want to shoot the whole thing then and there. The words of the script, I can see them spark into life, but there's a three-week wait before the filming schedule kicks in. When I'm done, I've effectively already shot the whole thing in my head.

Now the schedule's arrived and when it kicks off – that's when I come alive; I'm on the set (doesn't matter if we're in a studio or on location), I've got the actors, I've got the whole crew, everybody's waiting for the director to say, "Right, this is what we're going to do."

First things first – I have to get over my nerves. Am I going to get on with everybody? Will they enjoy working with me? Are they going to be on my side and make it all run smoothly? How are the actors going to react when they hear my ideas?

It takes me about an hour. At first I gabble at about 300 miles an hour, rattling off all the exciting things I can see in my head. We run through the dialogue, but I'm still hyper-tense, desperately trying to make sure everyone understands, urging them to see the script's possibilities and what I'm trying to get out of it.

Now the crew know what I want to do, they're up to speed on how it's going to play. The first scene's been broken down into shots, almost how I've planned it, but having seen the performance I can now see a more interesting way of shooting it!

Rehearsals are over, the order of shots we have to cover is locked down, and suddenly my nerves are gone. It's like they were never there. It's been three months since I set foot on a set, so the actual mechanical process of calling the shots has kind of gone. I've got to get back into the rhythm.

Eight o'clock in the morning, and everyone's on set, waiting with baited breath. By nine o'clock we are rehearsed, lit and ready to shoot. Now I'm blinkered, focused entirely on the scenes that we're doing and what we have to achieve this day.

It's the opening scenes of Episode Five. The TARDIS has crash-landed on an embankment outside Lambeth Palace in London, and already you can hear the 'Scooby Gang' inside, thanks to some strategically placed microphones.

"Why are we saying it's the first of February? Does anyone know? Obviously we're not going to be on at that time. This'll be going out in June, surely?" Noel Clarke's got a point.

"We're time travellers. We can do whatever the hell we like." Time Lord logic from David Tennant.

"But in an earlier draft it said April … ?"

Billie Piper must be watching from the crack in the TARDIS door while they wait for their cue. "I love joggers. They crack me up."

A balding guy wearing a red top and shorts shouts abuse at the politeness of the first assistant director, Clare Nicholson, as he runs through the shot and she asks him to stop.

"What was that?" David didn't quite hear what was said.

"He's moaning… 'F**k you! This is a public right of way, pal'…" Noel mimics the irate athlete.

"And action!" The first assistant has ensured everything's ready, and we're off…

Five takes on the first shot, keep up the energy guys.

Now a close-up on Billie, David flanking to her right. Three takes in and the sunlight is beginning to bleach out certain parts of the frame.

"That's just too cool!" Billie and Noel are caught up in reading the front page of a parallel world newspaper. The design department have gone down to the detail of even writing the copy for the headlines.

The edge of David's face and the outline of Billie's hair are beginning to merge into the background. Both are shielding their eyes. Every time the sun breaks cloud cover, the shot whites out. It's diffusing the picture, but we persevere.

Now tight close-ups.

"Is my eye line all right, Rog?" A provocative wink to the camera operator, Roger Pearce, from Billie.

You can adjust your camera depending on the intensity of the sun. If it's very bright, you close the iris down. Equally, if the location is very dark you need to open it up.

The length of the shot dictates whether Ernie Vincze, the director of photography, opens or closes the iris of the camera during the take. This depends on how the natural light changes during a shot. For example, the sun may start shining then several seconds go behind a cloud, causing a change in the light conditions and the stop he has chosen. Getting the timing right can be complicated, but if you're careful you can 'ride the iris'.

Another example: if you do a tracking shot from outside a stately home following action from the lawn in through the French windows, the exposure outside will be different to that inside. The director of photography can ride the iris so that you can see the action in the same light condition. This is usually done with a remote control device while he looks at monitor picture.

I've got to be conscious of the Zeppelins for this sequence.

There has to be enough definition of the skyline in shot for the CGI effects. The Doctor, Rose and Mickey all look over their shoulders and, bosh, a whacking great airship flies directly into frame.

They're in the elite end of town, the playground of the rich and infamous. The story dictates that there is a cultural divide between the wealthy and the poor, and there's nothing more nouveau-riche than a designer dirigible. John Lumic has set this benchmark of style, and no doubt makes millions from patenting, building and selling each and every one of them.

Dave Houghton from The Mill is present and correct, making sure that I get my shot, but also that there's enough room for them to digitally graft on the Zeppelins.

"Can you make the shot a bit looser? When you pan to the left, can you avoid the edge of that tree because it'll interfere, or can we move the whole shot a foot to the right?"

Everything's already been addressed with storyboards regarding what The Mill will create to complement the scene, so this is fine-tuning on the live set before it's enhanced.

There's a take with the actors going through their lines, then a 'clean plate shot', clear of any visual movement but showing the location in precisely the same way as before on a locked off camera. This will become the canvas that The Mill use to composite all of the elements you'll see on screen for no more than a few seconds.

In order to pinpoint the direction all of the light sources are coming from, a silver sphere's held up to camera for a few seconds – this is a Match Ball – along with a grey one, which separately performs the reverse of that, I guess, by illustrating the direction any shadows are coming into view from.

Moving on, we've got to tackle the living poster.

Rose's dad, Pete, still alive on the parallel earth, first seen advertising his own brand of health drinks via an animated holographic billboard. At the moment, all we're working with on location is a board with a green area to represent where Pete will be seen.

I'm blocking this shot so the point of view is between Noel and Billie's shoulders; they glance at each other briefly but I still have to keep the green screen clean between them. It's a medium wide shot followed by a tight shot through their shoulders. The difficulty is that the movement in the poster has to be matted in by The Mill. How are we going to get this to work?

Dave Houghton's agreed that we need to lock off the key framing. Once we've got the shot we want, I'll take the actors out of the shot and run the tape again for a plate shot of the poster area that is a green screen plus the area of location around it. It's the same working principle that we employed for the Zeppelin shots. There's quite a bit of shadow catching the left rim of the green screen, affecting about an eighth of the image, so we need to colour-correct in post-production, during the grading session.

Rose quickly angers the Doctor when it becomes clear that she wants to find her Dad. He's still alive here, and that's the immediate inner thought I tell Billie to focus on as we go through the scene.

We're off. The energy's intense. During the rehearsal, David grabbed Billie by the jaw, forcing Rose to look him straight in the eye, hammering home the consequences of what she's clearly contemplating, but it feels wrong. It's too strong a reaction from the Doctor, but I've lined up enough shots to cut around that, so the point of contact won't be seen on screen.

This is tricky. We're about an hour into the night shooting.

We've done the opening scenes and now, quite literally, we've got to do the closing moments of Episode Six. David, Billie, Noel… All of the highs, the chases, the energy, the exhaustion, the twists and turns that their characters' journeys take them on with this story. Well, none of that's happened yet.

In two or three minutes while the camera's set up, they have to rely on me to give them a sense of the heightened adventure I'm going to put them through. It's an enormous emotional leap to make without actually having played or shot the main bulk of the story.

Prior to the shooting period you don't get to meet the actors to rehearse anything, so you start to work on each scene in the studio or on location. By this stage the director and actors have full knowledge of the script and begin to block through and agree the way the scene should be played. My job is also to remind them of what has just occurred dramatically in the story. This will colour the way they play the scene and affect the emotions they will bring to the surface.

Those few minutes before a take, that's all the time we have to quickly discover the moments we want to get out of the scene, work it through and let the crew see where we're at. Then, if we're lucky, while the lighting, camera and props are being set, the director and actors will get ten or maybe 15 minutes to hone it down and cover any other points they want to get out of the scene.

They have to remember the emotional beats they have to find. Filming drama is like putting pieces of a big jigsaw together – everything has its place, there's a definite order to it and, when the pieces are slotted in, it's up to me to try and guide them towards what the eventual picture will look like, both now whilst shooting and then again in the edit suite later.

Day One is over. There are only a few hours before we start shooting again. Time ran out for some of the vital shots I needed, just to add colour and build up the pace of some sequences, so maybe there'll be a chance to pick them up later in the shoot.

Phil Collinson's been gone most of the day shooting second unit material and plate shots across the river from Battersea Power Station. It's the same for him tomorrow, filming on Westminster Bridge for ghost and Cybermen effects shots, and they've got a prime site lined up at GLC Annexe that should offer a great vantage point for the camera.

Everything he's got to complete has already been discussed, story-boarded and fine-tuned regarding what I need to see in the resulting footage, but Phil used to direct things like *Peak Practice* so I'm sure, if he gets the time, he'll line up and grab some other interesting stuff.

2ND NOVEMBER 2005

Episodes 12 and 13 – *Filming on the Brandon Estate, Kennington, London. This involves the arrival of the Doctor and Rose at the Tylers' estate and flat,*

*their reactions when they step outside and see the 'ghosts', and crowd panic
scenes as the Cybermen finally materialise.*

"That's really, really, really rubbish!"
In character, David is busily condemning the stream of nonsense that Billie
is ad-libbing.

"I know, but it's cool."

But is that Rose or Billie replying?

Bit of a schedule jump to Episodes 12 and 13. Three sequences that involve
Rose's home turf, and it's the only chance to record them at the original location
that's been established for the Tyler home.

The camera's focused low and wide, we're tracking alongside the Doctor
and Rose as they head across the estate's main quadrangle, holding hands and
aiming for the stairs leading up to her mum Jackie's flat.

A mental note for Billie and David: I want to see a high level of energy, a
kind of high exuberance radiating from both of them. That infectious glint in the
Doctor's eye – Rose caught it and embraced it. They don't know what they're
heading into, so we want to see them happy and carefree before the story takes off!

The sound recordist sits listening intently at his equipment bay, close by the
camera and the monitor screens. It's Simon Fraser's job to hear things before
anybody else. It's not like some strange canine intuition, just the fact that the
boom microphone can pick up the sound of a pin dropping.

"Got a nasty plane here, tell Clare would you?"

"Even if she shouts they won't hear her!"

The droll wit goes unnoticed. Clare Nicholson's busy ensuring we're ready
for the next set-up. David and Billie charge into the quadrangle and watch the
ghosts as the 'midday shift' begins; one literally walks through the Doctor and
Jackie joins them to watch in awe.

"But, no one's running, or screaming, or freaking out…"

Dialogue interuptus as David looks skywards.

"… or flying!"

Again, there's the distant rumble of a plane that seems to take forever to
pass. Sure, some of it can be resolved by redubbing the lines during post-
production, but it's the annoying distraction for the actors that you can't remove.

David's exercising his mouth between takes, making loud popping sounds with his lips. He's got to mime a physical convulsion, simulating the Doctor's reaction as a ghost passes through him. He has to hit his mark precisely to match his moves against a large green screen as it's carried into shot and held in place directly behind him. For this shot the camera has to be locked-off.

This is all building up the elements The Mill will need to polish the finished effect on screen. There'll be a clean shot of the same background on the locked-off camera, and then it's over to The Mill to add the 'ghost'.

"Hold it. We've got a helicopter heading over!"

Great. Take Seven.

"There's a plane, guys!"

Take Eight. David's ears prick up.

"Now we've got an ambulance."

Silence. Maybe it's parked. Onto Take Nine. The ambulance's reversing signal suddenly starts bleeping loudly just as another plane appears.

Camille Coduri is now in shot. Rose's mum has joined them watching the ghosts. It's a sense of wonder bordering on reverence for her, but confusion and disbelief for the Doctor and Rose. I give them all a cue to turn and head off as the apparitions start to vanish.

"Fade... and fade... and fade... They're gone... And cut!"

Reset the camera and it's a close-up on Billie and Camille looking over their shoulders at David. I say "Cut" in the middle of one of Jackie's lines and Camille feigns looking really hurt.

"Well, I've got to cut it eventually!"

I always shoot a little more beyond the actual dialogue I need on a particular shot, just to make things a bit easier in editing. Saying "cut" in the middle of someone's dialogue may seem a little unkind but it's not meant to be uncaring.

That's a wrap for the main artists, but there's still action to shoot across the quadrangle. High and wide, we'll see the ghosts appear and just mingle amongst the passers-by. They're easily accepted, just like they're a part of their daily lives. General moves are choreographed for the support artistes, including three boys playing football in the mid-foreground and two ladies crossing and chatting in the immediate foreground. This will require several passes using green screens behind the action, in order that a whole bunch of 'ghosts' can walk through the quadrangle and everyone else. These will be CG images inserted at a later stage by The Mill.

The process of staggering elements of the eventual image kicks in again, and the green screen is heaved in and out of shot several times. You'll never see the two riggers standing either side holding the support bars because The Mill will make them disappear. But their faces? Let's just say by Take Three it's clear they're dreaming of being elsewhere.

I let the kids ad-lib, building energy to the sequence.

"Hello Mr Ghost… How are you?"

The young girl watches as she imagines a ghost heading directly across her path.

"You can play too if you want to."

The boy at the rear of the triangle the three of them have formed offers the ball to another. It's tricky, and they have to be careful not to let their arms or the ball stray out of the boundary that the screen's created behind them, but we get there.

Clean plate for the shot with no one in sight? Check.

Same routine for the kids minus green screen? Check.

Final shots for the day. High up on the roof of the flats facing down into the quadrangle. Only a handful of Support Artistes, and this time they stop dead in their tracks. A squad of ghosts turning into Cybermen, and that's their cue to run screaming at what they see. Or what they will see eventually when The Mill have finished their stuff.

They don't see a shred of metal anywhere near them for the moment. Not a Cyberman in sight.

But, then again, we haven't seen them yet either!

3RD NOVEMBER 2005

David Tennant and Billie Piper are freed up from the filming schedule so they can to head back to Cardiff and record the Children in Need *mini-episode. This is directed by Euros Lynn.*

Episodes Five and Six – *Scenes of the first meeting between Mickey and Ricky are recorded, along with interior shots of the driver's cab of the pantechnicon,* *with Mr Crane talking to Lumic, sequences in the Preachers' van and their hideout. This is based around Tal-y-Garn Manor and Country House, near Pontyclun.*

"That was a bit fluffy. No threat, no edge…"
The camera's tight on Colin Spaul, cramped up in the passenger seat of a pantechnicon driver's cab. First shot of the day and his first day on the shoot.

Mr Crane's the right-hand man, the lackey, the guard dog in Armani who's John Lumic's eyes and ears in so many ways. He's playing him slightly gruff, like an East End gangster with a corporate sheen. He's not happy with that first take.

"We'll go again then…" Clare takes my signal and reads in Lumic's lines to cue him in.

Mr Crane is taking orders via a video link on a hi-tech monitor clamped to the dashboard. Its screen is blank for now. There's footage to grab of Roger Lloyd Pack's side of the conversation later on, which The Mill will add to the empty plasma during post-production.

The driver next to Colin, all mean and moody in profile, is just meant to turn and nod as he's told to drive on, but his eyebrows keep shooting up for the first few takes. Too Stan Laurel and I want more deadpan. A couple of takes later and we're sorted.

Onto the interior of the Preachers' transit van. Helen Griffin and Andrew Hayden-Smith arrive as Mrs Moore and Jake. The shot's simple. These are freedom fighters, guerrillas, who are meant to be experts with weapons. Mickey's sitting alongside them, watching nervously as, with great efficiency and skill, they assemble, then lock and load their machine guns. During this the van is being driven at speed to keep up with the large lorries that are carrying the Cybermen. In reality the vehicle was stationary and two prop men gently shook it from outside to give some feeling of movement.

The morning's been spent being taught gun-stripping and assembly by Faujja Singh, the unit's armourer. This should look mean and professional.

Take One – the gun jams.

Take Two – Andrew completes the assembly, swings the gun upright and rests the butt on the floor. There's a loud clank as part of it falls off.

"I think I can hear Graeme laughing..." Noel hears me, even though I'm by the monitor outside the van. I have collapsed into a fit of hysterical giggling.

Take Three. Clunk! Not again! Noel's now turning his head slightly, burying his mouth in the shoulder of his jacket, trying desperately not to laugh.

The Preachers' base is a strange mixture of ornate architecture and grime from their makeshift camp, with an added hint of hi-tech sheen thanks to their computer systems.

This is going to be complicated for Noel. He's got to be tied up and question himself at the same time. We've got a double in, wearing a replica costume for both Mickey and Ricky when the scene calls for it.

First things first. We lens up high and wide, focused on the ceiling before moving down to the centre of the room, where Noel's tied to a chair. Helen's got to hold her position for the entire scene working a laptop on a table, but Andrew's using a scanner on Mickey, trying to figure out who he is. We move the double in, who walks round the back of the chair; he's masked when he turns to face Noel by his left shoulder.

Next, we play out the same few moments, only now in a mid-shot, with a green screen being held up directly behind Noel. He matches his moves to what he was doing when his double moved behind him.

Dave Houghton's here and asks for a clean plate shot – just the chair and the fireplace in the background. He then steps in and removes the chair, allowing Mickey to be replaced by a white stick with a photo of his head on its tip, so Noel as Ricky has an eye-line to follow. Ricky then goes through his moves, with Clare reading in Mickey's lines off camera.

Still building up the scene, Noel strips off again and goes back on the chair, with the green screen now behind him at an angle, allowing the camera to shoot him in semi-profile. There's another clean plate shot for this angle, then the white pole returns with Noel back in his Ricky costume to play out his reactions.

One final shot of him tied to the chair as Ricky shoves some clothes at him, saying he's going to go with them.

"And cut... Can we do it one more time?"

I move in to talk to Noel.

"I think what you've just played is brilliant, but this man [Jake] has just rushed out of a van and grabbed you, dragged you here and tied you up... So, when he comes up and starts to push you around, I think you should be really worried."

Noel gives it just the right taste of meek fear. With The Mill compositing all of this together, it'll hopefully come together seamlessly.

I've been told that the first of two days' fitting for Cybermen costumes is under way at Neill Gorton's Millennium Effects studios. The first off the production line should be on set in a few days' time. To be honest, I can't wait!

4TH NOVEMBER 2005

Episodes Five and Six – *Piper and Tennant return to join the main unit during the night shoot, after dubbing the* Children in Need *mini-episode during the afternoon. Scenes are shot around the pantechnicon and the derelict area and streets at South-Side Roath Dock, Cardiff Docks. Various scenes inside the Preachers' van are also completed around nearby roads.*

Right, Mr Crane's out gathering in potential candidates for upgrading. Sort of a 21st century version of press-ganging.

What I asked for at the tone meeting was a massive wasteland, lined with scrap metal and debris, and that's exactly what the location managers have found. The horizon's lined with hills of rust across the river, and in the distance there's a factory, bleached white in the sunlight, belching out grey smoke from its chimneys.

I really want to generate a sense of bleakness for these scenes; raw industrial decay, rotting metal and starvation.

"Sixty nine… Or soixante-neuf take one!"

The clapper loader's in a French mood. On cue, the pantechnicon starts to reverse into shot.

Now, I want to use a combination of a top shot, to show a wide area of the dump and the lorry backing in, and then do a tracking shot to bring Mr Crane down and out of the vehicle. We'll hold on him and frame him with a burning oil drum in the foreground as he starts to give a lecture to the homeless guys, offering them free food, and then try something different.

Andrew's back as Jake, keeping out of sight, filming Mr Crane's activities with a camcorder.

"You've got lucky. You've been waiting to see this incident happen, you don't want to get caught, but you know that you've got to shoot proof that Lumic's henchmen are up to no good."

We've got a hand-held camera, which we'll cut into for Jake's point of view (POV) through his lens. We'll put a little recorder timer on the scene in post-production, just to make it look real.

Mr Crane spots what he's doing and calmly walks up, asking what he thinks he's going to achieve with the footage. The cops? The papers? Cybus Industries own them, so it's pointless even trying. I tell Colin there's no hint of violence here, just play it with a sinister edge, because he knows he's in control of the situation.

For moments like this, I love using low wide angles. I think the lens is a 4.8 – an absolutely amazing one to work with, which is heading towards a fish-eye effect. The basic rules are if you want a wide shot, the lens on the camera gets thinner the wider you go, and, equally, the tighter the close-up, the thicker the lens.

The cameras we use actually work with a multiple lens – a zoom lens which gives you a whole range of focal distances, so you can get from a very wide angle to quite close, depending on how far you are from the subject.

"We don't know when to go? Was that 'Action' or not?"

Helen Griffin is in the driver's cabin of the van and can't quite hear what's being shouted to her from outside. The walkie-talkie next to her crackles into life. I tell her what's wrong.

"We stopped because Andrew dropped out of shot. We can't see him."

Andrew's in the back with Noel, just to the far right of the shot. The scene rolls again.

The Preacher van's been mounted on a low loader, a towing vehicle, so we can control the van's movements on the road, and Helen just has to mime that Mrs Moore's steering it. All the driving's being done for her.

"And cut! Andrew, we need to go again, you've getting blocked."

Helen's got a clapperboard next to her to mark the scenes – there's no room for the clapper loader to hide – So, she starts moving it round in as many angles as she can think of, cueing in the next take, clearly lost over which way's the right one.

We're onto a night shoot… Still on the low loader, covering Mrs Moore listening while she drives, as the Doctor, Rose, Ricky and Pete are also now on board.

Onto the interior. Aggressive questioning from Ricky, but the Doctor slowly manages to kill off the tension.

"Any chance of getting Andrew a bit higher?"

"My head's already toughing the ceiling!"

Space is tight. There are seven actors, including Noel's double, and the camera and sound crew in here. The cast are having to work the clapperboard for each take.

We're focused on Andrew and Noel, in Ricky mode, with David and Mickey's stand-in flanking the right of the screen. Billie and Shaun are taking advantage of being out of shot by keeping their thick body-warmers on.

"How now brown cow."

Billie's warming up her vocal chords while we line up on her, leaving David in charge of the board.

"Eighty Two… Take One… A- and B-Cameras… Common mark…"

Right in the middle of the take, Shaun's right ear-pod falls out. He gets the clapperboard for the next slate.

"I didn't really think that was that good…"

David's teasing Billie and Shaun. Noel's now by his left side, and quickly joins in.

"Five… Five out of ten at best…"

A beat. He smirks at Billie.

"Maybe six and a half out of ten, because it's you…"

She rolls her eyes, but smiles…

They're teasing each other mercilessly and we're not even at the end of the first week!

5TH NOVEMBER 2005

While the Block Three crew take the weekend off, Russell T Davies and Julie Gardner travel to France to take part in a press junket launching Doctor Who *on the France 4 TV channel.*

David Tennant, still unseen as the new Doctor save for a fleeting appearance at the end of Season One's final episode, The Parting of the Ways, *attracts huge media interest as he attends the London premiere of* Harry Potter and the Goblet of Fire.

7TH NOVEMBER 2005

Episodes Five and Six – *TARDIS interior scenes recorded at Unit Q2, Newport. Phil Collinson sanctions the decision to abandon recording plans for 12th November.*

"Is it when was that, or where was that?"

Noel's framed at an oblique low angle, tilting up so the umbrella patterning on the TARDIS ceiling is in shot. Not something I think we've really seen properly before.

"It's where..." Non Eleri Hughes calls out from the side of the set, script pages open across her knee in a folder, as she continually makes notes across it. Continuity's her watchword, and she never misses a beat.

I really believe in something I call 'the hook'; the opening of any drama you direct. You have to feed information to the viewers: the dialogue, the drama, what the actors are doing. You have to grab the audience visually, and find the most interesting ways possible to lead them into the story you're presenting. Those first few minutes are the key to making them decide to stay with you, and see what you've got to say.

The audience is entitled to see something as powerful, colourfully rich or maybe as glamorous as I can make it. If they bite 'the hook', then they're there for the ride.

So, what about *Rise of the Cybermen*? We're straight in with a crisis. The TARDIS crew are relaxing mid-flight, then suddenly they're in trouble, way out of control and the jeopardy's instantly there – they're going to crash, and there's nothing the Doctor can do about it.

We're on the set, the lights are up and the gantry's coral girders and console are spread out before me. Big question: I can see the TARDIS, and I know other directors have shown it in all its glory before, but what can I do that's different?

We move the camera right up to the top of the support arches, slightly to the right of the console. What I want to see is a sense of scale, so, maintaining that height, we slowly swing round to the next girder, then arc down and close in towards where the Doctor and Rose are sitting. It creates a sense of depth and power visually, so hopefully that should do the trick.

Billie, David and Noel are all on the floor around the console, holding positions a safe distance from the console as small explosions detonate. They roll slightly and duck down flat against the floor.

"And cut!"

Special effects crew race onto the set with fire extinguishers and put out anything that's accidentally caught light. Ed's added a neat touch for the aftermath – oxygen masks drop down, dangling from feed pipes in the girders, just as they would during an aircraft emergency landing.

Slate 100. The clapperboard's lifted up in front of the camera. The 'one' has been drawn in as a champagne glass, and the zeros are fizzing wine glasses. You reach the centenary of Slates on any show, and you'll see something similar… No time, more's the pity, for the real thing to celebrate, or enough money in the budget, come to that.

We're onto a wide shot of the cold, dead TARDIS. Somebody points out that we're still lit… Ernie's forgotten to turn out one batch of lights, but we've quickly agreed that there's an internal logic to this – no matter what, the TARDIS should always have its own power residue for latent lighting, but nowhere near enough to get it going again. It's absolutely dead.

One of the notes I've given to David: this is the Doctor at his most worried. Not panicking, but deeply fearful. The core of this story concerns the death of the TARDIS, and everything that happens is a result of this fact. But there's a dim hope, a tiny light just under the side of the console. The Doctor and Mickey have to reach it.

Take One. David goes way too fast through his lines, and is the first to recognise that fact.

"Well, that was absolute rubbish on my part. Absolute with a capital 'R'."
What I'm trying to show is that you can step down into the engines of the TARDIS. The grille is about two feet off the floor, so there's just enough room to put a camera in there and look up. That's all. In reality, that's a two-foot drop,

but in the story I'm trying to show that you can actually climb down six to eight feet, so that's why I've done such a hard shot.

Take Two. The panels lifted, they get through the lines, but then...

"Yikes! Yikes! Yikes!" Noel's beginning to overbalance with the weight of the metal, and his fingers are caught up in the mesh. David quickly tries to help.

"I've got it! I've got it!"

Hands are quickly there to help. Clare's by Noel's side as he ruefully examines his right little finger.

"Are you all right?"

"Yeah, I'm fine... It just bit me!"

I could have lensed up an overhead shot on the chevron, and cut in with a close two-shot on the Doctor and Mickey, but this way I can show the height of the TARDIS and, with darkness behind them, create a real feeling of depth.

It's the same with a shot we stage using a camera crane, slowly running down the contour of one of the coral struts, gradually coming in to focus on the Doctor. All the time you have to remember scale and breadth of focus.

When you do something like that, you're addressing the show's mythology. It really is bloody big on the inside!

8TH NOVEMBER 2005

Episodes Five and Six – *Filming at the Riverfront Arts Centre, Newport to complete Thames/South Bank scenes is effectively rained off. This will be remounted on 16th November.*

"Could you rise on the line earlier?"

"Which one?"

I go over the dialogue with Billie so she knows exactly what I mean.

"Yeah, it felt a bit staged..."

"You see..." I'm talking while she tries to stop her hair being blown to bits in the wind. "That moment, it just feels better for you to get up then."

"I was supposed to – I don't know why I didn't. Anyway, I will this time. Thank you."

"I love the actual sense of what you're doing, it's just that moment... I think it needs to rock on."

"Okay."

Billie starts talking about how she's thinking the scene through. Noel and David stand listening.

"I think I'm quite scared to tell him I've been on the internet, and I've found out all this information…"

Rose has stormed off from the TARDIS. The Doctor and Mickey have followed, but she's already hooked up on-line via the Cybus Network and her mobile phone, and found some news about her 'parallel' Dad. I try to back up the way she's thinking the scene through.

"And also, I'm coming in close on that, so we'll get a sense of what you're feeling… You all right David?"

"Yeah, yeah… Absolutely, no, that's good… That's good."

He's backing Billie, supporting what she's trying to find for the moment we're blocking. I go on.

"But I'm going to bash in to all of this… It'll be great… Right, let's make it happen."

David and Noel start singing the few words they can remember from a KT Tunstall song. Lots of 'Da-da-da-ing' for the bits they haven't got a clue over.

"You know, that song's been in my head, I've been singing it to myself so much, but it's only the other day when you told me who it was."

I cut across Noel. "Loads of pace and energy!"

High and wide, we swoop down as the Doctor and Mickey find Rose, but the light's fading fast. Black rain clouds are closing in and the natural light is really being affected.

Take Two. David bounds off to take up his starting position for the scene, Noel races to join him, and the rain starts to fall as the half-remembered KT Tunstall song returns.

No choice. We've got to move on. The outdoor location has been washed out with rain. We'll have to come back. Onto the Preacher van.

Billie's yawning in the foreground, Shaun's sitting to her right, holding onto a support strap as we lens up.

"That's a nine???"

David's out of shot, but incredulous at the way the digit's been drawn on the clapperboard. Billie peers at it.

"That's really bad!"

"And action!"

Clare's ignoring them and cues in the scene. Billie stops the take about 30 seconds in. Helen, Noel and Andrew are just outside the van reading their lines in for the scene. So there's an eye-line for the others, their positions in the driver's cabin are being represented by different coloured spots taped into place on the dividing mesh grille.

"Sorry, I'm looking at different spots. Which one's Mrs Moore? Sorry, you guys. Mrs Moore is the white one?"

Take Two. Shaun's right ear-pod falls out just as he starts to speak. The words 'Encrypted wavelength six five seven using binary nine' make him get tongue-tied.

"Why am I calling them the Scooby Gang? I sound like Scooby Doo!"

Final shots to complete, and they're also the last ones for Episode Six, as Mickey and Jake head off to liberate Paris. Only problem is, when we frame the van low and wide, as soon as Noel starts to drive off it stalls and judders forward a few feet.

Noel quietly starts banging his head against the steering wheel, while in France a few more people get Cybernised.

9TH NOVEMBER 2005

Episodes Five and Six – *Zeppelin flight deck scenes are recorded at Unit Q2.*

"Ready?"

Noel's voice is no more than a whisper as he checks with Andrew.

"One... Two... Three..."

The doors leading into the conference room and flight deck of Lumic's Zeppelin get kicked open, Mickey and Jake drag in and drop an unconscious Technician, and head straight for the transmitter controls.

On the first bank of monitor screens, directly behind the huge table that dominates the set, Noel stops for a few seconds on each take and glances at a painting of the ship. He's secretly fulfilling a promise to concept artist Pete

McKinstry to look at his artwork, which has been framed and hung as set dressing. It's also won him a bet that dared him to do it.

"That's ten quid, isn't it? Ten quid, man!"

You can hear him claiming his prize behind the doors as we set up for the third take.

"Damn it! I was looking in the wrong place!"

When they reach the ship's wheel, Mickey turns and sees a Cyberman standing in an alcove directly in front of him. Noel's got the mark for his eye-line wrong.

"Awww crap! I was looking there too!"

Andrew's got the same problem.

Take Five... Noel turns round and jumps as he catches sight of the metal.

"Cyberman! ... Oh, bugger, I've done it again!"

Noel turns and looks into the camera, smiling manically while Andrew heads off cursing.

"But I got it right this time!"

Reset... They're now chatting off camera and laughing.

"I thought, shall I continue? Nah! He's got it right and my eyes are all over the place."

"You should follow the maestro's lead, man."

Only one solution. Time to put one of the crew in the alcove so they have more than a mark on the wall to look at.

"You're doing what? No way, man... As soon as I see him, I'm going to laugh... He's gonna have to face the wall!"

Noel's running back to the wheel to look at how we're playing this. Andrew follows.

"I've gotta see this... What if he stands sideways, then we just look at his ear?"

"No way, man... I just know I'm gonna laugh!"

A big yellow arrow made out of tape is put on the wall as a compromise, with a post-it sticker underneath saying 'Look Here'. They get it first time. High fives all round.

The first Cyberman that Neill Gorton's crew have completed is on set, and actor Rauri Mears is tentatively walking round in it, almost test-driving it I guess. It looks stunning. As soon as we get him standing in the alcove, lighting it low and wide, I can see that there's immense potential in the way they're going to look en masse.

We've got to build up the scene around Mickey trying to crack the computer locks on the Zeppelin controls; two-shots on Noel and Andrew at the keypad, singles on both of them in tight close-ups, and then wide as the Cyberman comes to life, staggers forward and lunges at them.

Time for some Frankenstein moments; ground level, looking up at the Cyberman, lit from overheads so its skull glints and its hands twitch, energy coursing through it, reactivating it.

Back to the chase. Mickey dodges out of the way, moves behind the wheel, then has the idea that the Cyberman crashing into controls might do the trick as it pursues him. Only problem is, Noel trips and lands on the floor.

"Are you okay?"

The Cyberman bends over and helps him back on his feet. Not the kind of thing its programming would normally let it do! Paul Kennington's now wearing the suit for the main stunt, as it smashes its fist through the panel concealing the transmitter circuits.

With purple lights inside, plenty of sparks and smoke, he convulses on impact and slowly falls to the ground, dragging his hand free from the resulting damage as it dies.

"And cut!"

Fire extinguishers quickly douse the area, just in case, and applause breaks out around the studio. Everyone's stopped to watch this. What's it going to be like when we've got the full squad painted, buffed and ready to invade?

10TH NOVEMBER 2005

Episodes Five and Six – *Zeppelin flight deck sequences continue to be shot at Unit Q2, along with boardroom scenes chaired by Lumic.*

Back on the set. Ready?

"Action!"

And off we go. Mickey and Jake are fighting at the wheel of the Zeppelin, trying to get control from each other – Mickey wants to save the Doc and Rose, Jake wants out of there pronto.

The camera could be locked off and we could just leave it to the guys to act it out, inter-cutting with close-ups to give pace and energy, but there has to be a way to show this on a grander, wider scale without resorting to The Mill for shots of the airship swinging from side to side.

Roger Pearce, the camera operator, has an idea. "I can lay a track round the outside of the flight deck," he tells me, "and every time they spin the wheel we swing round in a wide arc in the opposite direction we think the Zeppelin's turning, and counteract that when they turn the other way."

Roger is the saviour of the universe! The effect is terrific. Add some shudder to the picture and we're sorted.

Out of vision, there's some guys behind the flats representing the sides of the flight deck. They have sticks, which they poke at the cables and ropes hanging down to make them twitch and swing as we stage the wide moves of the ship. It's all detail like that which heightens and adds depth and reality to the scene.

Noel's ecstatic as we reach his final shot for the day: "Start the car! Start the car, man! I'll see you guys Monday!" And, with that, he's gone.

A screen's been erected at the far end of the conference table, with black crosses marked out at four points, all as reference for The Mill to matte on Lumic's animated presentation. The camera's on tracks, and we move across. Don Warrington's on the far side, Shaun passes in the foreground, and we close in on the wheelchair-bound life-support system's occupant, with monitor screens and pressure gauges lining the wall behind him.

Roger Lloyd Pack has arrived on set and, contrary to the press reports, his broken leg's not stopping him from working at all. If anything, the fact that all his screen time's spent seated has made it easier for him.

First thing we did before the cameras started to roll was record a wild track for his propaganda film, so as we play through the beginning of the scene now, pitching his upgrade schemes to the clearly horrified President, the voice-over can play in the background, giving the actors something to react to.

We lens up a wide shot, taking in all three actors, but positioned in such a way so that the detail of Lumic's chair can be seen. I wanted it to look hi-tech but with a strong retro edge, so it's not something that could have been bought in. Ed's team have made it from scratch, complete with functioning air bladders that inflate and wheeze as he breathes.

We focus on Don, with Roger's shoulder in the foreground to the right. Yes, it's out of focus, but that doesn't matter. It still creates a sense of depth. When Don leaves the scene, we move low in on the far doors, revealing a green screen floor to ceiling outside, so gas tanks and interior walkways can be added with CGI to give a sense of scale to the craft.

I still need to build up detail to cut into for the sequence we've been working on. The glass of the table-top offers a reflection of Roger, so we open with a three shot as the President and Pete get up to leave, and hold on what becomes a wide shot as Roger plays out his lines.

"Mr Crane?"

Roger spins his wheelchair round so he's in tight close-up, but hits the camera so the picture visibly shakes.

"Sorry, I came round too fast!"

I'm reading in Colin's lines. We haven't filmed his reaction shots yet, so I've got to stand in. Roger's blinking a lot and shutting his eyes between takes, mainly to stop them smarting when he's performing, as he's trying to have Lumic not blink at any point on screen.

We move low and wide again, looking up towards Roger at a sharp angle 45 degrees from the floor. Lumic's instructing Pete via ear-pod to come to the Zeppelin, in spite of the fact it's Jackie's birthday.

"Roger, can you make the first couple of responses mock-warm to him, disarming him slightly…"

Roger nods, scratching his nose thanks to the lining of the oxygen mask making him itch.

"Yes, yes. Of course."

Onto the last set-up for the day, lining up a wide shot behind the ship's wheel, taking in Lumic's crew as he instructs them to switch the Zeppelin to automatic and leave. The Bosun is dressed in navy-blue military fatigues, while the Captain and his second-in-command wear traditional naval uniforms, very much in keeping with the hint of the 1930s that I asked for right from the beginning.

Take One, Take Two… Both hampered by Roger having difficulty wearing his mask and controlling the wheelchair. By Take Three, we're there. I wonder whether Davros ever had the same problem?

11TH NOVEMBER 2005

There's a PR photo shoot of Rauri Mears in the Cyber-Suit on the flight deck set. This is planned to avoid any press leaks revealing the new design after an incident during Season One, when one of the extras reportedly sold a camera-phone picture of the new Dalek to the press.

David Tennant is away from the main unit and working at Unit Q2 on the TARDIS set, recording scenes for Attack of the Graske, *the interactive game due to be broadcast on Christmas Day.*

Episodes Five and Six – *Filming at Uskmouth Power Station, West Nash Road, Newport – which has a similar chimney to Battersea Power Station.*

This has got to look epic. We've blocked out a huge shot, moving from the entrance of the factory, panning right as a lorry (which is meant to be full of dead bodies heading for a furnace, but that's never really made clear) moves past in the foreground, revealing three Cybermen leading a line of humans towards the main doorway. As they cross the eye-line of the camera, we see Pete and Rose moving through the background shadows, making their way to hide behind a spent cabling wheel.

Clare shouts out last-minute instructions and we go for it, but the trio of Cybermen aren't moving in line, or in sync. Ailsa Berk is choreographing their moves, but it's quickly become clear that the visibility factor with the masks is far worse at night than anyone anticipated.

We go again. Shaun and Billie are both wearing radio mic's, and you can hear him quoting Peter Kay.

"It's the rain that gets you wet…"

"He's coming to do a *Doctor Who*."

Shaun's instantly jealous when Billie says this.

"Why couldn't they have brought Pete back for that one?"

We move in for a tight close-up of them hiding, putting in fake ear-pods, and then move to a wide shot showing them joining the line-up of upgrading candidates to try and infiltrate the factory.

By strategically placing the Cybermen at certain points, it makes it looks as though there are far more than we actually have. As the humans file in, one's tight in the foreground with a line of four others tailing away from him, making sure no one escapes. The logic is that there's another line of Cybermen flanking the opposite side, but with the space the closest one's taking up on screen, we can use the ones he's naturally masking elsewhere in the shot.

The poor guys inside the suits are having a really tough time. They can march up the pantechnicon ramp at the right pace when we shoot them, but between takes, thanks to a combined mix of drizzle and the cold night air, they have to be gently led back down to ground level in case they misplace a foot and slip.

We've got 30, maybe 40 extras charging past three Cybermen at the mouth of the factory, as they run screaming in terror from within. As they clear the shot, the Cybermen are left looking at each other. One shrugs, another rolls his head round and puts his hands up in despair, while the third breaks into a little dance.

We've got to abandon the rest of the night shoot. All storyboarded and recce'd, the majority of the Cyber Factory interiors were due to be recorded here. There was an agreement in place that the station would shut down for six hours to create the sort of disturbance-free atmosphere the crew would need. However, the autumn cold snap has caused massive power demands in the area and, as a result, we've been told there's no shut-down. They just can't afford to do it.

We're going to have to find an alternative site for later in the block. Over to Gareth and Lowri for that one.

12TH NOVEMBER 2005

The Daily Mirror *claims Billie Piper is leaving the series and plot elements of the scripts for Episode 12 and 13 are beginning to leak out to the media. There are rumours of a Dalek/Cyberman war.*

13TH NOVEMBER 2005

Billie Piper quickly responds by issuing a press statement laughing off claims that she's leaving the show.

14TH NOVEMBER 2005

Episodes Five and Six – *Mickey and Jake's infiltration of Lumic's Zeppelin, along with the climactic escape from the Cyber Factory, are filmed on the runway of Veritair Limited at Cardiff Heliport, Cardiff Bay.*

Bit of a geographical cheat going on here.

You're on the roof of Battersea Power Station, which is pretty high up, so what can you see? The London skyline… And, what with all of the action and camera movement we've got planned, it would be a nightmare for The Mill to try and matte in the outlines of any landmarks or buildings.

There's a simple solution – you see nothing. The set-ups take place at night, so you just shroud everything in darkness, but that in itself is another problem. If we're avoiding seeing anything of the capital, then we've got to avoid Cardiff as well.

During their recce for locations, Gareth and Lowri, hit upon the idea of using an airport runway. The nature of the beast dictates that there are no buildings surrounding it, so we've got a clear, untrammelled skyline. We're using Veritair Ltd's landing strip; they operate Cardiff's main helipad, which is right next to the coastline, so at least there'll be plenty of sea air to carry off the smoke from what we've got planned!

Ed's team have built a lengthy section of wall, only about three feet high, with a curved metal ladder leading up and over it. At night, with the actors ducked down and then rising into view as they climb over it, it's easy to believe it's the lip of the factory's roof.

"I almost danced into the flames!"

We're two takes in. Billie's laughing nervously after running past a flame bar as it spewed a sheet of orange up in front of her. The atmosphere is charged, adrenaline's already building up.

She's perfectly safe, all of the actors are. They've rehearsed their moves until they don't have to think about it, the action's become almost mechanical. Stunt Co-Ordinators have checked and double-checked everything's okay, and there's enough fire and ambulance crews on stand-by to tackle any kind of problem.

The location's been dressed with crates, wire cages and even the odd fire extinguisher. There's a low orange glow and smoke guns drift their vapour past the lens.

David, Shaun and Billie grind to a halt for a three-shot after climbing the wall, and stare straight ahead with a mixture of relief and disbelief – Mickey's flying the Zeppelin in to save them. Cameras are moved along and we open the scene wider as a rope ladder comes into the foreground.

"Rose… Get on the ladder!"

"And cut!"

Billie bursts out laughing, still dangling on the second rung.

"I know, I know, I know." David's beating himself up. "I didn't look up once. There's a ladder just hanging there, and I didn't look up! I am such a terrible, terrible actor! Did you look up?"

Shaun shrugs, like it was the most natural thing in the world to do.

"I looked."

Slate 200. All stars and champagne corks scribbled over the clapperboard. Noel and Andrew scramble over the wall. Eyes narrow on their targets; two guards, all white boiler suits and ear-pods, stand flanking either side of some metal disembarkation steps.

Take One. They charge up behind the guards, attack from behind using souped-up smelling salts and watch as they collapse.

"And cut!…"

"Sorry, mate… Are you all right?"

Noel helps up his guard.

"You're ear-pods flew out!"

It happens again and again. As soon as they start to fall, Noel sees them pop onto the tarmac. He turns into the shadows, desperately trying not to laugh.

Take Five. As soon as Noel's arm goes round the guard, his right ear-pod flies out. Noel just about holds it together until he gets half-way up the ladder, then the giggles win through.

Moving on. These things happen. No problem, I can cut round that and make it work.

High and wide, looking down on the wall in the distance, Billie, David and Shaun clamber over and weave through the belching flames. We've got lighting cranes and unit vehicles clearly in shot to the right of the frame, but that will all be wiped out courtesy of The Mill.

David's very interesting in the way he'll come in and approach a scene like this. He generally arrives on set as you're about to rehearse and go through it, to find a shape and visual structure with whoever's involved.

Some actors just stride in and say, "Right, where d'you want me?" He never does that.

The coat's on, the pin stripes and trainers will already be in place, and his hands rub together excitedly. There's a broad grin and a look that says, "Right, what's going on?" Only tonight he's wearing a tuxedo. One or two people are already calling him Dr Bond!

"What I'm after is this, Guv. You've just been and done this, you're about to go there…"

Now, they know all that, but you just have to confirm you're there with them, sparking on the same kind of level and singing from the same song sheet.

"When you did that and turned to him, I asked you to be really aggressive, so when we reach this moment, you're still carrying that anger while you climb over the wall."

Basically, you've got to guide them. One scene does not necessarily shoot directly after another. You might do, say, Scene 16 one day and Scene 17 could be done a week later, or it might have been done three weeks before. It's like you've had that last moment on pause, so it's now your job to remind the actors and bring to the fore what they've just done.

If it's really tricky, building round a special effects shot or something that's similarly complex, you'd offer them playback on a monitor as a precise guide, but that's a luxury.

To be blunt, you've got to make it all tally. That's part of your job. If you don't do that and just leave the actors to get on with it – don't get me wrong, it's not that they won't do it properly – then they may not give it the degree of intensity you want. The levels of hysteria, anxiety, pace and energy… That's something you'll discuss and agree with each other.

'Right, this is what you're doing, Guv. You've got to climb over that wall, run to this post here, hide, hold it there for a moment and check what you're going to do. Over there, you clock the explosions going off on the roof. What are you going to do? I'll cut in to share that, see that moment from your point of view, then you run like clappers!"

I always make sure they understand where the camera set-ups are placed.

"From over there, we've got a big long tracking shot with flame bars going off all the way. We've got bombs, flames and explosions all sounding off in the foreground. There's probably just three, maybe four licks of flame from different bars as you run. Loads of fierce energy, it looks as if you're right in the thick of some enormous fire. You've got one option, no alternative, you know you've got to get through it in order to reach the Zeppelin."

What I'm doing is effectively channelling emotions, trying to help develop how he'll externalise them and making sure they fire off in the right directions.

Now, David and Billie, they know that they've got to bring something to the characters during the scene, find a specific reaction for that particular moment, and, I promise you, I don't doubt that they'll both have thought it through.

They'll have gone through the motions of finding what they think the scene's about, but what they don't have is a sense of the location. Neither of them has ever been here before. Sure, as I said, they could go down the "Right, where d'you want me?" route – but that's just not the way they tick.

"We've got steps coming over a wall, leading to this area, which is a tiny section of what will be the parapet of the power station…"

I walk them through it, describe all the action, and all the time they're piecing it together mentally, visualising the scene, whether it works for them and if they can clearly see the mechanics of how to play it. All the actors, David, Billie and Sean, they've all taken it on board, they know the positions they have to be in, they know how fast they've got to tell the beat of the story.

Back to the ladder. David and Billie cling on, held with harnesses and wires rigged via the crane that's supporting them, shouting their dialogue against the noise of the wind machine that's blasting them with air. The camera moves in close, swinging round and moving in the opposite direction to the one they're twisting in, creating real visual tension. Lots of short, sharp shots. Hands clinging, feet balancing. Continual buffeting. We focus on Shaun as a 'stunt' Sonic Screwdriver is dropped to him, as he uses it to cut through the rope, and for the final takes we cover the reason why.

Paul Kasey's wearing the upper half of the Cyber Commander's costume, as he grasps the ladder's lower rung and slowly starts to haul himself up. He needs his footwork to be absolutely accurate, as he's having to be very precise about where his face is going to be – framed between the rungs of the ladder – so sparing him the costume's legs has given him as much physicality and freedom as possible.

This is framed as loose as I dare without seeing the bottom half of him. Initially it's difficult for him to see where to aim his hands for the ladder, but by holding it at the base and only letting it go as he moves into shot, he's quickly figured out a mark to swing his gloves at.

Sunrise is in 20 minutes, we've got to crack on, but nobody seems to comment on the fact we've just wrapped a sequence with a Cyberman wearing jeans!

Clare's let me know the stunt doubles are in place; James O'Dee, Derek Lea and Shelley Benison are wearing duplicate costumes for the Doctor, Rose and Pete, and they're wired safely into the ladder positions we established earlier on.

I want to get some clear long shots of the ladder flailing around as the Zeppelin moves off, just after the Cyber Commander's fallen to his death. The crane supporting it slowly turns and, with the wind machines on full blast, it looks spectacular as they drift out of view.

"And cut!"

It's been a long night. And expensive! The fire effects, the ladder work, it all costs.

Of course, Phil Collinson's probably been worrying that everything will get done on schedule, quietly watching as each explosion carves another slice off the budget, but he's never let it show. He's been there right the way through, supporting everything and only tactfully questioning decisions that he really thinks will cause a delay. And if he can see it's for the good of the programme, he'll fight as hard as everyone else to make it work.

You can't ask for much more than that, can you?

One final thought occurs as I'm heading home: thank God it didn't snow!

15TH NOVEMBER 2005

Episodes Five and Six – *Ely Papermill, Sanatorium Road, Cardiff; sequences are filmed for the escape from inside the Cyber Factory. And tragic news is heard during a scene on Bridge Street, which is also completed on Papermill Road.*

Noel's framed through the shattered windows of a burnt-out car as he heads towards a curfew checkpoint, staffed by soldiers.

"Just let this pass for a minute… Sounds like we're at the seaside!"

The air's suddenly think with seagulls, making an incredible racket that drowns out Noel for one of the takes. This is a simple scene, but we still need to frame one shot low and wide, clearing space over the railway bridge the gate's under to matte in a Zeppelin overhead. No Dave Houghton on set, but the silver and grey spheres still get their own takes for lighting references.

Flame bars line the ground at strategic points, and smoke's being pumped across them before each shot. The paper mill's been used before – last year, on the very first episode, *Rose* – so a lot of the crew are more than familiar with working around the site.

The Doctor, Rose and Pete charge into shot, trying to find a way out. The Cyber Factory's burning down around them, and whenever they look through a doorway, there's Cybermen everywhere. Only one option – the roof.

We lens up looking through the gap between steps on a metal gantry, trying to find a way into the sequence, but simply looking down the smoky corridor, with overhead lights casting shadows through some pipes as David, Shaun and Billie race towards camera, looks far more atmospheric.

"And action!"

The stairway leading to the roof, in terms of the story, is drenched with mist, heavily lit with deep red gels and a hint of blue, which turns the upper layers purple. It looks like they're escaping from the depths of hell.

Billie sprints up them first, followed by David and then Shaun. As they hit the mark so they're safely out of danger, the special effects team make a massive ball of flame erupt, billowing up through the steps.

Everybody's stunned by how good it looks.

Just one more short scene before we wrap for the night. The camera's set up on a side street by the paper mill. Andrew joins the group as Jake discovers that Ricky's been killed. It's an intense moment, and Andrew plays it brilliantly.

It's built up with a crane shot moving down towards the group as Jake runs to join the Doctor, Rose and Pete, then we work through two-shots and tight close-ups. Everyone's reacting, Billie's playing it slightly tearfully, but David has to calmly close down the high emotions and make them realise there'll be time to mourn later.

It takes a little over an hour and a half to complete, then everyone disappears into the night for some sleep.

16TH NOVEMBER 2005

Episodes Five and Six – *The previously 'rained off' Riverside sequences from the early part of Episode Five and the closing moments of Episode Six are finally completed at the Riverside Theatre in Newport.*

Episodes 12 and 13 – *Filming takes place on the front entrance steps of Tredegar House and Park, Newport for the brief sequence featuring TV psychic Derek Acorah. Final shots of the day are at the Unit Q2 studio for the Police Chief's briefing room scenes.*

"Two Three Two... Take One... Stand by then... And action!"
It's the first shot of the day, a tight close-up on Billie. We've got to complete this little scene, this moment that really triggers off the drive behind Rose's personal story for these episodes.

It's going to be really interesting, because I was originally meant to finish it in London, during the very first day. It was all planned out, the recce done and dusted, approved, rubber-stamped and green-lit, all just a short distance further down the river from where we were based outside Lambeth Palace. But we just couldn't do it in time.

Phil Collinson was reassurance itself. "Never mind, Graeme. Don't worry about it. We've done well and had problems with the failing light and weather. Right, look, we'll find an embankment somewhere in Newport, or maybe even in Cardiff. We'll go take a look and see if we can make it look as though it could double up for what you wanted."

But how are we going to do something which is meant to show the spot 150 yards further down the embankment, just across from where the Houses of Parliament are? From the outset, I knew I'd be a fool if I didn't frame them in the background during those opening moments for *Rise of the Cybermen*, but now I've really got a problem – how the hell can we make it all match up?

I didn't think about it much, I didn't have time to, until Lowri Thomas had to go off and find a substitute. She scoured all the riverside areas in Cardiff, Newport and I guess Port Talbot, but there was a clear vibe coming from the production office that they'd be much happier if it could be found somewhere close to base.

Bingo! The Riverside Theatre in Newport – a really modern arts centre and, as the name says, it's right by the water. This is good because there are so many modern buildings by the River Thames, thanks to the huge post-Second World War refurbishment. It's just what we need.

Thank you very much, we're sorted!

On one of my days off, the recce showed that it's got a fairly sizable towpath and good access for parking all the unit vehicles, which isn't normally something I'd have to think about, but we've got to set up pretty quick and move on to another location before dawn. No time to cope with miles of traffic queues, and, if there are problems, all our backup equipment is very close at hand, so that's great. We lost most of our first day here thanks to rain, now we're back, literally picking up where we left off.

Everything's being rigged up, we're nearly ready. Time to look at the geography. If you face one way, there's a bridge that's clearly not on the Thames, and it's the same if you look in the opposite direction... But that's the old city of Newport further along the banks. If I lock off the shots focusing in that direction and hold the frame wide, then we can matte in some CGI Zeppelins and put St Paul's Cathedral in the distance. That could work, but how am I going to do cross shooting – varying the shots on the Doctor, Rose and Mickey, while they stand together talking – and still not give away that we're not in London?

Okay, we'll use close shots to get them all in together, then top shots and crane shots to show the water, so we know we're still by the river.

The theatre that's just behind them, all glass plates and a steel framework, could easily pass for something along the Thames Embankment. Tight three shots on the bench with that as a backdrop. We've got an argument between the characters; Rose is all fired up, agitated and forcing the issue about finding this parallel world's version of her Dad. The Doctor's not happy and can't get through to her about the dangers.

Now, Mickey's clocked the fact that if Pete's still around, then so's his Gran, who died in an accident tripping over some loose carpet on the stairs in her house. He's also got wind of the fact that he's – how do you put it? – more tolerated than embraced as part of the TARDIS crew. So he's off as well, and the Doctor's caught right in the middle. Who's he going to follow?

Right, a lot of this requires background, so we've lensed up and taken the camera as far back as possible to get the size of shots I want – plenty of close-ups and medium close-ups.

By doing this, the backgrounds are completely blurred and the point of focus is on the actors, so we don't know where we are but you do get to see hints of movement. A bit of water maybe, sparkling and rippling, people in the distance, that sort of thing. The story's already told you we're in London, the shots immediately prior to these will show you we're there, so by shooting like this and cutting it in, we should get away with it.

We'll use a big wide angle at the start, bringing Rose into play, and then a fairly high angled shot when we see the Doctor and Mickey coming in. I'll do the same tonight when Andrew and Shaun arrive to stage the big farewells and departures.

We'll carefully put the TARDIS in place so that you can believe it's where it was in daylight, and that Lambeth Palace is out of shot to the left. I think there's only one two-shot of Rose and Pete with Parliament behind them in the can, so we'll cut in for all the close-ups and reverses on them as soon as it's dark. Same for Pete when he runs off. In a few short paces, he'll have gone from London to Wales. Now, that's what I call fast!

"Was that loud enough for you? Or am I being too loud?"

We've got Derek Acorah for about an hour. The unit's at the rather ornate Tredegar House, the lights are out inside and the stone pillars flanking the main entrance are austere, cold and very grey in this light. It's kind of spooky, so he must feel right at home!

I only need two brief sequences, shot so they look similar to the style of his *Most Haunted* series. It'll only be there for a few seconds on screen, just showing him protesting how he's been put out of business, now that so many ghosts have turned up.

We've got some of the Cybermen, out of their normal armour, playing the camera crew bustling around him, and I've come up with an idea that'll probably never make it on screen.

Why don't we have him charge past us, ranting, so you see the full crew standing there looking bewildered as he heads off into the night? Rather than just a few camcorders right in his face, opening it up like that will give it a bigger impact. We'll play his crew.

No harm in trying!

Take One. He's worried that he's shouting too much, but it's fine. I get up right in shot, earphones on and next to the monitors, shrugging and stunned as he goes. Non's right next to me.

Take Two. He hits it perfectly, with just the right sense of bravado. The crew play up the shock, all looking at each other in disbelief. In my heart, I know it won't get used, but it's been fun.

A simple set's been put up at Unit Q2 for the police chief's TV statements, trying to reassure the public. We just need two quick moments, one all spin-doctored calmness, the other utter panic as the Cybermen invade all around him. David Warwick's playing the role, and we manage to wrap in something like half an hour. Not a complex scene to set up in any way, and a very easy sequence to end the day with.

17TH NOVEMBER 2005

Episodes Five and Six – *St Nicholas, near Cardiff. This is the location for the Tyler mansion. It's a large private house, which was only found two weeks prior to the start of filming there. The first few scenes for Pete and Jackie are shot, along with night shots of the Cybermen arriving.*

Château Pete.

We're lensed up and low and wide as his car glides into view. Out steps Shaun Dingwall. This is *Doctor Who* does *The Thomas Crown Affair*. Check the cuffs, he knows he looks cool. Survey the Tyler domain at a glance, he knows he's loaded and liking it.

It's about 9.00 am, and already the sun is beginning to bleach out the paintwork on the front of the house. There's a slight hint of California about this kind of opulent wealth.

Into the house.

The main hallway. All polished and autumnal brown, a large wooden stairway lies straight ahead, branching up and splitting to the left and right to reach the next landing.

Jackie's lair. Servants rush around arranging celebratory flowers for all they're worth. Camille makes her grand entrance, very Gloria Swanson, in silk and spitting venom at Pete. She's really bringing depth and humanity to this character.

Take Two. Camille's cruel micky-take of Pete's 'Trust me on this!' catchphrase sets Shaun off. His shoulders are heaving.

"Cut!"

"You really set me off there!"

Camille's given him the giggles. Dangerous territory, and sometimes a place that's impossible to find your way back from.

The crew are hidden away in rooms flanking the hallway. The monitors are with me to the left; lighting, costume and make-up to the right. Space is tight. So's the time. Moving on…

Into the main room, which will soon play host to the presidential banquet. Jackie's irate – Pete's got a banner saying she's 40, but the official biographies knocked a year off. Beneath the chintz beats the heart of a 39-year-old, or else.

'My official biography says my birthday was born on the… Bugger!'

Camille gets tongue-tied. She hits it perfectly with the next take. Time for another 'parallel' character to make her debut.

We've set up on the right tier of the main staircase, so the camera can move down and focus on Jackie's pet, a small Yorkshire terrier – Rose.

Her trainer patiently moves up and down the stairs, waving a biscuit in his hand as he traces out the route she's got to follow. And you know what? Wide shot, mid-shot and close-ups, that little dog hits its mark every time. Everyone gathers round, petting the dog and congratulating the trainer as he goes to leave, but one voice pipes up and darkens the tone of the past few set-ups.

"Does the dog get turned into a Cyberman as well?"

Darkness. There's a lot of misty breath. It's freezing cold again. We're right on the far side of the estate, by one of the main gateways leading into the grounds. We've lensed up, holding tight on the back of the pantechnicon, which is positioned to the right of the frame while Noel and Andrew hide behind some bushes in the background.

I just need some shots of the ramp being lowered to the ground by Lumic's technicians, and then we can move the camera down to ground level. This is so we just get to see their boots as the Cybermen march out in perfect unison, hitting the ground hard, swarming out towards the Tyler house.

"I'll cue in the boys to start marching."

I watch the monitor intently and shout out the command. Instantly, I can see the shot's going to work. It's exactly what I wanted... But it's a slightly strange sight. The Cybermen just have the lower halves of their costumes on, with body warmers and balaclavas protecting the actors' chests and heads against the frost.

We move in tighter on Ricky and Jake staring in disbelief, with more Cybermen moving past, completely out of focus in the foreground. This kind of thing adds a sense of movement to even the most static, locked-off shot.

David and Billie had to leave before any of this started. They're turning on the Christmas lights in Cardiff tonight, and they're predicting thousands of people will turn up... I wonder if they've got any idea what they've let themselves in for?

18TH NOVEMBER 2005

Episodes Five and Six – *Filming at the house continues with scenes in the bedroom and downstairs interior hallway.*

"Freeze!"

Camille lowers her face-powder brush and stares into her dressing table mirror.

"Lock off... and activate."

She holds the look, motionless. I let the seconds tick by, so I know there's enough material there for The Mill. Metal arms will be added with CGI, sliding out of her ear-pods and forming a square frame over her head – just a hint of Cyber-design.

"And deactivate... cue the dialogue."

She breathes out, regains her senses and starts applying make-up again.

Clare reads in Lumic's line that plays over this.

"Thank you, Mrs Tyler."

Take Two.

"Could you make it a slightly bigger reaction, Camille, when you come out of the trance?"

As the ear-pods come alive, she drops the brush with a thud, and almost seems to have half-heard Lumic when she comes round, but quickly dismisses it and carries on. I'm not quite happy with the way the brush fell, so we go again, and again, and again... Sometimes it refuses to drop out of her hand when she freezes, then it bounces out of reach, lands on her lap and then just hangs in her fingers limply.

Take Eight nails it.

"At last... That thing must have an agent, the way it was performing!"

Camille's glad it's over as she heads off to have the full ear-pod structure fitted. Dave Houghton quickly steps in, armed with his ever-present silver and grey spheres, holding them level with Jackie's head position as the camera rolls.

"You could do your make-up while you're there, Dave."

The crew are merciless.

"Yeah, and get it right this time!"

The grey sphere shakes as he holds it up and starts to laugh.

Camille returns. We lens up a reverse shot facing her, sharing the mirror's point of view, only now she has the square pod-arms in place. She freezes as we roll.

"And cut... Ear-pods out."

"Let's just have five seconds on Camille holding that pose and then go..."

We've got it, but Camille's worried.

"Did I blink? I'm sure I blinked when I wasn't meant to."

"Paul, I'll tell you when to move, if I may. So hold when you hear action until I say 'now'."

There's a muffled 'okay' from inside the Cyber-suit.

We've been framing low, looking up on a wide angle as a Cyberman marches down the corridor towards camera. The trick with this shot is to add height and breadth that's not necessarily there. As a result, it looks immense.

An idea's struck me about getting a sudden reaction shot, with the Cyberman turning directly into shot. We've gone for a tight close-up from the start position of the scene, so when Paul Kasey swings round, the skull-like faceplate is right in the lens.

It works a treat. Moving on…

We're blocking out cutaways during the massacre of the guests at Jackie's party. The pace has got to move fast.

"Stand by then…"

A Cyberman standing in the background slowly rotates his neck and flexes his shoulders.

"And action!"

In the foreground, one of the guests holds his position facing a Cyberman, whose hands are on his shoulders. Right on cue, he screams as electricity surges through him and falls as Camille rounds the corner. She stands terrified, framed just underneath an archway as half a dozen extras run past behind her screaming.

"Now!"

Her cue's fed in so she doubles back and runs out of shot. The Cyberman in the foreground swings towards her and lumbers away in pursuit. On every take, Camille's screams as she runs off get increasingly loud, more hysterical and funnier.

She's playing to a captive audience… Namely us!

This is going to be tricky. A two-and-a-half minute steadicam shot moving right around the lower floor of the house. If we do it in a series of carefully choreographed moves, it'll work.

Move One. We hold on the kitchen doorway as waiters come through carrying canapés and champagne. There are two familiar faces! The Doctor and Rose in disguise, carrying trays. In they come to the main hallway and head past the stairs, passing through into a pink-walled lounge. And hold it there…

A quick dialogue exchange between them, while guests help themselves to the contents of their platter and glasses, gives the camera operator time to move round 180 degrees to their opposite side… And we're off.

Move Two. Out of the pink room and into a green dining room. We hold again. More dialogue…

Move Three. And they move on, circling round the President and his aides… Don Warrington's ad-libbing a discussion about various food crises in Europe…

And then they hold for a beat as Shaun is cued in on the stairs.

"Excuse me… If I could have your attention, please?"

Out they go through another door, and we swing round to focus on Pete as he introduces Jackie to the party crowd. A little thinly veiled bitchy banter later, and they head into the green room hand in hand… And we hold on the Doctor and Rose again.

That's the theory, anyway.

"Loads of pace and energy! You're having a laugh, enjoying the party!"

Take One… More of a run-through than anything else, but it works…
Take Two… There's a small collision with a retreating cameraman and a table, followed by language not suitable for broadcast… Take Three… It all begins to take shape and work.

To beef up the sequence, I'll get some shots to cut into, but the actual flow works brilliantly. Movie-style moves on a TV budget, he says modestly… And while we're doing this, we should probably pause for a second and raise a glass to David. While the party's moving through multiple takes, he's making his debut as the Doctor tonight with the *Children In Need* mini-episode. No turning back now!

21st NOVEMBER 2005

Episodes 12 and 13 – *Scenes around Rose's dream for the closing sequence of* Doomsday *are recorded at the Tyler House location. The second unit records the 'Ectoshine' advert in the kitchen.*

Episodes Five and Six – *The second unit records scenes of David Tennant at the computer screen in Pete Tyler's study. Work is also under way filming the Cybermen's approach to the house in the main front garden.*

Slate 300. Out come the streamers and champagne bottles on the clapperboard again, but the scene's hardly the right atmosphere for a party.

With light mainly being drawn from the flames in the fireplace, Billie's held in a close-up as she tries to relate the dream she's had to her family. She ad-libs most of her dialogue, because there'll eventually be a voice-over for this, and the others need something to react to.

Two-shots and close-ups moving round Shaun, Camille and Noel should give me enough material, before moving to what's been dressed as Rose's bedroom.

"Cue One."

Billie's eyes flick open as I speak.

"Cue Two."

She sits up, trying to catch her breath as she realises what's happening. It's exactly what I want. Some of the last shots on tonight's schedule involve the Tylers leaving the house in a Land Rover, setting off to help Rose find the Doctor.

Sure, these are all tiny moments, but vital to building up the ultimately heartbreaking closure she has to come to terms with.

While Camille and Billie go to make-up and wardrobe to change for their next set-ups, I've got to move on to work with the second unit and shoot David finding a computer in a side-room, where the Doctor sees Lumic's 'upgrading' promo film and quickly starts to realise what's happening.

"I think, David, what you're seeing for the first five seconds is this electronic wire-frame head, and all sorts of diagrams dissecting and analysing the human brain, and then we get to the promo."

"Okay."

Take One. The look slowly dawns on him…

"And Cut! That's what we need! One more…"

I'm not too happy with the animation. It looks very square-jawed, a bit too 'Health And Safety' public information films from the 1950s. I'm sure it can be changed.

Take Two.

"Cybus… Cybus!"

David spins round and crashes straight into the door, as his hand slips and it fails to open.

"Oh, now that's gotta hurt!"

Two costume changes later, and we're back to Jackie's party, with Rose following her outside onto the terrace and trying to chat to her a bit too informally.

"This dress has gone down a treat with the cold, let me tell you!"

Billie's finding that her maid's uniform isn't that protective against the icy air outside. As she sits next to Camille on an iron bench, we move to a two-shot and Jackie storms off.

On come the lights. What's that ahead? Shapes moving in the darkness? Time for the Cybermen to invade…

22ND NOVEMBER 2005

Episodes Five and Six – *Scenes of the Cybermen smashing through windows and storming the Tyler house's main dining room are staged as work goes on at St Nicholas, near Cardiff.*

"Okay… Party, party everyone!"
Jackie Tyler's party is informal and the height of style. Suited and booted support artists mingle, cocktail glasses glinting and lukewarm canapés clutched in hands, all adding to the reception's atmosphere.

Clare's cued them in. I shout one more instruction.

"Lots of chatter, please."

Cameras roll. David pushes his way through the social elite towards the window, face fixed in horror. As ever, you can hear him running on the spot just before the take, energising himself and channelling absolute focus on his performance.

Take One.

The Doctor's glasses are whisked off as he enters. Way, way too Clark Kent.

Take Two. He veers off the wrong way and gets caught up in the crowd.

"David, can you give me a pointed look… You know what's coming, you've just got to confirm that it's real and see it for yourself."

Take Three's exactly what I need. The point he's hit is marked so he can pick up his moves from there for the next set-up. Moving on…

Billie comes out of the kitchen with two glasses of wine on a tray, balanced at shoulder height. She moves into the main room, and as David sees her, holding the position for the 'look' I just asked for, that's his cue to move in and join her by the window.

"And action!"

The Doctor and Rose peer through the glass. Two problems with this;

Billie's tray is hitting the window as she leans forward, and the B-Camera focus puller is clearly in shot, peering through from outside.

"What shall I do with this?"

Billie's finding it awkward to get rid of the tray smoothly without looking too obvious. I move in to try and find a practical solution for her. There's a small table nearby.

"Just put it down there as you move in to join the Doc."

Roger Pearce is at the glass, mouthing loudly to the rather confused face outside.

"Turn your focus…"

"What?"

He mimes using the control that's being held on the opposite side of the glass. The signal from it is affecting the A-Camera.

"Your focusing my camera!"

It's decided that it's a more fluid movement for Billie to dump the tray before she comes into the room, so this runs on the third take and then…

"Bang!"

I shout out to signal the fact that the Cybermen have suddenly started smashing through the windows.

"And cut!"

We're going to go for another take.

"It's happening again… It's happening again… It's happening again…"

David's trying out different inflections on his line for the moment he sees the Cybermen outside.

"Stand by… Err, Graeme, you're in shot for the second camera."

I'll be gone before Clare says "Action!" Fourth time lucky, they meet at the window and duck right on cue as I shout out… We've got it.

Paul Kasey's now fully Cyber-suited and, along with one other Cyberman, we've lined them up for a relatively simple shot, as they march into the main party area through a doorway. Rose charges forward and skids to a halt, practically face to face with them, before being dragged out of shot by the Doctor.

There's a hollow thud as she crashes into Paul's chest plate. Let's cut there and try again. This time she's actually knocked him backwards slightly, and the Cybermen clatter together like skittles.

Slightly strange to see them muttering to each other as we reset.

You can almost imagine them bitching about how that would never happen with upgrading!

There's just one chance. One solitary take to get this right.

Two of the windows leading into the main dining room have been replaced with framed sugar glass, the theory being that they'll explode safely and spectacularly as we stage shots of Cybermen smashing through them.

Take One, Window One…

We lens up slightly to the right of the window. James O'Dee's in the Cyber-suit, and as he swings his right arm up at 45 degrees, the upper half of the glass explodes. The rest is demolished as he marches through into the house.

David's filming with his camcorder, everyone's standing a safe distance away watching, and there's a huge round of applause as I shout "Cut!"

Take Two, Window Two… Paul Kennington's playing the second Cyberman. The camera's low and wide, looking up at the window directly in front of the glass.

"And action!"

This time, two fists swing forward in unison. Shards fly everywhere, and the Cyberman kicks forward with his left leg as he marches in. More applause. The *Doctor Who Confidential* crew walk into view as I call cut, cameras on shoulders, as they're filming the action from outside.

Now I need a side angle. I want three Cybermen to step in with precisely the same movement, and arrive in a line blocking any route of escape for the party guests.

"Plenty of energy. This is pure terror, you know you're dead if you move past them!"

Roger holds on an angle at head height, so that to the left we catch sight of people backing away in fear, but the shot favours the Cybermen on the right, in the same move as before, only now we have face-plates moving away in a line-up from tight in the foreground to the wall in the distance.

"And cut! Well done, guys. Brilliant! Absolutely brilliant!"

Time to organise the chaos. Every guest, every waiter, every official and presidential aide is herded into the centre of the dining room by every occupied cyber-costume we've got. Space is at a premium.

First things first. General party chatter.

"Bang!"

On my cue, they spin round, Don Warrington in the foreground, watching in confusion.

"Cybermen!"

Another cue for screams and panic. There's no escape, but the President straightens himself up to face the enemy. My note to Don is to remember quiet dignity, presence and authority through all of this.

Nick Briggs is off camera reading in Cyber-lines and John Lumic's dialogue. We'll deal with getting Roger Lloyd Pack's voice track for this scene in post-production.

"What happens then?"

The President's facing the inevitable as he asks one final question, and the Cyberman gives the predictable answer.

"You will be deleted…"

But as the Cyberman clutches his shoulder, Don breaks into a broad grin.

"Oh, I'm sorry…"

He's forgotten it's the moment he's meant to die.

"Cut!"

Another take goes west as his left ear-pod flies out at a crucial moment, but, by building it up shot by shot, we get there…

The Cybermen have formed a ring around the guests, and start killing them with deadly efficiency. We've blocked this out so the camera slowly moves across the slaughter, catching sight of Pete shouting for Jackie, and following the Doctor and Rose as they break through the crowd and head out of the closest window.

The first take's not got enough energy, so we go again, only this time it's quite the reverse. The party guests are screaming like mad and charging around so much that David and Billie get caught up in the throng, and start laughing like mad as they realise there's just no way to get out of it.

"Cut! Cut, cut, cut!"

I move in to check they're all right. Everything's fine, but even the Cybermen got slightly winded by that one.

One final shot… The Doctor and Rose land outside, charge off in one direction, but run straight into a line of Cybermen rapidly closing in. As they race off, Pete emerges through another window and Rose shouts out for him to follow.

The extras have been instructed to run around inside, still keeping up the pretence of trying to escape, although they're actually more than safe. We've got all of the Cybermen outside in the line-up, so the only threat they're facing is if they collide with each other.

Ailsa Berk has worked out a formation for them to move in, running through the moves while the cameras were being set up in the gardens. Hopefully, they'll get the mechanical precision we're after and there won't be any replays of the collisions that happened last night.

Three takes in and we've got the shots I wanted. The Cybermen have marched right up to the wall of the house, and as they hear "Cut!" one or two start to jump up and down on the spot, rattling loudly as they try to get warm.

It's not really a sight the viewing public are ready for yet.

23RD NOVEMBER 2005

Episodes Five and Six – *Still filming around the house, the second unit cover Cybermen killing guests and Jackie's attempt to hide in the cellar. The main unit shoots outside with the Cybermen marching towards the house.*

"That one had the edge. We'll have some of that!"
Camille's on the run from the Cybermen as they start killing everything with a pulse in Jackie's house. Her only retreat is a cellar. I want a sense of absolute terror from her on this.

With the lights down to a bare minimum, I've asked for the camera to follow her as she races down the stairs, pauses for breath leaning against a wall, spots a cupboard to hide in and then dives for it as we swing back to the stairs.

We've got one of the Cyber-extras just wearing the lower half of the costume, so he can see to find his footing as he follows her into the darkness. Just a tight close-up on her as Jackie peers round the door where's she's taking cover, and then we move on to her being followed by the two Cybermen back to ground level, as she finally becomes possessed by the ear-pod signal.

There's a thin layer of frost on the ground outside, and everyone's wrapped up in several layers of thermals, apart from David, Shaun and Billie, who's probably quietly cursing whoever green-lit the decision to make her maid's outfit so short.

Got to build up the energy for this sequence...

The three of them charge round the corner of the house, straight into our full quota of Cybermen, marching in two lines of five. Take after take, as they swing round and move towards camera, their formation starts to break up.

They just can't judge their sense of direction because the visibility's so poor inside the masks. It's like trying to see out of two pinpricks. Alisha keeps trying to find ways to make it work, but it's near impossible. All I need is enough material to cut round it, and we should be all right. Moving on...

The pantechnicon's lights are full on, silhouettes armed with machine-guns run to help, but while Jake concentres on trying to shoot the enemy, Ricky's far from interested in Rose's delight at seeing who she thinks is Mickey again.

We lens up wide on the group and block the sequence so that, when Billie hugs Noel, they're grouped to the left of the frame. Now I'm happy that we've got that shot, Noel's double has to step in and hold Ricky's position, so we can get Mickey running in to stand by David on the right. The Cybermen start marching into the background of the shot, and the Doctor lunges towards Jake to try and stop him firing.

"Stop shooting! Now!"

"And cut!"

Billie starts telling Andrew off as well.

"You bad boy!"

We focus on Andrew as he opens fire, with the image fed back on the monitor screens as a mid-shot. The sudden gunfire makes both Noel and Billie jump.

"I forgot that that was coming!"

Billie's leaning against him regaining her breath.

On comes the green screen. First we need Rose looking towards Ricky, and then turning as Mickey runs to her side, so just Billie then Noel. To complete the effect, we just need Noel in full Ricky mode, with Shaun standing behind him with a natural background, which in this case is slightly misty darkness.

Phil's practically completed shooting some second unit material with Cybermen murdering half a dozen or so party guests. It's now nearing dawn, and we've got to finish. We go through staging the final set-up for the night, as David confronts the lead Cyberman.

Tight close-ups on David shouting that they're surrendering.

"Lots of urgency! You know you're dead if they don't go with this!"

We go for one long take that runs from the cliffhanger straight into the resolution from *Age of Steel*, with David blasting the circle of encroaching Cybermen with energy from the TARDIS energy cell.

"And cut!"

Just like a cowboy, David blows the end of the cell like the barrel of a revolver, and smirks as he mimes reholstering it.

24TH NOVEMBER 2005

Episodes Five and Six – *Work starts back at the airstrip, and the crew return to St Nicolas to resume work on incomplete scenes from last night.*

Back to the airstrip. The President's entourage arrive to meet Lumic's Zeppelin, and this is where we establish ties between him and Pete.

The air's icy, but the sky's clear. No overcast clouds or anything, but the natural light still has a slightly grey look. As the cameras are being set up, a helicopter with its landing lights full on starts to head towards us, slowly coming in to land. Roger's able to lens up on it and we grab some footage of its outline as it comes into focus, just in case we need it later on.

Don Warrington climbs out of the Range Rover as it stops, and strides across to Shaun. I want there to be a kind of cordial friendship here, but an unspoken joint wariness of Lumic.

The skyline's clear ahead, and we shoot low and wide, leaving about three quarters of the frame empty for The Mill to add the Zeppelin landing. The only part of it we'll see are the metal steps leading up to the entry hatch, which we position to the right of camera as the President and Pete move to go on board.

We were due to go to the Victoria Park Playground for part of the day and work on scenes where the Doctor's party find a lone Cyberman, which they manage to disconnect. The human memory within kicks in and returns as it dies, and the crunch was that we reveal it's actually a young girl called Kerry who's been Cybernised. However, the priority is to try and complete the scenes we started late last night, and build up more shots for the cliffhanger of *Rise of the*

Cybermen. So we're heading back to the Tyler estate. I don't think the scenes will be lost for keeps, though… Russell's saying he can rework the material for the Doctor and Mrs Moore, so she gets extra screen time. Helen's performance so far has gone down really well, and they're keen to see more if it can be worked into the schedule.

Clare's rushing backwards and forwards, trying to make sure everything's ready. We're set up in the same positions as last night, picking up shots on the Cybermen as they circle round and close in on David and the gang.

My dream shot would involve overhead crane work, building up shots of Cybermen that could be composited together, so it looks as though there's about 50 moving in towards the Doctor. Looks like that's going to stay as wishful thinking – there's just no time. I'm going to have to build up the idea that there are far more than just ten by showing line after line moving around the group, and then use tight close-ups on the dialogue shots.

It's a strange sight – Cybermen heading to block out the sequence with blankets over their shoulders. Not sure whether I'm imagining it, but that could be rattling from them shivering.

"And action!"

There's some frost on the ground, but we plough on.

"We've got snow!"

Phil's by my side. What can we do? We wait for it to clear. It's just light, and it probably won't settle.

Twenty minutes have gone. The snowfall's moving in thick and fast. You can't see that far ahead, the air's full of it. The crew have retreated, the actors are sheltering in one of the vans.

The only option's to keep waiting, just in case.

An hour's passed. It's stopped, but the ground's white. Brushes and rakes are being used to try and uncover the grass for a specific area we were working around, so hopefully there'll be no snow in shot.

We start rolling again. David in close-up, his breath thick with mist from the cold. Other days, he'd be chewing ice cubes or eating ice cream between takes to try and bring the temperature of his mouth on an even keel with the air, but there's no time. We just crack on.

That sequence wraps. There's just the escape in the Preachers' van to stage.

The script has them dodging Cybermen as they speed for the main gates, but the snow's made that impossible.

We can just about get away with framing on the van and moving around it fast, just to add some energy to the getaway. Thankfully, we're back in the studio tomorrow, so no more snow!

25TH NOVEMBER 2005

Episodes Five and Six – *Cyber Factory Control Centre scenes are filmed at Unit G12, Bridge Road, Trefforest.*

Technicians line the studio floor, drilling and fixing scenery securely, rigging lights and frosting the atmosphere with blue gels, checking that there's room to swing in the boom mic and that doors, switches and buttons all operate smoothly. By the computer banks lining the wall, three Cybermen, already fully costumed, shake their limbs trying to warm up; one even dances on the spot clunking loudly.

This is going to be a meeting of great minds. The Doctor meets John Lumic, or rather what's left of him. He's been upgraded to the rank of Cyber Controller and, although Paul Kasey's wearing the costume, we'll get Roger to dub the lines in later. For the moment, Nick Briggs is doubling for him vocally and playing the Cyber voices.

As the recording moves on, I realise that I've learnt a lot about David Tennant and the kind of actor he is from this scene. It's practically a monologue, three pages of dialogue aimed straight at the Controller while the Doctor moves right around the room, also feeding information to Mickey, who's watching it all on CCTV from the Zeppelin.

When we start to rehearse this scene, I say to David, "Look, I've got two cameras to play with, you've got three pages of dialogue, and I'd really love to see if we can do it all in one go. I'd rather not break it up but, if you want me to, I'm very happy to do just that. So you'll have to lead the pace of the page, but I imagine you'll wander around and use the whole room, so what I'd like you to do is fix specific points to aim for during rehearsals, so we know you'll be in certain places for certain things. Now, if and only if you're happy and it works for you, then I'll discuss shots with the camera operator, and we'll cover the way we think it will cut together beautifully."

David's really open and says, "Okay, let's have a go and do the whole thing." And that's exactly what we do. And David's word-perfect every time.

Working with Roger, we've come up with three camera positions: a high angle looking down on the whole set, which was meant to be Mickey's point of view via the security camera; then one facing the main controls, so we could favour David, Billie and Shaun in mid-shots and close-ups, and then a reverse on that to cover the alcove that the Cyber Controller's throne emerges from.

David's performance is extraordinary, word- and position-perfect and playing progressively better with each take, always giving us something else, adding and making his performance grow. I think that he's really learnt, over the years, that as a young actor coming up through the ranks one of the most important tools he's got is his ability to learn lines and learn them remarkably fast. You could turn to him and say (although I wouldn't want to try this too often), "Listen David, can we bring a scene forward from tomorrow?" Now, he may not have learnt it, but if you warn him – say over a lunch break of one hour if it was two pages long – I reckon he would get that done, so you could have a shoot at five o'clock in the evening and still pick up another two hours' work with him. His utter professionalism and commitment to making *Doctor Who* the best that he possibly can would not allow him to say no.

A kind of sign language seems to be evolving with the Cybermen. Shout an instruction to them, and ask them if they heard, and you get a thumbs-up. Ask them if they're okay and you get a similar sign, but it's a thumbs-down if they need to rest for a few minutes. It's simple and saves time for Clare, because you can't always hear them properly unless you lean in close.

The Cyber-controller's throne looks like it could have come straight out of *Flash Gordon*. Add some steel-blue gels to the lights, swirl some mist round as the door opens to his chamber, and the effect should be complete as he glides forward. At least that's the theory. Turns out that moving in a straight line isn't one of his strong points.

"Cut it! Firstly, he's veering to the left, and second, one of his feed lines fell of in shot!"

Take Three. He's heading right, and his left foot is getting way too close to the lens.

"Whoah! He's nearly on top of us!"

We move the camera, focus low and wide and I ask for his dialogue to start earlier, rather than wait for the truck he's sitting on to stop before speaking. But there still seems to be a bump he's hitting, which weakens the whole effect.

I confer with Roger Pearce. "Let's do a slow zoom in on the mask, close off as much background behind the throne as we can, and that should make it look as though he's shifting." It works. As we move on to the next shot, Nick Briggs' voice echoes through the set, still in Cyber-controller mode.

"Never knowingly underplayed…"

26TH NOVEMBER 2005

Episodes Five and Six – *Cyber Control Centre scenes continue alongside tunnel sequences at Unit G12.*

"Can we do one more? I'd love it if you took a big, deep breath, then just exhaled like you were blowing out smoke from a great cigar."

Roger Lloyd Pack's back in the wheelchair, cramming all of Lumic's scenes in the factory control room into one day. Lots of reaction shots, monitor shots and close-ups. Between takes, you occasionally see him shuffle forward slightly and produce a newspaper that's been wedged behind him like a cushion.

He's all unblinking, mouth-twitching-into-a-half-smile menace. There's something almost vulture-like about the way he's tilting his head and staring at people. "They will come to me… My new children! The immortal ones!" He inhales deeply as he swings his oxygen mask round, his shoulders rise slightly, and he quivers as he exhales, eyes bulging with satisfaction. I break down laughing first, then Roger goes along with everybody who saw what he did.

There was almost something obscene about it, but it was brilliant. And ever so slightly Dr Strangelove!

One corner of the studio's been turned into the tunnel hatchway leading into the Cyber factory. There'll be some location work for the middle section of the sequence in a few days' time, with a corridor full of frozen Cybermen, but, for the moment, entrances and exits have to be made.

Brightly lit overhead, the hatchway's thrown open and Mrs Moore and the Doctor descend. She hands out torches, and we focus on David's reaction as he sees the line-up stretching out ahead of them. I'll pick up shots of Cybermen to inter-cut with that, but for the moment that's all we need.

The hatchway set's doubling up for their escape route as well. David and Helen charge into shot and up the ladder as they reach the factory, with several Cybermen in pursuit. It's lit from above again, and we block the shot so only one Cyberman starts to climb up.

Ed's had the set built so we can film above the hatch as well, and get reverse shots as the Cybermen try to reach them, but the sonic screwdriver intervenes, welding the lid shut.

Colin's been put into a harness to stage Mr Crane's death sequence, as he disables Lumic's life-support system and gets thrown across the room by a Cyberman. The shot's cued in, the wires are pulled taut, and Colin lets out a scream of pain. I don't think anyone was quite prepared for how high and how fast Colin takes off. It makes the Cyberman's strength look immense, like he's flicking paper across a table. He's fine, completely unhurt, but as for his character…

As Lumic's wheeled off to be upgraded, his wheelchair passes too close to the camera, and it's side-light and cables bunch up together as they press against the lens. Not quite what I was after, but another take soon fixes it.

That's Roger finished. For a character whose presence is felt throughout the story, he's barely been needed on set, but the impact he'll make is immense.

28TH NOVEMBER 2005

Episodes Five and Six – *The reunion between Mickey and his Gran is staged, along with a stunt van sequence in Compton Street, Grangetown, Cardiff. Scenes are also completed with the Cybermen at Clarence Embankment by Hamadrayed Hospital, Cardiff Bay.*

Waterton Street, London SE15. Or that's where we're meant to think it is. Permissions have been granted, waivers have been signed, we're in the heart of Grangetown, and the crew are swarming around a specific old red-brick house, framing up for the afternoon.

"How many set-ups do you want on this, Guv, once you've rehearsed it?"

One of the assistant directors needs to get moving on this, so I talk to some of the crew.

"Right, I've got two singles to shoot, and there, that's the set-up, so the camera needs to go there."

Where you've put the camera, that's a set-up, but the thing to remember is that even if there are two cameras working, quite a distance apart on different parts of the set, that's still one set-up; it's a series of shots favouring the same angle, with both being achieved from a particular position.

Filming around Mickey's gran's house, we've got the whole scene played around the front door, and there's a way to save time here.

"I am so thrilled you got Mona!"

Noel's ecstatic that Mona Hammond's playing his Gran. I've worked with her before, years ago, on one of the first plays I did as a TV director, and just knew that she'd come in and give us a wonderful, irascible, semi-grumpy grandmother, who despairs of but still adores Mickey... Or, in this case, Ricky!

One camera will stay on the street focused primarily on Mona, while another goes in the house, and we'll lens it up for over the shoulder shots on her that favour Noel. If I roll both cameras at the same time, that's 15 minutes saved on setting up the shots. If we can do that two or three times, I've gained an hour.

We've got Mona for a day, and the first half of the call sheet revolves around her completing a good few pages of dialogue. She sparks with Noel immediately, it's exactly what I want to see and we complete everything with plenty of time to move on to the night shoot. This is where people will start to feel as though they've got continual jetlag!

We've got the Cybermen out in the streets, hunting down anything that's not under Lumic's control. David, Billie, Shaun and Helen all run like mad from a line of five moving in on them from the right, only to head straight into another batch marching in from the left. There's no choice other than to charge down an alleyway, directly past where we've set up the camera.

In my mind, I want to suggest the sheer power and brute force of what's heading towards them, so the sound of the Cybermen marching has to be heard well before they actually arrive in shot. This is like the footage you see of Nazi stormtroopers at Nuremberg, hundreds of jackboots sounding like thunder with each synchronised step. Like the marching hammers that Gerald Scarfe animated in Pink Floyd's *The Wall*. That kind of imposing, ominous threatening beat.

"And action!"

David leads everyone past the next set-up, further down the alley, allowing us to use a wide-shot as five Cybermen swing into view, moving in an arrowhead formation towards the camera, with the second five holding the same pattern as they merge in behind them.

Take One. Just as he reaches the point where he's meant to swing to his left and clear the shot, the closest Cyberman on the front line goes the wrong way, panics slightly and runs back to join the line-up he's just broken away from. Not quite the precise, mechanical killer I wanted to see!

The gang emerge from the Preachers' van and see line after line of people, completely under Lumic's control, drifting like zombies towards t he Cyber factory.

Take One. There's hysterics in the van as Helen manages to lock everyone in. The extras hold their trances and just shuffle on, oblivious to the transit-bound chaos.

Take Two. Noel runs ahead, while his double drifts in the background, waiting for him to head around the camera and appear back on screen, so he can duck out of shot. It's the simplest way I can think of to keep Mickey and Ricky in the same grouping.

Andrew Hayden-Smith shouts off camera to give David his cue, and runs out of shot to join him. Just as he does so, there's a loud thud.

"Are you all right, David?"

"I ran into a bollard!"

Yet again, it's going to be a long night!

29TH NOVEMBER 2005

Episodes 12 and 13 – *Torchwood's subterranean corridor #2 and Sphere Chamber scenes are shot at Unit Q2, Newport.*

"Remember, lots of tense energy."

"Stand by... And action!"

The bulkhead door slides open, Billie walks in, looking straight up and over the camera, transfixed by the sphere. The chamber's vast, one of the largest sets for this recording block, all copper metals, bronzes and sparse, clinical equipment.

As soon as Dr Singh approaches and asks for identification, the psychic paper's produced, but it takes off from Billie's fingers and skids across the floor. Another take fixes that slip.

"Right, I'd like to go from that very moment. If we can do a close-up on a long lens there, Roger, that will give some kind of sparkle to the metal in the background. Just to spice it up a notch?"

Raji James stands talking to Billie, almost doing ballet exercises with his legs, bending his knees up and twisting round to limber up. I wanted Dr Singh to look austere, very businesslike, and, topped off with a sterile white lab coat, he looks spot on.

Out comes the psychic paper again, Raji examines it. "That's all right, you see everyone here at... Sorry, I've forgotten where I work!"

When you move into the studio, I always try and plan everything very carefully; all the camera positions, specific moves we're going to use and the way I am going to shoot it so I have got a way in, a visual route into what we're going to play out. On the day, working with the actors, the kind of practical mechanics you need to sort are quickly worked out. Where are they going to come in? How long's the set? What distance have they got to move before the dialogue starts?

If you're not careful, the problem with a big set like the Sphere Chamber is that you can go from your entrance to your mark before you start your lines. Words have to flow on the move, unless you want to make a big moment out of showing off the set, but I want to keep the energy levels high.

Okay, so the doors slide open, there's the void ship, the huge black sphere just hanging there, so you want to take the audience in with you and share the impact with whoever's seeing it for the first time. You do it from that character's point of view as much as you can.

In comes Yvonne, leading the Doctor, and you need to travel fast. Maybe a big tracking shot, then eventually cut behind the point they hit. Tracy-Ann Oberman has to drive the scene. She strides in and takes us right up to the sphere so it's a big fast move.

I've given a note to everyone – walk quite quickly around this set, these scenes are pacy, only slowing down when there's a huge confrontation between the Daleks, the Doctor, Rose and Mickey. Most of them really rattle along fast, but those scenes have verbal sparring, so you pull back and allow the audience to enjoy them.

The scene lays in the Doctor's immediate suspicions about what he sees. I've got to build it up; high and wide holding on all of the dialogue right through, close-ups holding on each character.

"What you are going to look at is nothing – a gulf of wall going way up, reaching high above the main ceiling level of the room, and half-way up that height, there's going to be this massive sphere..."

I go in and, using my hands to give an eye-line for them of its shape, try and demonstrate the enormity of what they are looking at. It's 20 feet in diameter, just sitting there ominously. Originally, it was meant to half submerged into the wall, as if part of it had grown out, but that's been dropped in favour of having it just sitting there, hanging in space.

Jackie, Dr Singh and Yvonne stand, all listening to David, who's come up with ways to keep movement flowing. The Doctor sits on the metal steps leading up towards the sphere, quiet and solemn, then springs up and heads for the door...

As we rehearse, David plays out an ad-lib, turning in the wrong direction as he heads out into the corridor. Tracy-Ann shouts out "No, Doctor!" and a split-second later he storms past the doorway heading the right way, holding the same serious, slightly stooped walk.

I nearly hit the floor laughing, and, thankfully, we're allowed to keep it in. Take after take, I'm only just holding out, trying not to make any noise. Finding humour at such a serious moment... I mean, how brilliant is that?

30TH NOVEMBER 2005

Episodes 12 and 13 – *Torchwood's Sphere Chamber scenes continue shooting at Unit Q2, Newport.*

"Boom!"

Raji and Billie leap up from the desk they're sitting at.

"Boom!"

They nearly lose their balance standing by Noel, as the Sphere starts to become active, sending out ripples of shockwaves.

"Boom!"

Noel starts laughing. "What the hell? What is it with the 'booms'?"

He's finding it hard to take my impersonations of the sound effects seriously. I'm cueing them in to mark precisely where I want the real ones to be placed.

I had quite an involved conversation with Noel on the read-through day, discussing the three kinds of Mickey the scripts require. First, you've got the 'normal' Mickey, well established and familiar, then there's Ricky, the 'parallel Mickey', hard as nails and ruthless. And then there's Mickey Plus, the same, original Mickey, but different.

He's been fighting Cybermen and developed the strength, guts and energy that Ricky had, along with leadership capabilities and extreme combat skills. I told him I wanted to see a very cool, collected extension of the original character – nothing fazes him, he enjoys the fight and he knows he can win.

The wall behind the sphere has been built up to a certain level, and The Mill will add extra height later on, but for the moment it just suddenly ends. The pattern is layer after layer of golden, almost copper panels reaching across in strips of nine.

"I don't get which point we're meant to look at."

Noel's lost over where his eyeline should focus on the sphere. Billie points to it.

"The middle panel, right on the top row."

"Sorry, testing… Testing…"

Nick Briggs is on set, microphone at the ready for Dalek dialogue duties. Raji's perplexed.

"A Dalek that apologises? Wow."

Slate 501. Champagne and wine glasses still being drawn on the clapperboard. The camera glides down towards Mickey, Rose and Dr Singh, and only she knows exactly what's just hovered down from the sphere.

"Exterminate! Exterminate! Exterminate!"

Between takes, all three of them start giggling as they practice 'B-Movie' looks of horror at the Daleks, completely overplaying what they're actually doing.

Take Three. We cut in the middle of a Dalek rant and its voice slower peters out, getting weaker and weaker.

"Ex… ter… min… aaaaaaaaaate…"

The 'Big Sci-Fi Gun' that Russell tantalised Noel with, promising he'd get to use one as a mock incentive to sign up for Season Two, has finally been brought into play. Peter McKinstry's designed it so it's pure James Cameron; a big, bulky breach-loading blaster that could have fallen straight off the props list from *Aliens*.

Everyone's framed in a three-shot, with Noel gritting his teeth and aiming to the right. Raji starts muttering to him, like he was guiding him through a computer game.

"Left a bit, left a bit, down a bit… Right a bit, right a bit… Fire!"

Time for the Black Dalek to make his debut, eye to eye-stalk with Rose.

"Daleks!" Billie point-projects at them with such force, you'd think their lenses would shatter. She strides towards them with authority and confidence, certain she's got the upper hand.

Originally, Russell just wanted four of the bronze Daleks to come out of the Sphere, but the combined persuasive efforts of myself and Ed Thomas, who came up with the idea to make their leader distinctive, kind of swayed him round pretty quickly.

Nick's staying in character, so if I shout instructions to him, you hear and see the Black Dalek reply on the monitor screen.

"Nick, I need you to hold for a second."

"Affirmative." Or "Malfunction! Malfunction!" when the Black Dalek's headlights refuse to stop flashing.

"One… Two… Three… And go!"

The Daleks are framed in a wide-shot, moving forward in an arrowhead formation, with two bronze ones flanking the left and right of their leader.

"Exterminate! Exterminate!"

"And stop!"

They freeze. We hold tight on the Black Dalek, the blue light of his eye right at the centre of the screen.

We talked at length about how to reveal them leaving the Sphere, and there were ideas about lowering the four of them down on cranes. Cheaper than using CGI, definitely, but time-wise you'd be looking at maybe two thirds of the day just to get that one sequence. We need them to have a certain elegance, and chances are, no matter how hard you tried, they'd still land awkwardly on wires, or even a crane.

A crane's used for the last shot of the day. A high and wide point-of-view shot for the Black Dalek, gliding down and closing in tight on Rose. Billie gives it suitable wide-eyed terror.

"And cut!" That's a wrap.

1st DECEMBER 2005

Episodes 12 and 13 – *More work involving Torchwood's subterranean corridor #2 and Sphere Chamber at Unit Q2, Newport.*

"Well, that's where they were when we just rehearsed them…"
One at the front, pearl black and glinting in the studio lights, with three bronze subordinates flanking behind in an arrowhead formation. The Daleks have, quite literally, just landed.

It's barely past nine in the morning. Do Daleks need coffee as well to be this wide awake? There's a definite buzz in the air now they're here. Or is it just relief that we're in the studio and not trying to get them to invade across someone's front lawn in the dark? Trying to get a Black Dalek to see where he's going in the dark. It doesn't bare thinking about!

"Sound… Speed…"

"509 Take One. Camera A and B mark…"

"Stand by then… Action…"

I'm off to the right of the cameras, shouting out the cue.

"One… Two… Three… And go!"

In unison, they glide forward.

"Exterminate! Exterminate! Exterminate!"

"Sto-o-op!" I only need a few feet of movement. Susie Liggatt, the first assistant director for *Army of Ghosts* and *Doomsday*, is organising them for a second take.

"Okay, reset the Daleks. I think they need a little hand."

I dive in, helping to push the closest Dalek on the right back to his mark. The lead Black Dalek is slightly off course.

"Left a bit… Right a bit… Left a bit more…"

It sounds like *The Golden Shot*!

Billie's lines are read to them off camera, and their eye-stalks swing round slightly as they react when Noel's are fed in.

What's the internal logic that makes the Daleks frightening? They're slow, they can't move that fast, but perhaps it's the fact that they can be quite menacing because they glide. If they don't manage that and start bumping over lumps on the floor, it all starts to look a bit tame, so that's got to be avoided at all costs. It's just a shape. A lump with an eye-piece that looks around, a plunger that… Well, okay, we've now been told it can operate keypads and extract brainwaves from people's heads with it. And then there's the gun. As far back as I can remember, right back to *The Power of the Daleks* 40 years ago, people on set called it an egg-whisk!

They just don't look good when they're moving around, so you have to make it work for them and create their mojo by the way you shoot it.

Rule number one with a Dalek in shot? The best thing is to shoot tight on the features and details, or move low and wide. When you track it backwards, try and be as low, wide and close as you can. On a wide angle, low and tight in, that's quite threatening, but then you've got problems in a studio with the ceilings. The designer needs to know you're planning those kind of set-ups, otherwise you'll just be lensing up straight into the group lights.

The closer you focus on a Dalek, the better; spooky, creepy. You let them shout and rant, edging backwards and forwards, but the priority is to narrow the moves right down, get them to settle, then move the camera around them. The same applies with the Cybermen; low and wide angles add height and menace, because you're emphasising their sheer size and power.

I talk to Ernie and Roger, giving them a visual point of reference from *2001*; HAL 9000 watching silently as Dave and Frank talk in the pod, and the computer's lip-reading what they're saying in silhouette. That's the moment when you see the passive red glow that's still so creepy on Hal's red eye. When we do close-up shots on the Dalek's eye, just staring into Rose's face. That quiet, sinister unpredictability. That's what I want.

"Just have one more go. That was absolutely brilliant, now let's make it fantastic!"

Raji's going through the motions of having his mind drained. Billie and Noel stand watching helplessly and sucker arms close in on his skull.

"Loads of adrenaline, Daleks!"

Billie and Noel try desperately not to smirk during a take as Raji screams in pain.

"You've not quite hit your mark there, Raji."

"Well, that's because there's a Dalek on it."

Reset. Time to bring in a green screen and position it just behind the Daleks and their target. The plungers are removed for this take, just leaving bare poles to close in on Raji. The Mill will add the skull-sucking effect further down the line.

A dust-encrusted cadaver's been moved in to represent the dehydrated remains of Dr Singh, and the wig it's wearing is the first thing to go. Add a little bit of mist, get it to fall in the right direction, and we'll get away with it.

Just the Dalek's side of their argument with the Cybermen across monitor screens to stage now. Lots of close-ups and medium shots, it's the only way to energise this, because if you look at the bare bones of the scene, it's basically the Black Dalek shouting at a blank wall. No Cyber-leader being projected up there yet, that's still got to be filmed.

For the moment, it's Clare reading in Cyber-dialogue, while Billie and Noel stand to the side. This has all got to be completed pretty fast. Once we're out of the Sphere Chamber, the same space will be occupied by the Torchwood Lever Room. But before that happens...

2ND DECEMBER 2005

Episode 13 – *Sphere Chamber scenes continue at Unit Q2, Newport.*

It's been looming on the horizon for a while. When it came up during the tone meeting, the only question you could really ask was, "How the hell are we going to do this?"

Doors explode, Cybermen storm the Sphere Chamber, the Daleks open fire. The Doctor, Mickey and Rose try to escape, while Pete and Jake also turn up, backed by troops who are also caught in the crossfire.

It's the dreaded Scene 36.

David's back and has to carry the bulk of material scheduled for the morning. He's making no secret to anyone about how thrilled he is to start working with the Daleks.

"Are we going to do one of those close-ups with a Dalek staring right at me?"

"Yes, Guv."

Point-of-view shot, all blue with a fish-eye lens. Too good a trick to miss.

The Doctor makes his entrance at the far end of the room, nobody's seen him arrive and the Daleks instantly panic. The operators are so experienced now, they can make them shake with rage or almost twitch nervously, and that's exactly what they're doing. We hold wide on David, 3D glasses in place, almost silhouetted against the corridor outside, but I want to build up rapid cuts between him walking in and reactions from the Daleks. Plenty of movement, but only one or two seconds on each shot, building up a sense of tension and danger pretty rapidly.

As the Doctor moves between them, the plot unfolds about the Time War, and we're always keeping the camera moving, circling round and in between the Daleks. Key plot points? They're punched home with tight close-ups on David, or on the blue iris of the Black Dalek.

Lunch is over. We're into the afternoon, war's about to be unleashed. Andrew's behind the wall flat to the left, in front of a line of troops, waiting a few feet away from the side doors. Two Cybermen stand opposite them, briefed in just the same way – they've got to fight through a lot of smoke and noise when they hear "Action!"

The special effects crew have rigged up a barrel, tilted up from the ground to face the centre of the door. It's loaded with explosives and debris, so when the panels in front of them blast into the main set, they'll make it look as though there's far more than just plastic being blasted to pieces.

"Standby… And action!"

It's deafening. Thick smoke and guns firing. Both cameras are focused on the action. Nick Briggs' voice bellows over the speakers rigged high up the walls, giving the Daleks' voices as they counter-attack.

Just as the air starts to clear, we do it again, but from the right side.

The air's just as thick with smoke as before. We zoom in on every detail we can; Dalek and Cybermen guns firing, Mickey skidding across the floor and grabbing his gun, Pete grabbing Rose to drag her to safety. All cutting detail, all time-consuming to set up and shoot.

Between takes, upper Dalek casings and Cyber masks are quickly removed, and cups of ice-cold water are handed over to the rapidly dehydrating actors. Sweat is pouring off them, but the adrenaline in the atmosphere is high.

Susie Liggat is keeping an eye on everything, making sure we're keeping to schedule, and Phil's by the monitors with me, enjoying the spectacle just as much as everyone else. When there are big days like this, you can't help but notice that the main cast start producing camcorders out of their pockets. Shaun, David... They're keeping their own records as every explosion goes off.

David's keen to join in the action more heavily, and keenly suggests that we let him slide across the floor and slip to safety through one of the Cybermen's splayed legs. I thought about it, maybe it could work, but there's just no time.

On screen, you're looking at maybe no more than 90 seconds in the final programme, but it's well into the evening before we finally wrap for the day.

5TH DECEMBER 2005

Episodes Five and Six – *Street scenes are filmed at Clarence Embankment. Scenes outside the Cyber Factory are recorded at Grangemoor Park, off Cardiff Bay Retail Park, Cardiff Bay.*

"Let's move it in a bit this end. It's looking a bit thick towards camera." Susie's trying to organise moving the green screen into position, while Billie, Noel and Helen stand in a line facing left, shuffling slightly so all their faces are in shot. David and Shaun read in their lines off camera.

"Are you looking at Lynsey?"

"Yeah."

Billie's comparing where to fix eye-lines with Noel.

It's a composite scene as the group peer around a street corner, watching the Cybermen collecting more specimens for upgrading. As soon as we move the screen, Noel moves back into shot with Andrew.

If this works, there should be five people on screen with the finished effect, and Helen holds her hand up slightly to make it look as though she's gripping Ricky's arm, so that should help the illusion even more.

For the reverse on this angle, we split the screen up, so Noel and Andrew record Ricky and Jake's moves to the right, leaving the right clear, before we move the Doctor, Rose, Pete, Mickey and Mrs Moore in to finish it.

On go the thermal jackets between takes. I think Lynsey Muir, the third AD, is wearing a feather boa under her parka. Well, if it keeps the frost out, you can't complain!

Ricky gives out orders. Jake's next to him, with a line of Cybermen closing in behind them. "Okay, split up. Mrs Moore, you look after that lot. Jake, you distract them, I'll go right, you go left, then go right and we've left…" He's lost the plot. Andrew leans out of view behind Noel, laughing like mad. Noel just smirks, and the Cybermen keep on marching, oblivious.

"It's freezing, it's bloody freezing!"

David's singing to himself in a high-pitched voice as we set up a group shot. Everyone's either sitting or standing around a park picnic bench, looking at the schematic Mrs Moore has of Lumic's factory on her laptop.

We're working around the summit of a large hill, with the lights of the streets of Cardiff in the distance, and an empty gasometer framework on the horizon.

It's possibly the coldest I've ever been.

As soon as Susie calls "Cut!", blankets and parkas swarm in around the cast. We get to the end of Take Three, the Doctor gives Rose a hug, wishing her luck. Only this time, David squeezes a bit theatrically and lifts her up. Billie groans audibly and, although everyone else gets out of shot before they start laughing, along with Shaun, she doesn't quite make it.

6TH DECEMBER 2005

Episodes Five and Six – *Scenes in the mountainside nuclear bunker are shot at Brackula Bunkers, Brackula, Bridge End.*

Episode 13 – *Countryside scenes are shot at Heol Spencer, Brynceithyn, Bridgend.*

"Okay, we're rolling camera. We start in darkness… And action!"
On come the head and hand torches. Cybermen, flanking the left of the shot, starting in extreme close-up and moving away into the distance, lined up against the wall. This is tight, cramped and very claustrophobic. Tuxedoed and still in Bond mode, David moves up to the Cyberman immediately in the foreground and taps the faceplate. Even though there's an actor inside, there's still a hollow echo.

The Doctor and Mrs Moore head deeper into the storage tunnels, and suddenly the camera tilts. It's really proving to be far more difficult than we anticipated to get much done down here.

"And keep running. Go again… Start in darkness… Wait three beats after action…"

On Susie's cue, David enters the frame again. We track behind Helen as she nervously edges forward, then we stop level with the third Cyberman in the line-up and just hold on the Doctor and Mrs Moore, letting their lights disappear into the darkness as they move on.

Between takes, the strip lighting behind the heads of the Cybermen comes on, and you can see the actors inside stretching their legs. Can you imagine being in an uncomfortable costume that you can barely see out of, then having to stand motionless in a pitch-black concrete tunnel? Certainly not a job I'd want!

Now onto a reverse angle, so David's heading towards us and we pull backwards along the line. Two takes in and I move in for a quick word.

"David, can you hold back a little. Just a bit slower…"

He nods. "I got too far ahead of myself, didn't I?"

Both actors are freezing. The air's icy and cold. Brackula's an old nuclear bunker, buried in the mountainside near Bridge End, and it's austere, grey and exactly what the scene needs.

"Okay, guys, stand easy…" Susie's talking to the Cybermen. "Keep your heads on, but relax for a minute while we reset… We'll be moving you out in a couple of minutes…"

We need space to run the camera alongside David and Helen, so the space the Cybermen were standing along is freed up and used as a clear walkway to track along. The floor's damp, and occasionally you get a squeak from the Doctor's trainers, but that can be wiped off the soundtrack later on.

"Paul…" Susie cues in Paul Kasey, last in the Cyber line-up and closest to camera, to turn slightly towards the lens as Mrs Moore passes him. "Graeme, you happy?"

"I'm happy."

Susie moves everything on to the next shot; a hand-held camera, sweeping along the Cybermen as they start to reactivate, hands slowly clasping as they energise, reaching out and flexing. Then a similar move, but at head height as they half turn, some beginning to step away from the wall, all building tension as the Doctor tries to find a way out.

"Helen, can you throw it slightly over arm, so we can see it better?"

I race back into an old storeroom where the monitors have been set up. We're on an open platform area, with the Doctor and Mrs Moore heading along a side gantry towards it. Suddenly, they spot a Cyberman directly ahead, and she throws her homemade electro-magnetic bomb at it. Mist guns have layered the background, but the actors don't need any help producing their own with their breath. It must be almost below zero.

Take Two. The bowling action works a treat, but Helen's aim is slightly off and it hits the hood in front of the camera lens, making it drop down and black out the screen.

With the Cyberman dead, we move in low for close-ups on David, then two shots with Helen in the foreground as they remove the emotional inhibitor from it. While this is being rehearsed, the second unit are lining up a low angle on the Cybermen marching down the tunnel, backlit, ominous and echoing, heavy metal footsteps as they move. It's a nod to Douglas Camfield and what he did with *The Invasion* back in 1968.

With the main unit, there's only a high and wide shot for the Doctor and Mrs Moore's attack on the Cyberman, and then her death scene to do, along with close-ups on the dead Cyberman's chest and face before we can wrap, get out of here and get warm again.

Phil doesn't know what he's missing. He's been off doing second unit work for most of the day with Camille, Noel, Shaun and Billie, building up the shots for their characters driving across country, heading for her final moments with the Doctor. No dialogue, no heavy emotions to play out. Just daylight and relative warmth compared to down here.

Not that I'm jealous or anything.

7TH DECEMBER 2005

Episodes 12 and 13 – *Scenes in the Torchwood underground corridors #1, #2 and #3, along with a Torchwood office, are shot at Brackula Bunkers, Brackula, Bridge End.*

We've set up pretty much as close to the middle of a long subterranean corridor as we can, the idea being that whichever way you look, there quite a distance to natural vanishing point. The walls are lined with doors leading off to store rooms and offices.

Running for her life, Jackie charges straight into two Cybermen, whose arms rise, ready to kill her…

Paul Kasey and Rauri Mears are just wearing the upper halves of their Cyber suits. They're framed in a two-shot and, as they suddenly collapse, this makes it far easier and safer for them to fall. Pete's behind them. He's shot them with a blaster and, as the resulting smoke clears, we see him with the Doctor, Rose and Mickey standing behind him. Time for an awkward reunion.

The trick here's going to be playing on reverse angles until the right moment arrives. They're not seen together in the same frame while they talk, maintaining the distance between them as they do so.   Shaun's there, feeding cues to Camille all the way while we concentrate on her angle, and she does the same for him as we lens up favouring Pete. Russell's written the scene brilliantly, with Jackie double-checking just how wealthy Pete's become. It's clearly not something she's judging him on, just a slight edge of disbelief that he could be a success after her experiences with the 'other' version.

He's the first to move towards her, dropping the blaster, embracing her and lifting her off her feet. Close-up on Billie, overcome with emotion. It's a high point for the characters' story arcs, and hopefully for the viewers as well.

8TH AND 9TH DECEMBER 2005

Episodes 12 and 13 – *Scenes in the 'parallel' and normal Torchwood HQ Lever Room are shot at Unit Q2, Newport.*

Right from the outset during the first tone meeting, it became pretty clear that, although we're talking big broad sci-fi concepts here, Russell in no way wants

the Torchwood Institute to look like a cast-off from *Forbidden Planet* or
Mars Attacks. Yes, it's got to be modern, something like the interior of MI5,
all austere and kind of bare, but it should also still be a military establishment
and surrounded by elite security forces. The finished results for the Lever Room
look clinical, like something out of a Bond film, quite grand and with plenty
of open space to work around.

The script for *Doomsday* introduces the 'parallel world' version of
Torchwood and, both in terms of logic and economics, there was no need to do
anything other than dress it slightly differently. The scheduling's sandwiched all
of these scenes together on the first day and, compared to the other version, this
one's underlit and lined with hanging black power cables.

Straight away we're off with reintroducing Pete, now slightly perma-tanned,
suited and booted; it's obvious he's still doing okay in the years that have passed
since we last met. There are three main set-ups for these scenes; one by the main
doorway, one by the window and one by the far wall. Mid-shots and two-shots,
moving into close-ups as he tries to convince the Doctor to help.

Shaun's playing the character with a slightly harder edge. I want to see him
slightly weary, but with a ruthless side. Initially, he doesn't care about the other
Jackie, or that Rose is his daughter. That's the journey he has to make, coming
to terms with them and not only accepting they exist, but also wanting them as
part of his life. We've also got to tackle Rose being taken away from the Doctor,
becoming trapped in this alternate reality. I have to allow Billie plenty of room
to find how she wants to play it, drawing on all Rose's experiences and the fact
that everything's suddenly going to be different.

This scene's got to hurt, tearing into the viewer as well. We frame tightly on
Billie, leaning against the wall, tears and mascara streaming down her face. I
ask her to think about how isolated she suddenly is, how alone she thinks she's
going to be without the Doctor. We track across Noel, Camille and Shaun, all
standing in a line and watching, holding on each of them for a few seconds,
sharing their despair as they just don't know how to help her. It's the end of
Rose's journey, but not quite.

Overnight, the cables are removed, the lighting plot changed and the room
becomes all harsh whites and black suits. This is now Yvonne Hartman's world,
Tracy-Ann's domain, and the levers are soon being thrown as the Ghost Shifts begin.

10TH DECEMBER 2005

Episodes 12 and 13 – *London city street scenes and the Japanese street sequence for the Ghost Advert are shot around Mount Stuart Square, Bute Street, Cardiff Bay.*

Another Saturday morning shoot. Time's tight. It's two weeks to Christmas, so there are bound to be problems with crowds if we don't get out of here pretty quickly. We lens up high and wide, looking down on the street as Cybermen march in formation, turn and open fire towards the sky. This is the main battle with the airborne Daleks, and, as such, we've got to get as many multiple shots of the Cybermen as we can, so the images can be cut into, composited and complemented with CGI to create a vast army.

I don't know whether it's a dream come true for him or not, now that he's actually wearing one of the costumes he helped design, but Pete McKinstry's one of the battalion. As normal, Paul Kasey's working as the troop leader and leading the marches, but I've no idea which one's Pete. He's definitely in there somewhere!

12TH TO 14TH DECEMBER 2005

Episodes 12 and 13 – *Scenes in the Torchwood HQ Lever Room are shot at Unit Q2, Newport.*

We're filming in the Lever Room, the first of four solid days of work here, including the Cybermen taking over, and I'm looking carefully at its very long and narrow geography. Sure, it's quite high as you walk in, and the idea is that as you reach it, the far wall suddenly reaches up 80 to 100 feet. A bit like a reversed letter 'L'. Some POV stuff from the wall, that's what we need to create a sense of height and width for the room, and also distance when you're looking straight ahead to Yvonne's office, next to the main doorway leading in from the corridor outside.

The way to make the scenes varied and interesting is to use big wide angles, fast tracking shots passing foreground paraphernalia – which gives you pace and energy if you move fast enough, and from then on I'll try to keep the cameras moving as much as possible, finding all the different angles I can.

By the time we finish, you should know that room, all the main details of what's in it, where people's work stations are, and if I give it some fast and gentle tracking shots, the eye will never hold on anything for too long and get bored.

There's no David, Billie or Noel for the first day, just Tracy-Ann working the floor of Yvonne's world. Short scenes building the characters around her, ensuring that she's charismatic and clearly liked as a boss, developing the relationship between Adeola and Gareth, showing the excitement in the atmosphere as a Ghost Shift's induced.

"And we're into Ghost Shift…"

We hold high and wide from the far wall as Tracy-Ann marches forward, beaming with hands on hips as the levers are thrown, and we flood the set with light that bleaches out a lot of the peripheral detail. It's all vitally important. Even spending an hour or so getting the simple sequence right of Adeola texting her boyfriend over her computer's messenger system. It adds depth, makes it real, and all the more tragic when they die.

Is this a *Doctor Who* first? An entire scene that's driven by an actor talking to himself as two different characters?

The Cyber-leader's framed in the foreground, with the Doctor and Jackie in the background to his left. This is for the reverse shots of the verbal confrontation with the Black Dalek. That half's already shot, but this is for the monitor screen projected onto the wall of the Sphere Chamber as we move to close-ups.

During pre-production, sure, there were all the worries about what the Cybermen were going to look like, but the question about what they'd sound like was just as important. You look back at the old stories and you've got a wide spectrum to chose from, ranging from sing-song, slightly nasal voices to ones that get a bit too Darth Vader. We need a variation on that theme.

Russell and Phil both said the same thing. Nick Briggs is the expert on all things vocal for Daleks, so as he's already going to be needed for *Army of Ghosts* and *Doomsday*, he was the obvious choice to turn to. After a couple of chats on the phone, I think he supplied something like 14 different versions of Cyber voices on a tape, and we went for an emotionless, impassive, slightly monotonous style, which we'll treat in post-production to get the finished effect, but that's certainly what we're using live on set.

So for the moment, he really is arguing with himself!

15TH DECEMBER 2005

Episodes 12 and 13 – *Scenes in the Torchwood HQ Lever Room are shot at Unit Q2, Newport.*

Episodes Five and Six – *Near the Unit Q2 studio, Mickey/Ricky evading Cybermen are filmed this evening.*

The gang are all here in force today: David, Billie, Noel, Camille, Shaun and Andrew. And that guarantees giggles, lots of them, and all coming from that same core group.

The Doctor's at the window looking out of Yvonne's office. David's mind's eye can see the Genesis Ark spitting out Daleks in mid air, about 50 feet away.

"Time Lord science. It's bigger on the inside."

"You mean the Daleks put those Time Lords in there?"

Noel shakes his head, he's got it the wrong way round. Billie catches his smirk of shame and bursts out laughing. David's still focused. "We can start again… We can start again… We can start the scene again."

Camille's trying not to laugh, turning away slightly, her hand over her mouth. "Cut!"

Take Five… In they come… They get through the lines, but hold their marks when I ask for a shot on Billie, with Andrew flanking her. Shaun mutters.

"I could take on those Daleks…"

Billie flutters her eyelashes and takes on a Southern drawl. "What's that you say, Gemini?"

Pete's fake ID he used to contact the Preachers has stuck as a nickname. Noel chips in. "You're the man, Gemini!"

"Tonight, Matthew…" Shaun's gone all *Star In Their Eyes*. "I'm going to be…"

"Quiet!" Susie calls them to order, we get through another take, them move focus onto David. He hits his last line. "Millions of them." For some reason, his voice wavers on 'millions'.

"And cut!"

There's a whole chorus of impersonations around him saying the word, and he shrugs in mock-despair as he laughs. Another take rolls past, but only just. Shaun's out of shot, shaking as he tries not to laugh.

Noel rounds on him, grinning. "Who you laughing at, man? What's the matter with you?"

Don't think for a moment that these guys are anything other than completely professional when the cameras roll, it's just the bits in between takes when the laughter usually hits.

"Now come on, guys! You are blatantly talking during takes!"

Susie's telling off some riggers; Noel and Shaun look towards them and tut loudly as well. We keep working; two-shots on Jackie and Pete, then Jake and Mickey, tracking shots following the Doctor as he races round the room, moving from one of the computer terminals to the far wall. I'm thrilled with the level of energy David's driving the scene with.

We frame Billie in a mid-shot, tightly focused on her, isolating her from the others as she realises that she's got to go to the 'parallel world' – 'Pete's world'. To one end of the room, we've got David, while everyone else is by Yvonne's office as she stands in between. Visually, I'm trying to hint that her world's about to be torn in different directions.

Outside, on a road running between buildings on the industrial estate where Unit Q2's based, we line up cameras for about two hours' work as we move onto a night shoot. This is the build-up to Ricky's death, but first there's a scene to play out where he talks to Mickey. Noel runs down the road towards us, fast like an athlete, hits his mark on the left of the frame and plays out his lines. Susie reads in Mickey's responses. Three takes and I'm happy, with a pair of Cybermen closing in behind as Ricky runs off, carefully moving to keep the right side of the shot clear.

On the right side, Noel's now charging in, flailing slightly as he runs, making Mickey ever so slightly different, and Susie reads in Ricky as the scene plays out. Three Cybermen move in behind him on the right, the idea being that the two halves we've shot will be composited during post-production, and save the time that rigging up a green screen for the shot would have needed.

"I thought that was terrific. Brilliant! I'm more than happy."

Noel's released, and we wrap with a single set-up on all five Cybermen, moving towards camera through the shadows in an arrowhead formation.

I hear a story as we're packing up about earlier on in the studio. For the scene where Jackie is teleported to the parallel world, Shaun nearly managed to convince her that I'd told them she had to shimmy just before she vanishes.

He nearly got her. Nearly, but not quite. I'm sure she'll get her own back, and probably when he least expects it.

16TH DECEMBER 2005

Episodes Five and Six – *Near Unit Q2, Ricky's death scene (originally scheduled to be filmed on 5th December) is completed.*

"When you feel it grab your leg, that's when you get electrocuted."
Noel's clinging to a wire-mesh fence, and Susie goes so far with what she's describing that she actually grabs his ankle and provides sound effects to go with it.

This is a key moment. It's when the old Mickey vanishes forever, and he suddenly realises what he has to do. As he sees Ricky die right in front of his eyes, that's when it hits him. This is what he can do, this is his real role in life; he's got to take his alternate self's place and fight for everything he believed in.

Abbi Collins is going through his moves with him for his fall, making sure he knows how to hit the crash mat laid out for him without hurting his neck. She says he's a natural at it, but I think there's a side of him that's really enjoying it as well.

We lens up and go for the first take. The Cybermen catch up with Ricky as he fatally pauses too long as he reaches the fence, and starts to climb too late. Noel screams right on cue and falls like a dead weight. Just some close-ups, and we've got it.

For the reverse shots favouring Mickey, I talk to Noel about how I want to see this realisation. We've shot the Cybermen standing motionless, covered in shadows and lit so it looks like they're in moonlight, just staring through the fence impassively. Noel stares back. It's a medium close-up and, for one brief second, he changes his expression and it's Ricky's face. That's what I want, that says it all, he's got it!

There are some brief scenes that have to be done around the docks, but the crew are starting to wind down. This is the last day of filming for 2005, and everyone deserves their Christmas break. But it's far from over yet.

3RD JANUARY 2006

Episode 13 – *Scenes in the Torchwood HQ Lever Room are shot at Unit Q2, Newport.*

We're starting with the last shot of David in the Lever Room, where he goes up to the wall and can almost sense Rose's presence, then he quietly walks away. When an actor has to find this kind of emotional moment, you let them find their space and tell you when they're ready. You can't demand that they instantly conjure it up, and I never would, you just have to understand that they have to find it in their own way.

Once I've gone through the technical aspects of the scene, David asks, "Are you finished with me?" He then walks away, getting himself ready and into the mood he needs. The crew give him space, and he stays away from everyone. Just before the moment we shoot, make-up and wardrobe come in to check continuity, which he allows them to do. As soon as they're gone and he hears stand-by, he gets back into the moment. Susie's watching him like a hawk.

"Are you all right, David?"

"Yep. Ready."

Off we go…

"Eight Six Two. Take One."

"And action…"

Utter silence. High and wide, the camera's as far from the wall as possible, and we hold the shot for as long as we can. David walks to the wall, reaches out and touches it, then slowly turns and walks back. He plays the same moves again in a medium shot back at ground level, before we lens up against the wall and hold on him in a tight close-up. It's intense and works beautifully. If he'd asked for more time, I'd have had to give that to him. With scenes like this, you want the moment to be thought out and fully realised, otherwise it's worth nothing.

Billie's back on set. It's just the two of them today. None of the other cast members are needed. We've got to rattle through all of the scenes building up to the void being reopened, as the Doctor and Rose throw the lever room switches, and then cling onto the magna clamps they've fastened to the walls as all hell breaks loose...

A huge wind machine's aimed at David. He practises moving in towards the clamp and looping his arm round one of its bars, so he's got a firm hold. And boy, does he need it! The noise is deafening. I don't know how much of it's acting, but he seems pretty close to taking off! Paperwork's flying off the desk and whizzing past him. Susie suddenly charges in and grabs a panel of wire mesh. It's come loose from the upper wall of the set, and was getting blown down straight towards David. She's grabbed it, so thankfully no damage done.

Onto a wide shot. The curved arch holding the lever closest to him is just about within reach and, as the wind starts up, David throws his left leg out towards it and uses it to counterbalance against. He slowly lifts himself up and brings his right leg inwards, so it really looks as though he's being dragged in.

Billie's not as tall as David, so when we line the wind machine up on her side of the room, she can't quite reach the lever for a foothold, but still nearly gets blown away by the resulting gust. It'll be worse for her tomorrow, though. That's when she gets dragged into the void!

4TH JANUARY 2006

Episodes 12 and 13 – *Scenes in the Torchwood HQ Lever Room and the Ghostwatch Studio are shot at Unit Q2, Newport.*

Explosions are being detonated along the walls either side of Billie, who's facing the full force of the wind machine again. The lever's sliding back right in front of her, and Rose knows she has no choice. She swings forward and pushes it back into position, but in order to do that she has to let go of the clamp, and finds she's left with only the lever to hold onto against the draw of the void.

We've gone as far as we can with medium and tight close-ups of her desperately looking towards the Doctor for help, but what we need to see now is her being dragged away. Two lines of track have been laid out running up to the far wall. One's got the camera mounted on a dolly, the other's got a trolley on it, lined with padding, which Billie's been anchored to, so she's effectively lying down. By moving the camera alongside her as she moves, it'll create the sensation of the void pulling at her. Using the same track, we reverse the shot onto David and rapidly pull back, so we get a point-of-view shot for Rose as she's drawn in. It's tricky. Go too wide and you get the edge of the wind machine in shot, so Roger curves the camera move slightly and manages to hold the frame so it doesn't intrude.

Lensing up as wide as we can, David and Billie go through the motions, holding on to the clamps again, so we have a clean centre of the frame for The Mill to add the Daleks. The set-up's run again with the actors out of shot.

"Is that okay for you, Dave?"

Dave Houghton's on set, making sure he gets the shots he needs for the CGI.

"It's fine. That's fine, thanks."

Shaun moves down to the far wall and we rehearse with Billie, trying to find a move for her to swing into his arms. This is the sudden plot reveal, and Pete arrives to save Rose. She leans back as far as she can, then throws herself towards him. Roger arcs the camera round so it follows the move. We move in for two-shots as she looks over her shoulder, eyes filled with panic, as she realises what's about to happen, and then into a close-up. She plays it spot on, and I'm more than happy.

That's practically it. There are just a few brief moments of Alistair Appleton as the Ghostwatch presenter to record, working around a minute set that's been built in the corner of the studio, and then we're done for the day.

There are quite a few raised voices as we wrap. Nobody's angry, it's just that everyone's gone a bit deaf after battling against the noise of the wind machines!

5TH JANUARY 2006

Episodes 12 and 13 – *Scenes in the Torchwood HQ Lever Room are shot at Unit Q2, Newport.*

"There's a big whirring noise, I can't quite hear you."

Jackie's by the window in Yvonne's office, and quickly recognises they're in Canary Wharf, but Camille can barely hear anything that's being said to her, thanks to a nearby extractor fan. On comes the clapperboard, while she tries to blow a strand of her fringe away and hold her position. She rattles through a take.

"It must be Canary Wharf!"

Tracy-Ann cuts in, poking fun at her as I shout "Cut!"

"Oh, listen to clever clogs!"

Take Two. She plays it more clearly, as though you can hear the realisation forming in Jackie's brain.

"It *must* be Canary Wharf!"

Tracy-Ann goes all nasal.

"W-e-e-e-ll, could be!"

Camille looks over for approval, smiling.

"Little bit of variation there?"

I'm happy. Moving on…

David's got a page of verbal gymnastics to get through, explaining what the effects of the Ghost Shift are every time it opens. He uses the sonic screwdriver on some glass, and stands behind it as a web-like crack appears, slowly spreading out until it shatters.

The shot's lined up, he's off camera waiting for his cue. He quickly checks lines on some script that's folded up and hidden away in his back pocket. Just before Susie calls out "Action!", he dances from foot to foot on the spot, shakes his arms and puffs out air from his cheeks in rapid bursts.

Watching on the monitor, I can see he's energised and ready. He aims the sonic screwdriver at the first 'O' of the Torchwood logo in front of him, and follows the cracks in his mind's eye. The special effects crew have got a replacement sheet ready to rig and explode later on, but the main spindly web effect will be added by The Mill.

We keep building up the sequence. A two-shot on Yvonne as she rounds on the Doctor.

"The Doctor, lording it up with his alien authority."

Suddenly her face drops.

"Do it again!"

She walks out of shot, followed by David and Camille, and within seconds they pick up the pace, playing the scene out exactly as we've blocked it.

"Time for more pointy finger acting."

Tracy-Ann's taking the micky out of David, as he wags his index finger at her in the build-up to another take. If he smirked, he managed to hide it. The camera's positioned behind him as he faces the glass, pokes it, then steps back as everyone mimes their reactions to what this causes.

Now time for the real thing. No Doctor in shot, but Tracy-Ann and Camille are a few feet away facing the FX-glass.

"We're a bit close, aren't we?"

Camille's muttering under her breath, "It'll be fine."

Tracy-Ann's cool and collected. But everybody jumps as a sound like a bullet being fired goes off and shards of glass start falling to the ground.

"Oh, that's brilliant! That was amazing!"

She's the first to applaud, and the rest of the cast on set quickly join in. Pretty soon, the crew are standing round just staring at the remains like road kill. Susie quickly hustles everyone off to lunch.

"Guys, c'mon! We're shooting. Stand still!"

Yvonne's been put in an awkward position by the Doctor and cancels a ghost shift. David's sitting in a chair he's dragged out of her office, arms folded defiantly. As she storms past, he starts to shuffle it after her as he follows.

"You can't do that! You can't follow me!"

Tracy-Ann's laughing like mad.

"Is that what you do, like a little wheelchair?"

"Oh, they can cut me out in the edit!"

David waves his hand nonchalantly, dismissing what he's doing, lifts his legs up and spins round fast a couple of times.

"Lift your eyes up, Freema... Just look a little higher."

Adeola's about to die. We've lensed up on actress Freema Agyeman, David's right by her side staring at her left ear-piece. As she slumps down, Tracy-Ann pulls up another ear-piece that's out of shot and sitting in a cup of runny gel, moving her arm as though it's come free from Adeola's right ear.

Take One. It's not in shot as she swings her hand up. Way too high.

Take Two. Too much to the right, no detail.

Take Three. It swings too much. And through all of this, Freema's getting dripped on while she lies across her computer console, and doesn't say a word.

6TH JANUARY 2006

Episodes 12 and 13 – *The Torchwood top floor and 'No Entry' corridor sequences are shot at the HTV Studios, Culverhouse Cross, Cardiff.*

Yvonne runs down the corridor, excitedly speaking into her mobile. "Rajesh! He's coming!" As Tracy-Ann goes past the camera, she skips it slightly but doesn't cause any shake to the image.

"Can we go again on that one please?"

She winks at Roger as she heads off for a retake.

"Got ya!"

We're still running the camera between takes, and Roger's muttering, "Quick as you can. All this tape running through, it's enough to cover a football match!"

We've got a square of corridor, running around a central column, so to create a sense of height and depth I've asked for the camera to lens up high, looking down on the route David and Tracy-Ann take as the Doctor leads her round it, using his sonic screwdriver to track energy emissions.

Onto the next set-up. The camera's tight against the wall as a makeshift white flag's waved around the corner. David emerges, apologising for the fact it's not real, just a sheet of A4. On the first take, he gets completely tongue-tied, blows an enormous raspberry and retreats.

"Cut! We've got a microphone hovering around the corner!"

It looks as though it's peering round at what's happening.

Susie reads in David's lines on the reverse shot, showing three Cybermen standing over two of their dead troops. They look up, turn and move forward with gun arms raised as soon as the Doctor approaches.

Between takes, Paul Kasey moves backwards and forwards, rehearsing and rehearsing the few steps he has to make as the lead Cyberman. He's memorising where the mark he has to hit is, as there's no way he can see it when we roll.

Final moment of the sequence? A tight profile two-shot, the Doctor and

Cyberman eye to eye. David almost seems to be looking straight through its eye sockets. It's just like a stand-off in a western.

Financially, this must be Phil's dream set – interlinking corridors created through plastic sheets being hung from an overhead framework. Tricky to light, but it creates the opportunity to play with distorted shapes lurking behind them.

The Doctor leads Yvonne and two Torchwood soldiers into a trap, as Cybermen loom out from where they've been hiding. David pulls Tracey to safety as the soldiers swing into action and open fire with their machine guns.

"Oh my God!"

Tracey's shocked by how loud they were in such a confined space, but grinning like mad at the same time. Lots of shouting between takes, as people have got ear-guards on and forget they're wearing them. One or two of the special effects guys are crouched down behind clear protective shields, just like riot police, in case any wadding from the bullets flies at them.

"Remember, full-on terror! Loads of fear and energy!"

Camille's arrived on set. Jackie's with Yvonne as she's led off for Cyber conversion. Tracy-Ann's completely focused on what's about to happen to her character, finally breaking down the confident exterior as she tries to convince herself it's all been for Queen and Country.

"I did my duty! I did my duty! I did my duty!"

We line up so we see Yvonne walk into the makeshift upgrade chamber the Cybermen have built. But she stops just in front of the camera.

"Cut! Sorry guys, she can't stop there, she's not cleared shot."

"Yeah, there'd be blood flying everywhere if she held that mark!"

We lens up on Camille for a reaction shot. We've got a saw making a hell of a racket just to the right of camera, so sparks fly into the foreground. Susie has to shout at the top of her voice to stop it.

"And cut!"

Camille's eyes widen, thinking about what's happened to Tracy-Ann's character.

"Ooooh, now that's gonna hurt!"

"Go on, enjoy yourselves!"

I want Freema and Hadley to look a little less worried and more enthusiastic. Their characters are about to die, thanks to accidentally wandering too close to the upgrade unit, but they have to seem a little less worried about being caught doing what they originally planned – kissing.

They quickly play the dialogue out just as I want it. Freema's got scenes today switching between being possessed by Cyber-technology and back again, and she hits it brilliantly each time, and as for Adeola's last moments before she's attacked, creeping through the plastic alleys of sheets, she hits it spot on.

It's her last day on set, and there are rumours about her auditioning for *Torchwood*. I hope she gets it. She deserves it.

"Cyberman to the far right, just step forward about four inches."

It's a corridor of plastic sheets. The shot's no more than three seconds, if that. Two rows of three Cybermen facing each other. I need them to turn in sync towards camera, then just move their right fists to their chest plates.

"That's Matt."

Susie identifies the guy inside. He shuffles forward.

"Whoa! Then you!"

"And three... Two... One... Go!"

It's a mess. They're all moving at different times and only two hit their chests.

"Lets try everybody move on 'Go', then three... two... one... Chest plates..."

They all swing round brilliantly, but the second in on the right hits his chest plate on 'Two', then shakes his head in frustration as he realises what he's done.

"Reset!"

"Matt, shuffle forward three inches again. Then you!"

"Don't anticipate the 'Go', boys."

It happens again, same Cyberman, same early move. We keep running, time's running out fast.

"And Three... Two... One... 'Go'..."

Perfect.

"Three..."

All of the Cybermen bar the middle right hit their plates on Three!

"Two..."

There's middle right, just as he was before, but later than the others now! One last try...

"Matt, move forward again three inches... And action!"

They've got it!

"And cut! Excellent! That's the scene!"

"Well done, boys…" Susie pats the closest Cyberman on the shoulder as they head off. He rattles slightly.

7TH JANUARY 2006

Episodes Five and Six, **12 and 13** – *Scenes in the shopping street are completed on Mount Stuart Square, Bute, Cardiff Bay.*

Episode 13… Scene 75… People begin to emerge from hiding. Something extraordinary's happening overhead.

"Everyone's got to look up at a set point, otherwise your eye-lines will be all over the place…"

Susie's standing in front of the extras – soldiers, policemen, road sweepers, pedestrians, we've got the lot in today…

"And action! Soldiers!"

A squad of six soldiers run past, heading away from the gathering crowd, who stare with a mixture of awe and disbelief as the Daleks are dragged back to the Torchwood across the skyline.

"Look happy!"

I join in with the directions Susie's calling out.

"Come on, give one big cheer!"

Got it in one!

We're ready for David and Billie.

The silver people-carrier ferrying them from their trailers glides up by the roadside, the door slides open and Susie peers out, almost checking that the coast is clear. With her shades and walkie-talkie, she looks like a CIA outrider for the US President… Does that mean she'd leap and take a bullet for Russell? Is that in her contract?

"Go again, guys! It's looking very good!"

Back to Episode Five. The Doctor and Rose wander through the busy streets talking about Mickey's childhood. The camera's on a track behind some metal railings, following them as they move, so there's plenty of detail in the foreground of the shot.

"I've fluffed a line!"

Billie's apologising, we reset and go again.

"Excellent, guys! Well done!"

The camera's now at near-roof height on a mole crane. In one fluid movement, we sweep down and close in on David and Billie, holding on them as the extras around them suddenly freeze on the spot. Download time. Cybus Industries are feeding data directly into the public consciousness via their ear-pods.

"And cut!"

"I was crap!"

"I was dreadful!"

Neither of them are happy with the way that take went. They move back to their starting positions for the scene with the extras.

"Simon, surely you can hear that bike?"

David's talking over his microphone to the sound recordist, Simon Fraser. He holds his arm up, everyone's quiet.

"We've got a moped nearby."

It sounds like a loud asthmatic bee. Radio mics aren't really the preferred choice to work with. They pick up clothes rustling and have to contend against the howl of the wind, hence the fluffy sock you see on a boom microphone to stop that happening.

"We're clear!"

"And action!"

Only three or four seconds pass.

"Sorry, hold it there!" Susie flies out from behind the monitors. "When I shout 'Background', that means you all start to move. Don't just wait until you think you're in shot, we can see everyone!"

Off we go again.

"Background!"

Tentative shuffling starts.

"Cue David and Billie!"

They head towards camera as we close in, but something's not feeling quite right for David.

"I'm sure we could stop further back?"

I let him play the next take out how he feels it should go instinctively. Rather than stop directly in front of the camera and play out his lines, he starts weaving around people as they freeze on the spot, staring at them, peering into their faces until he reaches his original mark. It works a treat.

"I'm having that, thank you! Right…"

Susie closes in to confer.

"The shots I need are a decent single on David from this side."

I point out where I want the lens to frame-up.

"I've already got Billie, so I need a tight single profile on David from here."

She's made note of the different camera positions, we rehearse and move on.

Russell's here chatting to David and Billie. There are questions about how they are, how things are going – and gossip to catch up on. It's one of his rare appearances on set, and everyone's genuinely pleased to see him.

Phil's not too happy. There's a lot of people watching from the security boundaries today, and it's a bit of a mystery how they found out we were here. Letters were dropped around the street saying the BBC would be filming here for the morning, but there was no mention of *Doctor Who*. But then again, there was a TARDIS letterhead at the top of the page! Big clue or what? Any frowns soon pass, though. Phil's good humour wins through and he's laughing about it now like the rest of us.

9TH AND 10TH JANUARY 2006

Episodes 12 and 13 – *Torchwood subterranean corridor, loading bay and hangar scenes are shot over two days at RAF St Athan, Barry. The TARDIS arrives, Jackie and the Doctor are captured, and the war between the Daleks and Cybermen really begins.*

"Ernie? You happy?"

Susie has everything ready for the camera to shoot. The TARDIS has been positioned against the wall, crates and boxes surround it, and Torchwood Soldiers are waiting off camera to the left and behind a small door. They're all due to storm in and take aim as soon as they hear "Action!"

Everywhere you look, you can spot the distinctive 'T' logo for Torchwood. Ed Thomas' team seem to have gone out of their way to ensure it's always in shot.

"I can't get a picture on B-Camera." Ernie's on the walkie-talkie. Minutes pass and it's fixed.

Two takes of the action, and that part of the scene's sorted. We just need a clean plate shot for the TARDIS to materialise into, a reverse angle on the soldiers and then it's time for Yvonne Hartman to make her entrance. Story-wise, it's her first encounter with the Doctor. Two clapperboards mark the scene, as two cameras are rolling from only slightly different angles. We focus on a close-up of David as he comes out of the TARDIS.

Take One. The door really creaks as he pulls it shut. Slight problem; he's already got his hands up, but quickly realises his mistake.

"Hang on, I don't put my hands up until I'm outside, do I?"

Take Two. David's spot on as Tracy-Ann runs in, applauding his arrival. "Oh, how marvellous… Oh…"

David suddenly grins. That's definitely something loud and metal everyone can hear, and it's not a Cyberman.

"Now you hear that?" Susie's on the case. "That's definitely the sound of a truck going past… And they know they're not meant to."

I wouldn't want to be in their shoes! Onto a two-shot of the Doctor and Jackie by the TARDIS. They're clearly enjoying this.

"That was lovely!" Camille's more than happy with the take.

Now high and wide from the roof of the TARDIS, looking down as Yvonne rushes in. All the time, we're building up different layers of visual information. It'll all add pace and energy to the scene when it's cut together. On paper, this bit seems pretty simple. The soldiers level their guns as they flank round the front of the TARDIS. The Doctor emerges, they cock their guns and that cues in Tracy-Ann. Well, that's the theory.

"Okay, plenty of energy, soldiers. And action!"

Tracy-Ann runs in and passes through the centre of the troops.

"Oh, how marvell… Oh, bugger!"

"Sorry, I haven't come out yet," David apologises.

"No…" I think she can tell.

There was no loud click of the guns breaching.

"Wait till they've cocked their guns," Susie explains.

"I thought that was a cock…" Tracy-Ann turns to the front three soldiers.

"Show me a cock?"

Two of them obligingly arm their weapons. Click! Everything's lined up again. I call out instructions.

"Tracy-Ann, you've got to come in after the clicking of the guns."

"Yep... The cocks..." She's heard.

"Otherwise known as the 'cocking'..." Susie joins in.

"I've got it, on the 'cocking'..." She's definitely heard.

I just didn't like to say that. Take Three. She comes in too soon.

Susie shouts out, "No cocking... No cocking... Go back, there's no cocking!"

Tracy-Ann grinds to a halt at the back of the troops.

"Does it take that long for the cocks?"

"Give it ten seconds at least..."

I ask for the scene to go from the top again. Take Four. The set's clear, and Susie calls out again.

"Now don't be premature, Tracy-Ann..."

"Yeah, pre-cock, and then cock..."

Take Five nails it.

"Plain shot... Five seconds of this..."

Packing crates, some against the walls, some flanking the aisle, marked out with yellow painted lines on the floor between them.

"In you go, boys..."

Two Cybermen amble in and stand one behind the other, just in an alcove between crate stacks, all of which bear the Torchwood logo.

"And standby... Action!"

The first one strides forward. Suddenly he physically jerks and falls face down on the ground. The one behind him swivels round and crashes down.

"And cut! ... You all right?"

The front Cyberman kneels up, a human face grinning under his balaclava. As soon as his head hit the tarmac, his mask flew off, but thankfully out of shot!

"Loads of energy!"

I'm standing too close to Nick Briggs' microphone, and my voice echoes like a Dalek's. That's clearly Billie laughing as a result, waiting behind the doors we're focused on.

David peers out, Shaun behind him, standing in shot with Billie. He races in, picks up two magna-clamps and barrels back through the doors. We open the shot, move back and frame it wider with a crate in the foreground.

The action's replayed, David races in, ducking down as the Doctor dodges post-production laser fire, grabs the clamps and crashes to the floor, nearly falling right over them as her tries to make it back. There's the distinctive sound of Piper laughter from behind those doors again as the take ends.

Okay. The big one...

Daleks enter the hangar at the base of the Torchwood tower. They come face to face with a line of seven Cybermen, backed by troops and all opening fire at once. There's a huge green screen draped down the wall to their rear – in my dreams, I'd love to see a CGI effect making the Torchwood storage hold stretch back as far as the eye can see, just like the scene at the end of *Raiders of the Lost Ark*.

"And action!"

The troops run in, take up their firing positions and let rip. There's a camera operating to the side of the hanger so we can maximise coverage, and the noise from the machine-guns is deafening. We get it in two takes. Even firing blanks is expensive and, with that amount going off, the costs would rocket if we kept going.

This has got to look huge, really epic. We need to build up quick shots to cut into; Torchwood troops taking cover behind a crate and opening fire, a line-up of Cybermen marching in, then turning in unison and firing at the Daleks... Singles on Cybermen hitting the ground dead, close-ups as soldiers get caught in the crossfire...

For the reverse on the main shot, the Black Dalek glides in, leading the other three and the Genesis Ark. They stop in the immediate foreground and open fire, turning slightly from side to side, gun sticks twitching as they exterminate.

Just time for one master shot, as far back, high and as wide as we can get, showing the Daleks and Cybermen fighting at close range, right up until the moment the Black Dalek says "Elevate." Thankfully, that's where The Mill take over, and we don't have to worry about making him fly!

David Tennant on location, waiting between scenes. When I started working with David, Russell T Davies said he was rapidly finding his feet as the Doctor. Now, two years down the line, he's honed it to perfection.

ABOVE: The Scooby Gang at the National Television Awards in October 2006. David is standing behind the usual suspects: Camille Coduri, Noel Clarke and Billie Piper.

ABOVE: Billie Piper's assured performance and professionalism are incredible, and her leaving scene was just as upsetting to film as it is to watch.

Freema Agyeman, the one and only Martha Jones, but also very nearly the President, maybe a Preacher, and definitely an Adeola... and look where that lead her!

Executive producer Russell
T Davies and producer Phil
Collinson. No matter how
complex the problem, or how
late you need to talk to them,
they're always there for you.

ABOVE: Russell T Davies with the Best Screenwriter BAFTA he won in 2007. I still can't get over the fact that we both won Welsh BAFTAs for *Doomsday*.

ABOVE: Julie Gardner, *Doctor Who*'s other executive producer and part of the triumvirate who make the show tick.

LEFT: Neill Gorton, from Millennium Effects, with one of the finished masks for his Art Deco-influenced Cybermen.

ABOVE: At Television Centre with Adrian Rigelsford, making plans for *The Dark Dimension* in 1993.

RIGHT: Battersea Power Station is a great location, but impractical for days of filming when you're based in Cardiff. We had to use various tricks to get round this.

ABOVE: During shooting, every evening is taken up with planning my camera script for the following day.

ABOVE: A camera scrutinises David Tennant on location. David is full of ideas and energy, always striving to make each scene the best that he can.

ABOVE: *42* guest star Michelle Collins, promoting the new series at a press launch in London.

LEFT: For *Rise of the Cybermen*, we asked guest star Roger Lloyd Pack to play the villainous John Lumic like George Orwell.

John Barrowman, who plays Captain Jack, and Freema get the giggles between takes. There's never a dull moment when John is around!

11TH JANUARY 2006

Episodes Five and Six – *Sequences of the Cyberfactory corridor and Upgrade Chamber are shot at The Brewery, Wilcrick, Magor, Monmouthshire.*

When we first started filming them, it took a while to get each actor into their Cyber suits, but now, after all this time, the crew have got it down to a fine art and they're getting them ready pretty quickly. I've tried one of the masks on, and once the front and back plates click together, it's horribly claustrophobic. Not for me, thank you very much. But I did try, and at least I have a sense of how difficult it must be for those guys.

The leggings are a bit like a wet-suit which comes up past the midriff, and the arms are like sleeves made from the same material. It's all been painted and finished, so the detail increases as the layers go on. Each actor is wearing a black balaclava to conceal any sign of skin tones, and a thick rubber collar for the neck sections pulled on over that. It's all held in place with straps and clips, and after the pelvic plating is secured, the sections of leg armour slide on and the feet are tied tight with laces, because they're basically boots underneath. With the chest plate, arm sections and gloves quickly fitted after that, the heads are left clear until just before we start a take, allowing the actors to rehearse and get a sense of where they have to move before their sight is well and truly restricted.

Tonight's the remount for the scenes we lost at the Uskmouth Power Station, and the brewery we're in is just as effective. We've lensed up down a walkway between hop vats, which must stand at least 15, maybe 20 feet high. The idea is that each one is an upgrade chamber, and, as the extras file past them, we're moving the Cybermen around to create the impression there are far more on patrol than just the ten we're working with.

The tension has to reach a high here as Shaun plays out the sequence where Pete's confronted by a Cybernised Jackie. He's in a line of upgrade specimens with Rose as they're recognised, and we frame in on medium close-ups, moving between Pete and Cyber-Jackie. The lighting's almost metallic blue, and the vats are thick with shadows and strategically placed jets of mist.

Parts of the plant are a labyrinth of unending feed and drainage pipes, and there's something very clinical about the way it all looks. It's ideal to get some shots to cut into the sequence where Mr Crane instigates the first batch of conversions, holding low and wide, all the time thinking of how creepy they'll look as 'The Lion Sleeps Tonight' plays across them.

12TH JANUARY 2006

Episodes Five and Six and **Episodes 12 and 13** – *Alleyway sequences and shots of the Tyler estate are completed at Louden Square, Bute Street, Cardiff Docks.*

"Loads of pace and energy! Here we go… And action!"
The TARDIS door flies open, David hurtles out…
We're holding the shot low and wide as he races across the playground where they've landed, and starts to set up a triangle of hi-tech cones. If you look closely, there's careful detailing on them, thanks to an idea Peter McKinstry had, so their bases look like roundels from inside the ship.

The Doctor's trying to triangulate the point of origin of the ghosts, by jerry-rigging a detector he's built from cannibalised TARDIS equipment. We've already shot what's meant to be footage of it dematerialising, shot from high up on a wide lens to try and make it look like CCTV footage. So we go in for a similar angle, setting up on a crane so we look down across the TARDIS roof and hold on the Doctor as he works frantically.

The ghost effect and the energy triangle that captures it will be sorted during post-production. During planning, Russell made it clear that he didn't want even a hint of what they really are, and compared the shape and look to the figure seen during the opening titles of *The X-Files* – sort of a black silhouette surrounded by a crackling field of energy.

How do they physically move, though? Well, that's going to be down to Ailsa Berk. There'll be a day of studio work with green screens flanking all the main walls, so performers encased in black body-stockings can go through all the ghost moves we need.

Susie will have to crack the whip to rattle through the large number of set-ups, but she knows that. She's more than savvy enough to judge which days are going to be more intensive than others and, when they're as complicated as the 'Ghost Day', she'll go at it with a strategy and make sure everything's in the can.

We'd never have got through the Cyber-Dalek battle in the hangar without her keeping everything moving. Definitely one of the best Regimental Sergeant Majors around!

13TH JANUARY 2006

Episodes Five and Six – *Exterior Cyberfactory roof and Zeppelin ladder sequences are shot at Unit 878 Picketson Site, RAF St Athan, Barry.*

About a week after you've started filming, your video editor begins to look at all the rushes as they come in. So, let's say he has what? Five or six days of material to work with? Well, what he does first is methodically watch and digitise them. Every frame, every take that's been completed, it's all logged and loaded on his computer system.

Now, once he starts, a really good editor will recognise when we're missing a cutaway or close-up for a specific scene, and he'll flag up that fact to Phil pretty quickly. If he approves of the idea, he'll get in contact with Susie, who's out working on set, and explain, "We need a close-up on David's head in this specific light." It might be something that the second unit could handle, but whatever the case, the Editor can actually ask or sometimes demand that the scene requires the material, otherwise we'll be left with a very weak sequence. And we all have to take notice of that.

The sequences featuring the Zeppelin escape from the factory were done near the end of November, but it's become apparent that the pace and speed of the scene … well, if we could only add this shot here, or have that moment there… So that's what we're doing. Small moments, yes, but vital to build up the excitement. Definitely.

RAF St Athan has the ideal facilities to stage the last shot we're missing, of Rose falling into the void. Technically, it's got to be a high angle looking down at green screen to get the effect. Abbi Collins has planned a stunt fall and had some overhead wires rigged up, so Billie can do a carefully controlled drop for about 30 to 35 feet, landing on a green trampoline below. If we shoot it in slow motion, it should create an eerie effect as she reaches out, legs flailing behind her while she claws for help with her hands, desperately trying to reach for the

Doctor. When it's combined with the plate shots we've already got of the Lever Room, it should look terrifying.

15TH JANUARY 2006

Episodes 12 and 13 – *The sequence with the Cybermen storming the barricades on the bridge are shot at Cardiff Dockside, Cargo Road, Cardiff. Scenes are also completed by the second unit in the Torchwood subterranean corridors #1, #2 and #3 at the Basement, Capitol Arcade, Churchill Way, Cardiff.*

I've got one day. That's all.

Every shot of the battle on the bridge, as the arrowhead of Cybermen march on the soldiers. We're working from 8.30 am to dusk. How on earth are we going to make this one happen?

It's barely past nine o'clock in the morning. The air's icy, there's still a slight trace of mist coming from the river. Paul Kasey's in costume, along with nine other Cyber actors, rehearsing them over and over, drilling them so they march in perfect battle formation. The masks are off, but their heads are covered with black Lycra hoods, like balaclavas, so they do look a little strange. By the prop lorries, the armourer is going through the motions showing the military extras how to fire pistols and machine-guns. There are gun shots going off, and the distinct, hollow plastic echo of Cyber marching. There's definitely going to be a ruck!

No two ways about it, I've planned this out as an epic fight. Every shot, every angle, every special effect, it's all been meticulously storyboarded by Shaun Williams, so everyone knows precisely what I'd like to see. I've sat with him, describing who's going to be facing where, what direction the camera's going to move towards, and a rough schematic's evolved, sketching out key scenes like a comic strip.

What's interesting for me is that when you're planning action scenes like this, you often feel you don't give enough details, when it's actually quite the opposite. How do I explain that? We've got to switch channels to and look at something I did for ITV.

Steel River Blues, seven episodes of big-budget, prime-time drama exploring the lives and working challenges of Blue Watch, a team of fire fighters working in the heart of Middlesbrough. (It was broadcast in September 2004. In fact, being involved with that show was what led to me being unavailable for the first season of the new *Doctor Who*.) One episode I directed featured a sequence with a car going out of control, and rolling free down a hill towards a load of pedestrians. One of the show's main characters chased after it, managing to steer it through the open driver's window and trying to career it to safety.

Now, I shot it exactly the way I storyboarded it, matching every frame. Technically, we couldn't film it the way I'd originally planned, but because that visual information had been laid out by working with an artist like Shaun, the crew could see exactly what I'd dreamt of. Working together, we found ways to make all of it happen, using tricks and techniques that you wouldn't necessarily have thought of employing.

An example? You've got a car, rolling over and over, but you can't afford to stage the stunt. Time, money, extra rehearsals, you know the routine. Well, if you use a hand-held camera and move it all around the stationary car, swinging it at wild angles, during the edit you've got snippets of visual information that'll help create the impression it's tumbling in exactly the way you wanted. Cheats like that always enhance and never detract. It really is a case that the audience doesn't know what it can't see.

Back to the bridge. It's all iron girders, heavy with rivets, probably used for freight trains shunting into the goods yards when the docks were more active. There are grooves for rails running along the surface, which Danny Hargreaves and his special effects technicians have lined with bullet swabs to detonate in the foreground as the Cybermen close in.

"Loads of energy, complete terror. This is an invasion!"

"And action!"

Susie cues in the Cybermen after I shout directions to the extras. Some are done up as soldiers, some are cowering pedestrians, petrified and caught up in the crossfire. There's ten Cybermen in the distance, framed low and wide, marching in perfect sync towards camera, arms rising into a firing position. Metal chimneys and a large red crane line the background of the shot, thanks to the industrial estate in the heart of the docks where they're headed from. Several large mist-guns are trailing vapour across the road to add atmosphere.

"Let's have them grind to a halt, spread out into a mish-mash and reform as two lines, marching forward, arms raised and shooting."

Onto their targets. This is one long take that can be cut into the main action. The camera's moving along track that's been laid down, following people running for their lives, weaving round the burning wreck of a car…
Lots of flames and smoke in the foreground.

Closer, closer…

Soldiers leap out of a jeep in a medium wide shot, breaching rifles, taking aim and scrambling for cover.

Closer, closer…

Strafing laser fire effects from the Cybermen as they get within range. And then they're right on us!

Burning debris, screams, more troops arriving at great speed and charging into position behind some sandbags and firing, trying to hold them back. But the Cybermen are an unstoppable force, like a tank, crushing everything in their path.

The budget's only allowed enough money to blow one car up, right at the centre of the bridge, so I've framed it wide to get the full visual impact. We've got to generate pace, energy and fear. When you've got pyrotechnics going off left, right and centre, the rules are incredibly strict; walkie-talkies and mobiles get switched off around the whole area, to stop their signals setting anything off accidentally, and people have to stick within safety zones, all cordoned-off and well out of reach of any flying debris.

With something like this, you've got to push what you're staging to extremes, and, first thing in the morning, going through the shots for the day with Phil and Susie, that's when I emphasise how far I want to go. Normally, you get reined in, but with today, everyone's pulling out the stops to try and make it happen.

A Cyber suit's been rigged up on a support framework, positioned with its firing arm raised, and packed with explosives so we see what a bazooka shell can do on impact. The camera monitors are tucked away in a small black tent, Phil's alongside me watching the screens. Susie's outside and cues in the detonation.

Boom! Armoured plating, limbs and wires fly everywhere in a ball of flame that ripples outwards. Did we get that? Everything's fine. Phil emerges into the daylight with me, and I don't know who's grinning more. We're both thrilled. Two cameras, a mad flurry of flames, guns and set-ups later, and we've actually done it!

Let's fast forward to post-production, and the edit for this specific scene. The cut's done. The battle runs for about one minute 30 seconds, all very exciting and driven with a hell of a pace. Russell, Julie and Phil sit through it, and it's Russell who makes the most surprising comment.

"Just take your six favourite shots of the battle. Make the sequence out of that. I think you can make it just as exciting by being shorter, and the impact would be stunning as a result…"

I've got to admit, I'm not happy.

"Are you serious? You have all these terrific shots, and you want to let some go?"

But Russell's very clear in his reasoning. "I think by making it shorter, you'll leave the audience wanting more, rather than giving them too much all at once, because we've got other areas to spend the money on and the episode's already over-running time-wise.'

So I have to take stuff out. We've just got to be pretty brutal and cut it right down by about a minute. But it works. None of the impact's lost and, if anything, it works far better by being shorter. He was spot on. You still get the information you need, it's still exciting and you're not holding the audience up, making them wonder what's going on.

16TH JANUARY 2006

Episode 13 – *Beach scenes for the finale of* Doomsday, *and* Army of Ghost's *establishing shot for the 'alien world', are shot at Southerndown Beach, Ogmore Vale, near Bridgend.*

I've woken up far too early. Not the easiest day ahead.
Both for Billie as an actress and Rose as a character, they've got the most harrowing, disturbing and ultimately romantic scene to get through. She's literally tearing herself up emotionally. It's the end of her journey, and I don't know quite how to do it.

I'm driving out to the main unit location. We are about to shoot Billie's final scene in *Doctor Who*. Yet when I finish this block she and David have to shoot two more stories which are due to appear earlier on in Season Two. This is going to be quite a wrench for both of them. We've got a beautiful beach at a place called Southerndown. You can see right across the Bristol Channel. Somerset is on the horizon, but for the purposes of our story this will be a beach in Norway.

Questions are racing through my head. 'What's the best way to approach shooting this?'... 'Who do I film first? David or Billie?'... 'Is that going to put too much pressure on them if I offer them that choice?'

With any TV show that's got a long shoot ahead of it, it's always the same. It seems to take forever to reach that first day of filming, but once it starts, the whole thing just flashes past. Weeks merge into months and, before you know it, it's over. Because I've been filming with Billie for something like 40 to 45 days now, I know the emotional range she can call upon when she's acting. She can build up tears and emotions very easily. Knowing her, she'll cry very easily on Take One. Take Two, more difficult but I don't doubt it'll be just as good.

I've got to allow her space. Got to give both her and David plenty of time to gently find a way to play this out for themselves, without me interfering until I need to tweak the moments I feel I have to. I've talked very little to them about how to confront this scene. It's been there all along, looming up on us, but it's not going to be something they'll enjoy as it ultimately marks the end of their time together.

I'm having breakfast. I'll ask the third assistant director to find out when would be a good time to go and quickly nab them. They'll both be in make-up for a while. Time ticks by too quickly, everyone's nearly ready. The crew are strangely quiet. No jokes, no noise, no bustle... They've all been together for a long time, and they know exactly what's got to be done today. There's a strange, palpable sense of sadness in the air – Billie's still got five episodes to do after these, but it's still a goodbye no one wants to make, and there's a clear determination to do her proud in every way they can.

"Look, Billie, David, can we have five minutes to chat?" I've found them in the make-up trailer, talking. "We need to discuss how we play today, because I want to make sure I give you both the amount of time you each need to reach the emotions that the script's asking of you."

Which way do I go? Do I shoot David first? My instincts are telling me to frame him over her shoulder, a long lens shot maybe? Or do we favour her because she's going to have to break down?

David – ever the gentleman, Doctor and diplomat. "To be very, very honest with you... Billie would like to go first, because we've discussed this. And that's what I think we both feel would be best."

"The problem is, just thinking about it makes tears well up in my eyes," says Billie. "So it's going to be very hard to hold back, but I will and I know I can. But there's one moment where I know tears will start flowing. The problem is, if you want to go a second time, I know the emotions will be there but I don't know about the tears. I don't know that I'll be able to... First time, yes. Second, I just don't know. Third, you'll be very lucky."

I know I've got to be spot on. This has to be right for her. Billie's the kind of actress who gives her lines all the emotions and resonance she can, on each and every take without fail. And she will even do this when she is just feeding lines to David or the other actors when it is their shot. David's like that too. He'll give all of his cue-lines to her off-camera exactly as he would if the lens was focussed on him. He'd never let her down on that score, or any other actor come to that. It's great for all actors to have a full-on performance given to them off-camera.

We've rehearsed and blocked it out. The camera is in place. The wind is harsh, freezing and wet.

"And action..."

The first take is brilliant.

"Absolutely magical. Gob-smacking and moving, that was just fantastic."

Every word of it's true, but I spend about four minutes, while everyone else stands there freezing, discussing it with the script supervisor and Phil. Unfortunately, a bit of fluff or something landed on Billie's lip and hung there for the last part of her speech. I have to go again for that reason, and that reason alone. I agree to go in and do it straight away, rather than hang around and do other shots and expect Billie to be able to muster all that emotion again from cold.

"I put money on Billie being able to do it again."

Reassuring words. I have to be the diplomat now.

"Look guys, that was beautifully done, and I've got to cover David, but we need to do that again."

Billie's honesty makes everyone move quickly.

"Well, you'd better do it now, because if all that's got to come out of me again. I can do it if we go for it now…"

Very quickly, briskly, we're ready to go. David's watching Billie like a hawk, making sure that she's okay. This is just as difficult a scene to play for him. The Doctor knows that he's lost Rose forever and it's his last chance to say goodbye.

Billie does it exactly as, if not better than, before. The only problem was that it's so windy her fringe falls across her face several times, But in character, she manages to pull it to one side.

Between those two takes, I've got enough to show everything we need. "Are you really happy? Because I can do it again."

There's a look from David as if to say, "No way, you don't need to." And he's right.

I was absolutely thrilled and moved by her performance, as were the rest of the crew who were on the beach that day. There was not a dry eye in sight, and every time I see that sequence I am still moved to tears.

David's there for her, as soon as we cut, hugging her tight. Then it's his turn to give his performance. In the scene Rose tells him tearfully that she loves him, and the Doctor seems in all his shyness to be about to say the same, but his image fades away just at the crucial moment. Rose will never know what he was about to say, although the audience gets to see the Doctor in tears inside the TARDIS so I guess they realise how he feels. What a performance from David, brilliant for every take. What a team.

That was the day. That freezing cold day. When Rose Tyler died on that lonely, isolated beach. And yet, at the same time, she also came wonderfully alive. This was one of the greatest moments I have experienced both in my career and, indeed, my life.

17TH JANUARY 2006

Episodes 12 and 13 – *TARDIS scenes are shot at Unit Q2, Newport*

You're bound to see it sooner or later.

You walk across the back lot at the studio and there's a line of trailers. Each door sellotaped with printed paper, saying who you are and what you're playing. Costumes are being dressed, last-minute rewrites carefully memorised, mobile phones are buzzing with activity and coffee's being drunk, but mostly, there's a lot of waiting being done.

There's the third assistant director politely knocking, calling whichever member of the cast is needed to the set. The results are always the same with one particular person.

"Coming!"

One, two, three and bang! The door flies open, slams shut in an instant and he's off, running to the studio as fast as he can. Completely focused and more than eager to crack on, you can see that playing the Doctor is an absolute joy for David Tennant. And he just races to get to the TARDIS, the spaceship or wherever he's meant to be.

David has an absolutely clear idea in his mind of where he wants to go with the dialogue in any given scene, and he usually has an idea of, maybe not exactly where he's going to move or walk, but certainly where the Doctor should be heading towards on a particular line or when he should react in the way he does. Without fail, he always has an idea of what he wants to present at any given point in the story. He's pinpointed the precise mechanical structure of how it all unfolds, and knows exactly where the trigger points are that lead the Doctor towards the finale of the episode we're making.

My attitude with all actors is the same; I want to see what's on offer first, what they've got in mind, what the script's made them think of and the way they want to play it. Then I can help to mould and develop that. Ultimately, all the actors have a gut instinct about what feels right, because they're in charge of that character. David has been for two years, so he's still protecting where the Doctor might want to go, where he might want to take him, and as the director I throw one or two ideas to him that I think might enhance the scene. He always listens and he always tries out the ideas. If they work well for his character and the scene then they stay. If it feels uncomfortable then the ideas are dropped and we move on, but at least we tried.

I usually know from Russell if there's anything special about the Doctor at any particular moment that we want to bring out, but then so does David, because he's had a similar conversation with him. So we effectively join forces and merge our ideas. David finds his way round the set in character, and I tell him whether it works for me visually or not, which he's always very flexible about. There are certain things we have to lock onto, certain places you have to go to in a scene – you could have a book being put near a computer screen where the Doctor suddenly notices the information it's displaying. The script's already laid down the basic plan, so it's clear you have to achieve these positions, but how do you get there? That's where we negotiate.

When we've worked that out, finding how the scene naturally evolves and rehearsing it until it's locked down, that's when we show the crew. Then I call the shots out that we're going to do to cover the scene, choreographing the angles I want to see the scene from, all the time assembling a kind of mental jigsaw, slotting the pieces into place and visualising how it will ultimately play when it's assembled. All the time you have to remember that you want the audience to have the same reactions you did when you first read the script, to share the sense of excitement it generated, and now the actors are giving you their take on that same feeling.

As we progress, you find that David will absolutely rely on the director's discretion over whether a take is good or not, but that he will also know in his heart whether he's ultimately happy with it. If it's good enough for me and David's content with what he's done, I'll call out, "That's brilliant! Moving on…" He'll trust that, but sometimes he'll make a request – David never demands, he's always an absolute gentleman. "Is there a chance I could do that again? I think I can make that really so much better; I'm not quite happy with that, Graeme."

You don't even think about it, you go "Yes." Even if you're really pushed for time, you make it up and adapt the next scene if that's what's worrying you, and concentrate on getting this right. It's not rocket science. If I hear the magic words, "I can do that better," I have to go again if there's enough time, especially when it comes from the Doctor!

18TH JANUARY 2006

Episodes Six and 12 – *Scenes involving Jackie Tyler's flat are staged at Unit Q2, Newport.*

There's a simple wrap-up scene for *The Age of Steel* to do, showing the TARDIS in Jackie's front room as the Doctor brings Rose back to her reality, and reassures her that her mum's still alive in this world. Singles on David as he leans against the TARDIS, and on Camille as she comes out of the kitchen, then close-ups as Billie embraces her. Well, we're sorted in about an hour on that, but the scenes for *Army of Ghosts* are going to be a bit more complicated.

We lens up wide on the kitchen as Camille mimes watching the 'ghost' of her father suddenly move through the wall and circle round to her side. The image of the figure can be added in post-production, but for the moment we're relying on her acting.

Working round the settee, as the back story of when the ghosts arrived and how people reacted is laid in by Jackie, I just hold on tight close-ups and two shots of Camille and Billie. No foreground detail or moves on either of them, or David. The focus for the viewer has to be on what they're saying. It's a key moment, no time for distractions.

19TH JANUARY 2006

Episodes 12 and 13 – *The interior and exterior scenes of the Cybermen storming the suburban house are shot in Broadstairs Road, Canton, Cardiff. Brief shots of Rose Tyler are completed on a London bus, and sequences in the surrounding city streets are also completed at The Hayes, Cardiff.*

This has got to be one of the scariest moments of the episodes. The Cybermen break down the front door of an average house, and we see the family – mother, father, son, daughter – cowering in terror on the stairs.

As the son breaks away and tries to run and hide in his bedroom, bang! Too late! A Cyberman swings round at the top of the banisters. There's nowhere to hide now, and we've just taken away that safety barrier kids have to hide from monsters. No point in running behind the sofa or trying to make it to under your duvet, because the Cybermen are already upstairs!

20TH JANUARY 2006

Episodes 12 and 13 – *Pick-up shots of scenes involving the sky above London, Jackie Tyler's Flat, Torchwood HQ Lever Room, the 'No Entry' corridor, the Sphere Chamber and the Tyler estate are all shot in and around Unit Q2, Newport.*

Editing's well under way, and it's become clear that additional shots – maybe a close-up of a hand operating equipment, a door opening, a phone being answered, things like that – are needed as extra visual information to build sequences up. It's not a case of not completing enough material during the shoot, because generally these things only come to light when you're structuring the cutting.

You want an example? The Doctor's machine he uses to trap a ghost. When it was originally done, the dials on the prop were clearly repainted earpieces from Episodes Five and Six. Russell howled with laughter at that one, and Phil quickly sanctioned a re-shoot. Now, that's nowhere near as complicated as it sounds. No David Tennant required, no need to go back to the location, just a brief shot, no more than a couple of seconds, of a hand reaching in and operating a redesigned version of the switches.

It really is a case of just spending a few hours, carefully mopping up the final bits and pieces you need to complete the jigsaw.

27TH JANUARY 2006

Episode 12 – Trisha *studio sequences were shot at Teddington Studios in London.*

Down to Teddington. Last time I was here must have been, what, six years ago? That was for a sitcom I was directing, but this is something rather different.

The *Trisha* production team have been brilliant. We've got about 20 minutes. That's all they can spare us and that's all we need. The audience is already in for the show that they're recording anyway, so they're already fired up and ready to join in.

I talk through the shots I need. One set up on Trisha Goddard herself, one for an audience reaction to what she's saying and one for the actress we've brought in, who's sitting on the stage talking through her particular crisis. I go up to the control gallery and go through everything with the director.

Fast, professional and brilliant. It couldn't have been easier. The audience fall about laughing when they hear our mock-up show is about a woman falling in love with a ghost, and the lady herself? Trisha's thrilled to be a part of *Doctor Who* and couldn't have been nicer to work with.

It's just the same with Barbara Windsor. It's strange being back on the *EastEnders* set. It's quite a while since I directed it. When I did, the episodes involved Barbara, so there's a nice little reunion for half an hour. When I walk in during the morning to meet her and say "Hi," she tells me it was one of her dreams to be in *Doctor Who*. I get the feeling that she's pleased it's me doing this, someone she knows, because we've always got on, and thankfully I have enough time to explain to her what we need to get out of this. With Russell's blessing, she tinkers with her dialogue to make it 'more Peggy'. Secretly, I think he's quietly thrilled that he'll be able to say he's been rewritten by Barbara Windsor!

On the Queen Vic set, all I need are three shots to get in and out of the sequence. She's quick, very precise and clearly loves every second of it. In an hour, it's over. Time to move on.

18TH FEBRUARY 2006

Episode Five – *The revised/new pre-credits sequence for* Rise of the Cybermen *is shot in a work room at Gwinnut Ltd, Electrical Engineers, Foreshore Road, Cardiff.*

A decision's been made.

Episode Five's been assembled. It's been viewed, reviewed and analysed repeatedly, but Russell's still not happy with the opening 'hook'. Something just doesn't feel right about it.

We open with the TARDIS crash-landing, the Doctor, Rose and Mickey emerge, think they're in present-day London, cue the Zeppelins then bang! We're off into the title sequence.

The nagging doubt has been that John Lumic's introduced a bit too late in the story. His presence has got to be felt sooner, outlined and painted more broadly as a clear threat. As we stand, he comes across as slightly tragic, and the notion that he's dying kind of outweighs the fact that he's been working on creating the Cybermen for years, maybe even a few decades.

Russell comes in armed with a few pages of script. He's written a new two-minute sequence. The initial TARDIS scenes are a movable feast, they'll work just as well after the title sequence, but this? This adds a real punch.

We're shooting in an engineering workshop at the back of a large engineering works. Ed has quickly added some cannibalised equipment, I guess retrieved from other episodes, to give the room the right kind of edge. Some looks stripped down and some has been rebuilt, but it all combines with what's already there to create a slightly run-down laboratory. This is Professor Kendrick's base of operations. Paul-Anthony Barber's been brought in by Andy Pryor to play him, not long after he cast him for *The Chatterley Affair*, which Julie's just finished making for BBC Four.

Roger Lloyd Pack's back in Lumic's chair, and he's thrilled with the scene. I think he agreed with us over the fact that it really adds to the character, clearly defining layers of motivation very early on.

Lensed up low and wide, I want the opening shot to draw slowly across the lab benches, with equipment energising and lights powering up as Kendrick prepares his demonstration. Paul Kasey's in a Cyber suit, but I'm keeping him in the background, backlit by a stack of six lamps so he's blurred. You know damn well what he is, but there's no definition of focus. There's a hint of life, a soft-focus touch of blue as it speaks, but there's no reveal yet, not till the end of the episode.

Onto Roger; tight in on his thin pale lips, half-smiling, before we see him edge forward from the shadows, then we move right in on his face for the bulk of his dialogue. Just as before, he's unblinking, cold and subdued. I know I told him "Think of George Orwell" while we were filming his early scenes, but he's admitting that he had Donald Rumsfeld, the United States Secretary of Defence, at the back of his mind as well.

Finally, we frame Kendrick in the foreground as a hint of Cyber gloves grab and electrocute him. We've managed to wrap everything up in about three hours, just a morning's work, but when that's cut together and in place, I think it'll achieve everything Russell wanted.

22ND FEBRUARY 2006

Episodes Five and Six – *Unit Q2, Newport is used for pick-up shots on Kendrick, Lumic's scientist.*

The opening 'hook' for Episode Five is still not quite there. We need some close-ups on Professor Kendrick as he realises Lumic doesn't care about getting his experiments ratified by the United Nations. Paul-Anthony Barber's back, and we're done in less than an hour.

9TH MARCH 2006

Episodes Five and Six – *More brief pick-up shots; the Cyberfactory and Control Room, the Newsroom and the Upgrade Chamber are all staged at Unit Q2, Newport, with a street scene exterior completed on the same day.*

Episodes 12 and 13 – *More pick-up shots in the Torchwood Sphere Chamber.*

Another day of snippets and cutaways, mainly tiny details that have come to light as being needed during the editing; close-ups on the Black Dalek, locked off shots on Rose's mobile phone. It's fiddly, but if it's going to visually make the stories more complete, then it's a necessity.

31ST MARCH 2006

Episode 13 – *The closing seconds of* Doomsday *with Donna, 'The Bride', are shot on the TARDIS set at Unit Q2, Newport.*

That's it. The main unit's done. They're at the wrap party, slowly unwinding after nine months of shooting, but where am I? Back on the set and about to roll the camera again.

A couple of days ago, I got the final scene of *Doomsday*. Not Billie, she's on the other side of the wall. This is something entirely different. 'The Bride' makes her fleeting appearance on the main TARDIS set, and it's only in the past day that I've been told she's being played by Catherine Tate. The whole thing's being played out around me like an MI5 operation. There were questions and curious faces from some of the crew as they left.

"Hello Graeme! What you doing back here? You coming to the party?"

I'm all smiles and nods. Just popping by and, yeah, I'll be there later. Russell's put George Smiley to shame keeping this one quiet. There's a skeleton crew running the set, Phil's helping me run the floor and tea's being made by someone. Maybe it's Russell?

Catherine arrives. She's seriously incognito, using her maiden name at the hotel after being smuggled into Newport, and only coming to the studio when the coast was clear. I tell her it's a real thrill to meet her, even if it only involves about an hour of working together.

Shots are lined up quickly, we play the moment through a few times, and before it feels as though we've really started working, she's being driven away into the night.

If this all works and the secret's kept, nobody will see this one coming!

11TH APRIL 2006

Episodes 12 and 13 – *Final pick-up shots are completed at Enfys Television Studios, Unit 31, Portmanmoor, Cardiff. These involve the Torchwood Sphere Chamber, the Tyler estate and the Torchwood Underground Hangar.*

Finally, the last bits and pieces are complete. A couple of shots of Cybermen crashing to the ground, the Black Dalek against some green screen and it's done. The battle's won on set, and there are about three months to broadcast for the season's finale. *Rise of the Cybermen* and *The Age of Steel* are about a month away from being screened, and I've got weeks of post-production ahead. I can't help but wonder what people are going to make of it all.

EPISODE THREE: HOW IT USED TO WORK

NOVEMBER 1966

Thursday.

Another damp church hall, another gently steaming tea urn sitting in the corner, flanked by standard-issue light-green BBC cups and saucers. Strips of white tape on the floorboards mark out corridors, laboratories and offices. There's a rumour the radiators actually work, but the actors' jumpers say otherwise.

Scenes start and finish, bare furniture stands in for futuristic equipment and, for the moment, guns are fully loaded coat-hangers. The floor manager calls out what the next set-up is, where we're meant to be, and guides the actors onto the next makeshift set. We're in Saint Helen's Church Hall. Patrick Troughton is still finding his pace and style. The Second Doctor's only just arrived.

Christopher Barry is calling the shots, a bundle of energy, intense concentration and enthusiasm. A heavy ring-bound script folded in one arm, his free arm almost conducts the moves.

Friday.

The upper management are in, all eyes intently watching the final rehearsals. The producer, the script editors? Normally only invoked when there's an emergency or seen in the BBC club; lots of pipes being smoked, a handful of cravats but countless blazers and ties. All very RAF, but then again, so many of them fought in the war.

Tomorrow, everyone moves to Riverside Studio One, slap bang in the middle of a street of houses, right next to where the Thames passes through Hammersmith. There are only two studios there, and the pub over the road's been rechristened as Studio Three! *Doctor Who*'s being recorded only a couple of weeks ahead of broadcast.

So where do I fit into all this?

I'd just joined the BBC. Acting wasn't for me. Been there, done that. This was what I wanted, training as a floor assistant, working my way up to floor manager, passing lots of *Doctor Who* stories on the way. *Colony in Space*, *Planet of the Daleks*, *Planet of the Spiders*, *The Seeds of Doom*…

Then *Warriors' Gate*, working with John Nathan-Turner as producer, who kept an eye on what I was doing when I went on the BBC Directors' Course. When the phone call came, and he asked me to direct a fantastic script by Robert Holmes, I was thrilled, but looking back, it was a very different way of working then.

The Acton Hilton. How many memories? Not a hotel, that's just what it earned as a nickname. Could have been due to the uniformed commissionaires standing outside, flanking the main doors, or maybe it was the quality of the catering, I don't know. It was 13 floors of rehearsal rooms, stretching up in a long, thin tower, with each level holding different-sized spaces for every level of production. It still belongs to the BBC, but it's now open-plan offices and the days of white sticks and tea urns are long since gone.

Let me explain. Certain floors were designated to drama series and serials, some were for sitcoms, some for light entertainment, and then there was also stuff that the children's department made, and even the occasional current affairs show. Parking was at a premium, and people generally tubed in as the station was directly over the road. So for *Doctor Who*, the guest actors came through the revolving doors into the minuscule reception area and were greeted by a large pin-board. You know the kind. Silver letters carefully arranged in rows against some black felt. *Doctor Who* was normally on the fourth floor. The actual rehearsal room might shift around a bit, but as a rule you'd be locked off to that level for the whole of the series.

Now, let's go back to 1984 and *The Caves of Androzani*. Peter Davison's Doctor bites the dust, 'hello' Colin Baker, all wrapped up in a four-part story, right? We've already spent three days filming around a quarry in Gallows Hill, a couple of miles outside Dorset. That's only involved a few scenes. The TARDIS arrives, there's the entrance to the caves, wallop! Lots of gun fire and bullets hitting the sand as mercenaries try to kill the Doctor, then the final struggle to get back to his ship as poison seeps through his body. But that's only a fraction of the story.

The rest was broken into two recording blocks, one handling episodes one and two, while the second cleared up everything you needed for the final instalments. Yes, there might be the odd scene from the latter block that you needed to shuffle forward and stage during the first, but the general rule ensured you stuck to that set routine. Rehearsals for each block ran for five days, and the director would have planned out quite meticulously a way of shooting everything, so he or she would go in and expect the actors to move through the scenes following what had been mapped out. That's how you'd plan it.

You also had to work out a studio plan, showing where all the cameras were going to be. Five different cameras automatically fed live footage to the Control Gallery – some people called it 'The Gods', sitting right at the top of the studio, overlooking everything – where the director worked with the vision mixer. With the cameras now offering a choice of shots, as they were called out, they'd be recorded directly onto the master tapes.

So you'd be going from close-ups to wide shots and back again, instantly editing the sequence, if you see what I mean. Piecing it all together bit by bit.

In those days, you'd go into the studio at ten o'clock in the morning, maybe 10.30, start rehearsing a scene and then shoot it. Yes, sure, the actors all knew their moves and lines, but this was the first time they'd been on the finished set, or had to use working props, but the routine remained the same. You'd rehearse the next scene and shoot it, rehearse the next scene and shoot it, working your way through everything you'd blocked out at the Hilton.

Let's rewind a little.

You'd arrive, you've got you're coffee, you're in Rehearsal Room 403 and it's the first morning there. What happens next? Well, that's when you had the read-through. Nobody hits the floor running yet, it's just a gradual process as the actors begin to find their way round the script together and bring their character ideas to life. By the afternoon, you'd start choreographing the shape of the piece, and by the same time the next day, you'd hopefully be in a position to run through the recording block's two episodes with some sense of structure and pace. Certainly by mid-morning on Day Three, it would be reaching a point where you could start going through each scene and dissect it a bit more, investigating the key moments, defining the highs and lows that you had to find. All of this was practical, helping you to resolve any issues and figure out precisely how you were going to present it from a dramatic point of view.

Roll on Day Four, and you'd be ready for a production run for the technical crew. Costumes are being made, monsters vac-formed and painted, let's take all that as read. For this, the heads of department would come to the rehearsal room and mark up the floor with white tape, making the basic shape of the sets that the action would have to take place in, giving the actors a rough approximation of the space they'd have to work within. Pretty battered tables and chairs represented the TARDIS console, laboratory equipment or even spaceship flight decks. Bits of old rubbish and tatty old sofas would make up the set for you, and doors were represented by white poles on counterweights.

Sometimes, if you looked at the room from certain angles, it could easily look like a sea of flag poles. But what about the Daleks? How did we rehearse with them? Well, the operators shuffled round on chairs, and maybe got the lower half of the casings for producer's runs, but if your character had to shoot at them before being exterminated, the best you could hope for was a coat hanger. There wasn't a machine-gun in sight until you stood in front of the camera. It all bore no relation to what you were going to present visually in the studio, but it showed how the cameras could be placed without moving things around too much.

Now, as the cast went through their paces, you could take a look at the flow of the story and figure out where to get the cameras in, where the booms would be, where actors would have to make entrances and exits, where a specific door would open and whether there was scenery behind it to mask that you were in a studio. All of that had to be sorted out.

Day Four's also D-Day. The producer's run. Always a movable feast, sometimes swapped round with the technical run from an afternoon to a morning, but no matter what, you always had to be ready.

This was the first time the producer could stand back with the director, and quietly watch everything play out that you'd been working on. The first assistant cued it all in and ran it, unless something went seriously wrong, because you had to concentrate on the performances, and replicate exactly what was going to happen in the scenes in studio, even though you were in a bare-walled version of the set.

He would be watching intently to ensure the overall shape of the story was correct. Does the dialogue work? Are the actors in the right place on the set? Is something clearly not working? Should it be cut? The director would have to show the whole run-though as fast as he could, to gauge a sense of pace and energy, and then at the end the producer would sit down with you, after sending the actors away for a coffee, and for 20 minutes or so have a discussion about each scene, what was wrong with it, how to put it right, what was missing, etc.

Time to call the actors back. That's when the producer would say "Thank you for a lovely show, and see you on Saturday when you're in the studio." I'd then give out his notes, where I'd explain what he thought we should alter. If there were scenes affected drastically by this, then any actors directly involved would stay behind, and we'd look at the action and see how we could polish it. Chances are this would go on until six o'clock in the evening; that was the cut-off point when everyone went home.

Day Five. That was my day for fine-tuning. The actors would run through it very slowly so I could check all my camera angles are working, that everything I want to do is correct and that the producer's notes have been addressed. That's a morning gone, and, at the end of it, I'd turn to the cast. "Lets have lunch, then come back and just do one run for ourselves and let it go, and then we'll finish early because tomorrow, we move into the studio."

The block starts. It's two, maybe three days of rehearsing a moment, showing the crew, then committing it to tape. The cameras would practically fall over themselves trying to get all the shots. They had them all written down on a card, so they'd move from one shot to the next, locking in on where they were meant to be, finding what they had to focus on, where they were meant to be, what they were suppose to be looking for.

Scene by scene, the first studio rehearsal was always pretty raw, but that was forgivable. By the second, you'd start to panic that it wasn't working, because the shots were all over the place. But on the third rehearsal, then it started to come together, and, boy, was it good!

"Shall we have a go, or shall we have one more rehearsal?"

We do it, then we either agree to do another take, pick up several shots or simply move on to the next sequence.

That's how we made *Doctor Who* in the old days.

EPISODE FOUR: MASTER SHOTS

29TH APRIL 2007

I still can't quite believe what just happened.

Russell won Best Screenwriter for it, David Tennant won Best Actor for it, and I won Best Director for it. *Doomsday* went down pretty well at the BAFTA Cymru Awards.

Phil cried, Russell certainly got tearful and the wine flowed freely. Together, we'd survived the war that brought Torchwood to its knees. But that was for last year.

There's been a long haul abroad directing episodes for a new series of *Robin Hood* since then, and we're only a few weeks away now from screening another two episodes of *Doctor Who* that I've completed.

There was barely a month between arriving back, fresh from the arrows and unending heat of the makeshift Sherwood Forest in Budapest, and having to head for Cardiff for more *Doctor Who*. No ten weeks of pre-production or 50-plus days of filming this time. I don't think there'll ever be an attempt to mount a production block like that again. It worked, but the strain and the pressure was intense.

This time it's two self-contained episodes. Originally, there was an idea that I'd be doing a two-parter – *Human Nature* and *The Family of Blood* – but as can happen with production schedules, things got moved around and Charles Palmer was allocated those episodes.

For me? *42* by Chris Chibnall and *Utopia*, penned by Russell himself, and I couldn't be happier. *42* is about a spaceship called the SS Pentallion which is spiralling out of control towards a sun. When the Doctor and Martha arrive on board, they find the crew – Kath McDonnell, Riley Vashtee, Orin Scannell, Hal Korwin, Dev Ashton, Abi Lerner and Erina Lessak – all fighting for their lives. Things get worse when Korwin, then Ashton, become possessed by what is eventually revealed to be the sun itself, which is a vast living creature.

Utopia is Russell's magnum opus, the opening salvo for a three-part story.

Captain Jack is back with the crew, and the TARDIS lands at the very end of the universe, where Professor Yana is working alongside his insectoid assistant Chantho in an effort to save the last surviving humans. Feral predators called the Futurekind are closing in on the rocket silo they're hiding in, but there's far more to the Professor than meets the eye... He's another Time Lord, and as his memory returns, he becomes more like his old self – The Master.

The pre-production's over and done with, the locations are locked off, the tone meetings are a thing of the past. We're ready to shoot.

SEASON THREE RECORDING BLOCK FOUR

15TH JANUARY 2007

Episodes Seven and 11 – *All the opening TARDIS interior scenes for both episodes are staged, along with the initial scenes involving the Airlock/Escape Pod for 42. These are completed at Unit 1, Trefforest Industrial Estate, Trefforest.*

"I just fancy a bit of a skedaddle!"

Day One, Scene One, Take One... Well, Scene Two actually.

David sprints across the gantry leading up towards the console at a frantic pace, throws the appropriate lever and we're off.

"Freema..."

Freema Agyeman, who has returned to the programme in the role of new companion Martha, is left standing, caught in the breeze from the Doctor's coat as he passes.

"Can you shoot him a glance beforehand, as he goes past you, like 'This is odd?'"

She gets exactly what I mean. She's got to share the audience's confusion over what's bugging the Doctor.

Picture this, the 'hook' for *Utopia*; Martha and the Doctor are chewing the breeze, taking in the sun outside the TARDIS as it sits on the rift recharging, and bang! Panic stations! He spots a familiar figure charging across Cardiff Bay towards them. Captain Jack's back, she's none the wiser, and the Doctor really doesn't want to know.

There's questions and answers time at the console – "What's the matter?", "What's wrong?" – but the Doctor's avoiding the subject. Now, on paper, this could be played as just static dialogue, but now we're shooting, I want energy, movement and urgency. Even though David and Freema are holding their positions as they speak, I've got to keep the camera moving; foreground information, plenty of movement, static background details. It's a bit different this year. The TARDIS set's been moved. We're in new studios with a wider space to work around and improved access points up to the console, but something's not quite right. Every piece, every nut, flat, chevron and bolt was meticulously deconstructed in Newport for the move, then carefully reassembled to fit its new home. But now the central column audibly shrieks and groans as it moves up and down. The upward movement, well, it's almost shrill, while the downward, that's kind of baritone. I think Ed Thomas is as perplexed as everyone else. Nobody knows what's causing this, and there's no real time to fix it until the season ends its shoot. It's not impossible to work around. You can do close-ups, vary the angles and movements around the controls so that you don't end up framing the centre of the console, and that gives you a bit of freedom. If you don't see it moving, then there's relative peace on the set. Everything else can be fixed during the dub.

We lens up a low-angle shot. I want to move the camera around the perimeter of the metal framework supporting the seats by the console, so it passes tight in the foreground. It creates a real sense of depth.

After well over a year of playing the Doctor, David's certainly mastered the art of TARDIS in-flight acting. I wonder if he's figured out a set pattern of switches to throw, like a plane's take-off procedure?

"Right, we're buffeting backwards and forwards. Bit of a roller-coaster. Plenty of energy…"

The TARDIS is in trouble. It's got an unwanted passenger. Captain Jack's clinging to the exterior, and it doesn't want to know. No matter how it tries, it just can't flick him off. As a result, we're out of control.

Some tiny explosives detonate inches away from David's hands. Freema throws herself backwards, quickly scrambling back to his side. The time rotor's speeding up, screeching so much you can barely hear the dialogue. The Doctor crashes down onto the floor.

"And cut!"

Freema's quickly helping him up.

"David, are you all right?"

The scene's set up again. David's chatting about actors, and mentions Patrick Stewart. Freema's face visibly lights up. She's the first to admit to her Trekkie past.

Take Two. David doesn't just grip onto the edge of the console, but sort of twists his leg up and braces himself with his foot against it. There's something slightly spider-like about it.

We need to see the scanner screen on the console as he stares at it. Plenty of pre-recorded graphics played back onto it via a DVD. Symbols showing the sheer speed that the TARDIS is hitting as it hurtles towards the end of the universe. The camera's positioned just behind David's left shoulder.

"So, Graeme… Are we matching lines to this or just jiggling about?"

We just need a quick shot of the action.

"Jiggling about!"

Next scene, and we're there. The lighting's toned down. Slightly cooler, darker, all adding to the Doctor's solemn reaction as he realises where they've ended up. I tell David there has to be a look, just a smile to Martha after he says they really should go, sort of admitting "I know damn well we're not meant to be here, but let's take a quick peek!"

Right at the end of the take, David produces a huge, slightly manic grin. It's a purely instinctive reaction to the moment… and brilliant. It actually kind of sums up what the Doctor's really like in one brief shot.

Just one more shot for Episode 11. The Doctor dragging a power cable out of the core of the TARDIS, and outside to Professor Yana's laboratory… But that's not even been built yet! It gets knotted, twisted and tangled round David. Maybe power cables should be added to the 'don't work with' list next to 'Animals, Kids and Daleks'?

Costume changes all round, onto Episode Seven and more opening scenes, which will ultimately build to *42*'s 'hook'.

Just as before, we've got to keep building up the momentum on screen.

The Doctor's adapting Martha's mobile phone with the sonic screwdriver so she's got 'universal roaming', and moving round the TARDIS so he's directly on the opposite side of the console to her. What I want to achieve is a 'whip-pan', following the phone as he throws it across to her. Roger Pearce, the camera operator, has got to literally 'whip' the camera in a move from David to Freema, physically panning it as the phone is thrown, and then land on his focus mark on Martha as she catches it.

Sometimes, if you see a similar sequence on screen, say going from a bus to a house that's miles away, well, that's achieved during editing by assembling shots to create that fluid transition. But this is being done live and it's very tricky.

Rehearsals crack it with several practice runs. Roger knows exactly when to move. Take One, Take Two... Not quite there yet. Freema accidentally fumbles catching the phone on the third take, but by the fourth I'm happy.

Freema moves round so she's in front of David, her back to the camera so that the focus is primarily on the Doctor, as he holds up a TARDIS key on a chain and lets it trickle down into her open palm. Right on the first take, David desperately tries to keep a straight face as it slowly falls through the gap between her fingers and lands straight on the floor!

Right, now we're onto the spaceship, the SS Pentallion. Apart from the ship's medical centre scenes we've got scheduled in a few days' time, the only other material we need to complete in Unit 1's studios for *42* revolves around its airlock and escape pod. The pod's a self-contained unit that Ed Thomas has had built, complete with a porthole window on its entry hatch. The actual airlock it joins onto has a second hatchway, painted with burnt metallic browns and scorched reds to emphasise the building heat that's searing through the ship, and beyond that there's a back-flat covering the eye-line looking out onto the ship's corridor. It's all cramped and slightly claustrophobic, but that's exactly the kind of feel we need.

During the tone meeting, I talked about the idea of creating a harsh colour contrast for inside the pod. Throughout the rest of the Pentallion, we'll have reds, fiery oranges, yellows, and crimsons. All building up the burning, savagely hot and sweltering atmosphere, almost as though everything around the crew is beginning to melt. But here, it's full-on icy blue saturating the screen, heightening the fear and sense of isolation for the scenes we're blocking.

Only a few brief shots are slated for today, with Freema and William Ash as Riley, and both of them have been doused down with fake sweat and grime.

Take One. The airlock door grinds open. No smooth hiss and whirr of mechanics until later, just wood against wood for the moment. Freema charges in, near-hysterical and right on cue as Riley punches at the pod's controls. The hatch opens, she dives in and lands flat on her face, legs flailing with her lower half hanging out.

Take Two. In they go, the porthole slides into place and Martha's bathed in harsh blue. The energy levels are crackling. She hammers against the glass, panic-stricken and crying out for help. I'm thrilled – they've hit a real high in a very short time.

"And cut."

You almost don't want to leave it there. The day's ended on a real cliffhanger. No theme tune and trailer for 'Next Time' though…

16TH JANUARY 2007

Episode Seven – *Spaceship Escape Pod and Airlock Scenes are filmed at Unit 1, Trefforest Industrial Estate, Trefforest.*

Back to the Escape Pod.

We lens up on Martha at the porthole, shouting and crying out for the Doctor to help her. As she hammers on the window, her rings tap loudly against it. Between takes she starts tapping out a drumbeat.

"Freema, take the volume up a pitch so we can hear the cues. Real panic, real terror…"

She's slightly muffled inside the pod, but by Take Three she's loud and clear. Martha's utterly helpless, and so's the Doctor.

There's barely any light on David, just a slightly muted yellow and orange. We line up the reverse shots on the Doctor, shouting to her from the corridor outside the airlock. It's quite eerie as we shoot over his shoulder, catching echoes of his reflection and Martha in the distance, all in the same frame.

"I'll save you… I'll save you…"

Ed's designed the pod so that it actually works as a detachable unit from the main bulk of the set. This allows camera track to be laid down leading away from the airlock.

Right, onto the next shot. Focus on David, framed on the opposite side of the chamber's main door, silently shouting out as the pod pulls away from the Pentallion. The key to this is silence. Deadly, impenetrable silence... Just for a few seconds. It'll cut through the main pace and noise of the action like a knife, because suddenly the only information you've got is what you can see and not hear. It's got to be a shocking moment, complete despair.

Roger operates the camera, creating a point-of-view shot from the pod, slowly detaching and revealing the exterior hull. On screen, The Mill will add CGI effects so we get the whole spaceship, and not just a small section of scenery with the rest of the studio clearly revealed on the sidelines!

Onto Freema. The same trick, but now favouring the pod. We pull back along the track focused on Martha, shouting against the porthole, growing more and more distant, heading towards the sun. As before, The Mill have got to remove the technicians and light-stands clearly in view, or they'll get burnt to a crisp. That's definitely a phone call Phil Collinson wouldn't want to make to the union!

I need more detail, more information to build up the sequence. A camera's set up inside the pod so I can get an angle over Freema's shoulder. She's looking out at a green screen, rigged up a few feet away, so that The Mill will be able to add the shots of the Doctor as the pod drifts off.

"These jeans are, like, seriously cutting into my leg!"

What do they call it in America? A wardrobe malfunction? Sounds like Freema's having one.

Moving on... The front of the pod's been finished with a texture like decaying rust, all brown and mottled. We hold and slowly close in, almost at a painful crawl, on Martha and Riley framed in the haze of blue inside. They're as good as dead, and they know it. You can almost sense that their lives are flashing before them as they lament their past, their present and their clear lack of futures. Take after take, the dialogue's intense, intimate and laced with a sense of doom. They both play it with a deep raw edge. We move in hard, working with close-ups, two-shots and singles, all immediate and personal.

Take Five's called to a stop.

"That was lovely, that one."

Freema clearly agrees with William.

"Yeah, that was the best one, I think."

The schedule's allowed just enough time to add more shots to the sequence we did last night. Fast and furious. Pace, pace, must create energy and pace… The action's remounted, Freema and William hit the floor running, doors slam shut, keypads lock them. There's a distinct adrenaline drive behind the story, and there's a key thought the cast must always have right at the forefront of their minds.

"All the time, you've got to remember, if you stop, you're dead."

One of the make-up assistants waits until we're ready to roll cameras and dives in with a fine water spray, dousing down faces so the sweat's always fresh and registering on camera. Freema's smacking her legs between takes, shaking her head, loosening her mouth, trying to keep the buzz of energy going that the scenes are creating. She clocks Roger's distinctive jacket.

"I like the get-up today, Rog! Very samurai!"

Riley furiously punches out codes on the pod's computer read-out screen. Both actors are rattling off their dialogue when, quite by accident, Freema suddenly moves the location of the airlock, saying they're stuck in Area 13 of the ship instead of 17.

"Maybe it should be Area 13. It's unlucky!"

David's back. More shots of the Doctor as the escape pod ejects. All of his lines today, they've just been exactly the same three words, the promise that Martha just can't hear. He suddenly brings up the Doctor's anger and frustration with a deliberate bluster, breaking up the words with a staccato beat, causing me to interrupt the take laughing out loud.

"I… WILL... SAVE… YOU!"

He milks it a bit more.

"I really, really, really will save you!"

All of the pod scenes have been shot in story order, mainly to increase lighting effects and play on the fatigue factor as they get closer to the sun. It's been very confined for them, very claustrophobic.

Last set-up for the day. We zoom in to a tight two-shot. Nothing but smiles and relief at the fact the Doctor's managed to save them, magnetising the Pentallion's bulkhead to draw them back to port. And maybe also due to the fact that it's a wrap, and Freema and William can go home.

Tough day. Hot as well, technically speaking, for both of them in the pod. Unlike Icarus, they got back from the sun without getting their wings burnt.

And it's David's turn tomorrow.

17TH JANUARY 2007

Episode Seven – *Spaceship airlock scenes are staged alongside the stunt sequence involving McDonnell and Korwin's death at Unit 1, Trefforest Industrial Estate, Treforrest.*

"Could you just turn the steam up a bit more?"
David's got to contend with wearing a space suit, and also cope with the fact that his hearing's blocked off. Barely a word's getting through his space helmet. Shouting instructions just translates into a dull mumble for him. How's it going to be trying to direct him when we turn the wind machines on?

Mental note: on all the shots we're about to do I've got to build up the absolutely critical danger the Doctor's facing. One false move, one tiny slip-up and smack! He's dead, and he knows it. The physical risk is immense. But this isn't quite what it was meant to be. The script's original version of this scene involved a space walk right along the ridge of the ship's spine, but things have just weighed too heavily against even trying to stage that. There's the actual build of the set you'd need, studio time for pretty complex green-screen work, and then the sheer workload it would create for The Mill. Much as I dreamed of it, and much as I knew I could have shot the hell out of it, it's missing in action.

These things happen all the time. Sure, you're disappointed, but then you just channel your energy and imagination towards what's replaced it. Now, the Doctor's got to lean out of the airlock that's just ejected Martha and Riley's Escape Pod, and hit a lever that's almost impossible to reach. Will he fall? Will he get dragged into the sun? Yep, we can pile on the tension with this one. Bring it on!

We move in tight on a close-up as David enters the airlock set, with steam trailing from the corridor outside. The Doctor waits, bracing himself while the chamber de-pressurises. This could be suicide. The space suit Louise Page has assembled has internal lights round the perimeter of the visor. They're icy blue, so it makes him look cold, kind of chilled with apprehension.

Onto a low and wide shot, looking up as he moves to the outer shell's exit, looking out of what's actually a double-glazed perspex door. Someone mutters that he looks like Dan Dare. Thank God I'm not the only one here who's old enough to get that joke… At least they didn't say Buzz Lightyear!

Right, this has to look huge, epic, but we've only got about 12 feet of the Pentallion's hull surrounding the mouth of the airlock. It's thick with scorched blistering paintwork.

Here's the plan; I can build up the sequence moving tight in on David as he leans out, put the camera in close, then move against the wall, taking the lens high up so we're looking straight down on him pressed against the hull… But that's just the technical side. What I have to rely on is David literally throwing himself around, clinging on to the frame of the hatchway and struggling furiously as he's nearly torn apart and dragged outside.

The wind machines are pointing directly at him. Mist-guns are feeding in smoke, spreading the vapour wide and fast as the blades spin and radiate it out across the set. The Doctor's got to stretch hard, arching himself out, trying to hit the boxed-in lever to demagnetise the bulkhead. Initially, this is just a fraction too close and pretty easy for David to reach, so one of Ed's team unscrews the unit and moves it several inches across, just to make it that bit more difficult.

"Lots of buffeting, David."

Take One. As soon as he edges round the side of the hatchway, his space helmet starts to visibly turn round and unlock as it presses against the scenery.

"Cut!"

Take Two. David throws himself backwards, only just avoiding falling as he clings onto the framework. Those gloves he's wearing are pretty bulky. It's difficult to feel where the buttons are, but he's doing it.

"Come on! Come on! Go on, my son!"

The lever's thrown. He crashes back into the airlock but catches the rim of his right leg's boot.

"Bloody hell!"

Take Two. He stretches out, twisting and practically hyperventilating with the effort. Oh, there we go! He's fallen out onto the studio floor, but quickly scrambles back, picking up the moment precisely before he lost his balance.

"Are you all right, Guv?"

I check quickly between takes. He's sprawled out, exhausted. A grin and a thumbs-up from the airlock floor – it's like watching old NASA footage of Neil Armstrong. I can easily work round what we've got there.

Now we need detail. The buttons next to the lever. We've got to see what he's trying to do.

David gets a respite. For the moment, we just focus on his hand struggling to activate them. Then we're high and looking down, framing the lever box tight in the foreground, angling the camera to visually suggest there's more distance separating it from the hatchway than there actually is.

"I can't reach. I don't know how much longer I can last…"

Take after take, he's hitting exactly the right pitch. He throws the access panel open, and one of the buttons on the keypad by his head falls off, bounces on his faceplate and lands on the floor. We can act zero gravity, but not recreate it, more's the pity! Camera tracks are laid down, running up tight against the bulkhead wall. It's a moment of realisation. I want to go straight in, focusing right into the heart of David's eyes as the Doctor realises the sun is alive.

Yellow-gelled lights add streaks of colour to his space helmet's visor, emphasising the volcanic heat directly ahead. The Mill will add a hint of the reflection from the sun – all swirling orange molten lava – during post-production, and hopefully we'll get a taste of that movement as it's cast onto his pupils. We have to hint that it's reaching deep inside his mind.

"David, if we make the agony exhaustion… That's what I think it should be, then we're not giving anything away."

The Escape Pod's back, its hatchway flies open, Martha and Riley bundle out. The Doctor's crawling across the floor, and I want David to offer a confused image of what's actually wrong with him. He's not exhausted, he's been possessed, and Freema can't show any hint that she knows what's wrong. Well, not yet, at least.

It's a quick change for those guys. Charles Palmer's waiting for them on the TARDIS set. He's got to complete a handful of quick scenes for his two-parter that's been shooting while I've been in pre-production.

I really don't know how David's still standing after all of that!

Imagine this is you. It's your first day on the set, the very first scene you record and it centres entirely around your death. There's been no build-up of your character's story arc prior to that, and no real chance to talk it through, let alone meet the actor playing your husband, who you're about to drag off into a joint fiery suicide. It's tough. That's what the job can be like, and that's exactly what's facing Michelle Collins.

We block it out, rehearse the sequence as much as we can. I offer an emotional pointer, what I want to see as the drive that's making her do this. McDonnell's not evil, she's not a bad woman, the nature of her job's forced her into this situation. She's the Pentallion's captain, and she accepts what that means: full responsibility. If there's a way for her to save her surviving crew, then she's going to do it. The tragedy is that it's also the only resolution where she can be back with her husband, or what's left of him at least.

"Was that all right? Can I do another one?"

It's a simple shot. McDonnell is crouched in the corner of the airlock, lying in wait as Korwin enters. She just slides up against the wall until she's standing, and already Michelle's driving hard to find where the character's at.

Matthew Chambers is wearing the deep red welding mask Korwin uses to conceal the intense heat radiating from his eyes. He moves forward, ready to kill her, but she lunges towards him, hugging him as the airlock activates.

"Absolute fear. Here we go…"

This has got to be intense. Heartbreaking. Her eyes are smarting from tears. Her hand reaches for the airlock control pad on the wall… And a large chunk of it falls off!

We line up the final set-up on tape.

Michelle and Matthew are wearing harnesses that can jerk them backwards out of the airlock, throwing them out of shot and onto crash mats. Plenty of smoke, red gels are saturating the hull with light, the camera's rolling…

"And action!"

In an instant, they take off.

"I didn't get a chance to say I love you!" Michelle protests as she scrambles back onto her feet, then leans against the bulkhead wall. "What a way to earn a living!"

Now we're onto 16mm film stock, utilising a camera that can be under-cranked to create slow-motion effects. McDonnell and Korwin are going to slowly spiral towards the sun. It has to be balletic, graceful and strangely peaceful. Michelle's face to face with Matthew, suspended on a Kirby wire rig in front of a large green screen. They're holding each other in a final embrace as they slowly rotate about five or six feet above the ground, with a wind machine to their left making her hair billow slightly and adding movement to their clothes.

All of the footage is mute and looks slightly eerie out of context, but the finished effect? It's going to be one hell of an emotional high! Not an easy day for any of the actors. David's been blown to bits, and those Kirby wires can really dig into places you don't want to mention. And we haven't even got to the location yet!

18TH JANUARY 2007

Episode Seven – *Initial scenes in the SS Pentallion's Engineering Room are staged at St Regis Paper Company, Caldicot, Monmouthshire.*

It's seven o'clock in the morning. The air's freezing and crisp. It's winter… Why is it always a shock to the system?

Sarah Davies, our third assistant director, picks me up and we drive to the location, Sudbrook Paper Mill. We've all been warned that the whole site, which is vast, has been empty for quite a while. No wandering into areas unaccompanied, no leaving litter, and wrap up warm, it's like the Arctic in there.

Over the humped bridge, through the gatehouse and into the car park, right next to an echoing and very empty warehouse. Grillo's, the on set-caterers, are already dishing up breakfast to anyone who's awake and, as with any set, there's the distinct whiff of bacon butties and coffee drifting amongst the crew.

Freema's here and in the make-up trailer, David's on the way and Michelle's with Lindsay Bonaccorsi, who's supervising the wardrobe department while we're away from the studio. Every night, no matter how grimy they're meant to be on screen, costumes are meticulously cleaned and presented fresh and ready to wear the next morning, only to be suitably 'distressed' so they match the state they'd last been seen in.

The main entrance is on the side of an adjacent building to the warehouse called 'Rewind'. There's got to be a reason for that, but nobody seems quite sure. Stairs lead down from there into the bowels of the mill itself. Thick with engine grease, burnt-out cables, chains and steam, Ed's team have done a staggering job. We're literally underneath a gigantic grid of metal rollers, filming in what's effectively the access tunnel engineers had to use when this company was still up and running.

Red emergency lights line the area; it's dank and freezing. This could almost be *Das Boot*, the submarine's been hit and we're sinking. There's a palpable sense of danger here, both on the monitors and for real. Hard hats, luminous yellow jackets. It's dark and some areas with low-hanging pipes are lost in the shadows. We're supervised for every step we take.

We've got to break the back of a big scene; two and a half pages of dialogue at least, loads of exposition and nearly all of the main cast on set. We'll end up with six of them grouped together for some shots, and that needs an awful lot of coverage. Singles, two-shots, loads of energy and plenty of reactions. You've got to keep the information moving on screen, even when the words are taking their time. Looks and glances between the crew, it'll all build-up detail about how they function as a team... We've got to believe that these guys can fly a space freighter together.

Right from the outset, I wanted everyone to be clear on the internal logic of how the Pentallion works. There has to be a kind of practical geography of where various sections of the ship are, and why. We've been thrown in with a fully functioning freighter crew. Yes, they're a bit weather-beaten, but they're professional right down the line.

One of Ed's design assistants, Peter McKinstry, has plotted out a blueprint of the ship's design, going into exacting detail regarding how it would all work. This, in turn, has gone towards creating the on-screen graphics for the ship's computer monitors. Everything's been thought through... I wonder how many people will spot the brand name on the side of the space helmet David's been wearing, and the irony of calling it Icarus?

Take One. Down the stairs and into the engineering room. The Doctor's in the thick of it already, quickly concocting a back-up plan to use the ship's fuel supplies as a way to break free from the gravity pull of the sun. Plenty of wide shots, and then into close-ups. David's firing on all cylinders and can't resist ad-libbing reactions to Anthony Flanagan's dour attitude as Scannell, who basically gets landed with making the Doctor's wild theories work.

Hands on hips, aiming her best withering stare, Michelle cuts him down to size. Take One comes to an end.

"Oh, believe me, you're going to make it work."

David smirks at her.

"That told him!"

Take Two. McDonnell's line ends, and David's straight in again as Scannell slumps off.

"Bundle of laughs!"

Take Three? No wit, just drawing breath sharply across his teeth, like a builder giving a dodgy estimate, and then rolling his eyes up in despair as he looks at the Captain.

Onto the Doctor's happy prime number speech, rattled off down the intercom at Martha. It's verbal pyrotechnics from David. He just has the knack of being able to learn it all perfectly, gauge its speed and keep it all clear and perfectly defined. If you listen, I promise you, there's not a syllable there that's been missed.

That's a wrap for the day. I leave in the dark, spend all day working in the dark, then go home and it's dark. Strange thing is, it's not even a night shoot!

19TH JANUARY 2007

Episode Seven – *Spaceship Engineering Room scenes are filmed at St Regis Paper Company, Caldicot, Monmouthshire.*

"Erina, you got those tools or what?"

Gary disappears from shot. Ashton's lying underneath a section of the sabotaged ship's engine on a flat trolley, trying to repair it. We've framed the shot to track alongside the framework of the drive section, before coming in to focus on him as he works.

"Drill…"

Gareth Williams, the first assistant director, cues him to pick up some equipment.

"Door…"

That's a reaction shot. He looks right. Is that Erina? The lighting's quite subdued on him. His face is clear, but there are plenty of shadows from pipes and wiring. It's not quite working.

"Gary, when you lift your head up, don't move it as high and hold it in that position as the trolley's pulled out."

That's got it.

"Cut! Yes please."

Onto a top shot looking down on him as he sees that it's Korwin who's pulled him out. The camera's high enough to allow Matthew to lean in and lift him up by the lapels. For the reverse angle, from Ashton's point of view, we look right up at him. His hands reach either side of the lens as he looms into a tight close-up.

Pipes have been fed into Matthew's welding gloves so, as we frame up a two-shot, he clutches either side of Gary's head, who screams in pain as smoke's fed through them. When this is backlit with a red gel, it looks as though Ashton's head is burning.

"Nothing coming out, is there?"

Matthew looks at his smoke-free gloves. Gary smirks.

"Maybe you've changed your mind?"

Michelle's backing away from Matthew as he closes in towards her. Korwin's intent on killing his wife. We're holding her in a medium close-up as she passes through vapour trails of red smoke.

"What are you? Why are you killing my crew? … Oh, I'm sorry. I'm not even looking at him!"

Take Two. Matthew's feeding in his lines and moving alongside Roger, who's operating a hand-held camera for the shot.

"Sorry, can we do one more? I can't hear when you say 'wife'…"

Michelle's not hearing her cue line. The voice inside the welding helmet is a bit too muffled, so it comes off for the next take. To show Korwin stalking towards her, we stage an equally long take, which I'll be able to cut back and forth with so we see McDonnell as well.

"Okay, guys. Bring up the smoke."

As Gareth shouts out to the special effects crew, Matthew stands some distance down the corridor underneath an archway of pipes. He's soon drenched in vapour, red back-lighting kicks in and he strides towards camera as we pull back, stopping as he moves into a close-up directly under the mouth of a vent pipe from the cooling system.

"Matthew, at a given point I'm going to bellow 'Drop!' So fall to your knees please."

I've relayed the moves I want to see, and Gareth makes sure everyone's clear over what has to happen.

We've got shots of Anthony spinning the wheel of the valve controlling it, so all we need is a low shot looking up, at a slightly oblique angle on Michelle as her character faces up to Korwin and the coolant blasts out and freezes him. Fire extinguishers mounted overhead belch out a thick jet of billowing, noisy white spray.

"Drop!"

Gareth can barely be heard. He checks Matthew's okay as soon as he shouts "Cut."

"How was that?"

"Cold."

20TH JANUARY 2007

Episode Seven – *Spaceship Engineering Room scenes, sequences in corridor areas #11, #10, #7 and #6, #4 and #2 (in that order), along with the central corridor locker area are staged at St Regis Paper Company, Caldicot, Monmouthshire.*

"That's it! That's cool. When you do that, it sort of breathes."
Roger's lensing up on Matthew's hand. He's lying on the floor, his right welding-gloved hand in tight close-up, and the movement of his fingers as he slowly reaches for the red mask is the first indication that he's still alive. We're picking up the sequence just after McDonnell thinks he's been frozen.

"Watch your shadows, folks, on the floor."

A last request from Roger as Gareth cues in the scene.

"Okay, everyone. And action!"

The smoke swirling round him as he stands is red, thanks to the lighting, and his stiff, almost robotic moves make the moment just as unnerving as I'd planned.

"We're crashing into the sun, and everything's about to blow up unless we get a move on! And action!"

Michelle runs into shot down a smoke-drenched section of the corridor. The red paint on the pipes, valves and pressure gauges is glinting in the light. She freezes as Korwin swings into the frame, and then runs back the way she came.

Suddenly, there's a slight yelp and she falls to the floor. I'm there as quickly as Gareth. She's tripped over some pipes, But apart from swearing a bit, she's fine.

We move on, and Michelle's got some questions about the way her character's reactions, and why. We're able to get Russell on the phone during a recording break, and he takes us through her concerns. Everyone's happy, and we get the takes rolling again. That's the fantastic thing about working with Russell. If there's a problem, no matter how late you might be shooting into the night, if you need something answering, he's there 24/7. Even if you have to wake him up, after giving him a few moments to get his thoughts together, you'll never hear him complain.

The same's true of Phil, but chances are, unless there's something really pressing to be dealt with elsewhere, he'll be there on the set with you. But if you're shooting, even if his mobile's taking messages, he'll get back to you within ten or 15 minutes to talk through the problem.

With one camera positioned sideways on, filming Rebecca as Erina moves to a tool locker and starts collecting what she needs, we've got another focused on her from inside, so we catch the action in mid-close-up as she goes through her final lines.

As the locker door shuts, Matthew's in position so Korwin's suddenly revealed standing there, waiting, ready to kill her as she backs away. We go in for a tight close-up on the welding mask as the door shuts, totally impassive, just staring… And then frame Rebecca as she backs against the wall. Harsh blue filtered light hits her on cue as she screams. The token black silhouette is all that's left. Most serial killers in fiction have a calling card, so I guess that's his!

22ND JANUARY 2007

Episode Seven – *Spaceship Central Corridor Area #30 sequences, along with a scene in the Central Corridor, are completed at St Regis Paper Company, Caldicot, Monmouthshire.*

Most of today's scenes build up the detail and highlight the threat that's being faced, as the Doctor and Martha find their way into the ship's central corridor and meet McDonnell and her crew for the first time.

It's the 'hook', the pre-title grab that makes you want to see more. As soon as they realise they're crashing into the sun, the TARDIS is out of reach and there's no escape, we're off.

Michelle, Will, Rebecca… Between takes they all get the same treatment, as make-up artists move in and coat them with a sheen of spray-can sweat, even though it still feels like it must be close to zero down here. Huge gas heaters are either side of the area we're working in, but the wind chill of the air moving through the factory, due to its sheer size, still gets to you.

Freema's the first to show real panic as she looks out of the porthole that's been rigged up along the side of the set, and sees exactly what they're heading towards.

I only heard Freema had been cast while I was in Budapest making *Robin Hood*. The offer had already been made for me to go back to *Doctor Who*, so I knew that I'd be working with her again. And I sent her a text congratulating her, and asking how the hell she'd managed to keep quiet about it for so long!

She came in to audition for the Cyber stories last year, and you just knew there was a presence about her, and a wonderful sense of humour as soon as she came into the room. The idea at that stage was that the president was going to be a woman, so she read for that, and a part that later got dropped for another member of the Preachers. I think it was a girl who was a serious martial arts expert, but whatever the case, she gave us two very distinct and completely different interpretations of the roles. You honestly wouldn't have thought it was the same actress doing them, so everyone knew that she was good, but those parts didn't work out.

Don Warrington took over the president when Russell decided it should be a man, so, working with Andy Pryor, we got Freema in as Adeola. Not a huge part, but key and one that she clearly caught people's attention with.

And now it's what, just over a year since she finished filming *Army of Ghosts*? That's a hell of a journey for anyone to make, but she's still the same; bright, inquisitive, funny and eager to learn. You ask her to try a line or an action a different way, and she hits it spot on, as soon as the cameras roll.

23RD JANUARY 2007

Episode Seven – *The main Spaceship Central Corridor along with Areas #30, #29, #28 and #27 all have scenes completed at St Regis Paper Company, Caldicot, Monmouthshire.*

Gareth's trying to get out of shot, after setting some chains swinging to show the ship's moving, before any of the actors charge out of the Medicentre and straight into him. "I'll do it as fast as I can without tripping over," he says.

David, Michelle and Anthony all move past camera and race up a rusting stairway, but there's no clearance space for them at the top, so they end up cramped together on the top three rungs.

To create something to cut into, and stop that being seen, we move the camera tight against the outer railing, and shoot David shouting out his last line sideways on as the Doctor follows McDonnell.

"Gareth, I still can't see the cross from here."

There's too much mist, and Michelle can't find the point off camera where there's a tape eye-line mark. The Doctor's just run off to help Martha and Riley, and we close in tight as McDonnell slowly realises they're being picked off one by one.

"He's picking us off. I don't like that. Sorry, that was crap... Sorry, sorry..."

She heads off and finds her starting position for the scene again, determined to get it right. She's driving herself hard, trying to gauge how to play the moment with a growing edge of fear.

"Do you want a bigger swing on this, Graeme?"

Freema's by the hatchway door with a heavy magnetic clamp, which feeds data via the mobile computer terminal Will's got, to try and over-ride the codes that are holding it shut. She's lifting it up in and hitting a circular panel in the centre.

"Yeah, that would be lovely, and if you could turn your back as you do it, then look at Will over your shoulder?"

We get the two-shot, with Will typing at the keypad in the foreground.

"Freema, we're moving in for a close-up on this shot."

"Lovely."

Will stays on his mark and feeds in his cues for her, while Freema plays out the scene exactly as before. She practically throws the clamp at the door, and there's suddenly the loud sound of bits of scenery falling down behind it, thanks to the impact. Freema puts her hand to her mouth in horror.

"I didn't do it! I didn't do anything!"

How can you not laugh at such an instant denial?

Close-ups on Will as he works.

"Could you give just a few more looks back and forth to Freema as you type, Will? Here we go…"

Onto another hatchway and another question. Gareth has to read in David's dialogue off camera, and rattle through the 'happy prime numbers' speech. Freema stops the take.

"I'd swear there's a line about recreational mathematics, then the door opens?"

Gareth's missed it. I think he'd be the first to admit he's happy as the first Assistant, and wouldn't want to swap jobs with David after a speech like that!

24TH JANUARY 2007

Episode Seven – *SS Pentallion's Central Corridor Area #17 has scenes completed, along with one in the main corridor, at St Regis Paper Company, Caldicot, Monmouthshire.*

"Loads of energy, guys! The ship's about to crash!"

It's still freezing outside, and still burning in the belly of the ship. Lots of smoke from the heat, and nearly as much from the crew's breath.

"Actually, I need you to look something up for me. Good start to the bloody day!" Freema's angry with herself for losing her way on the first take, but we're still running the cameras and keep going. I shout out a character note for Riley.

"More agitated please, Will…"

Gareth reads in lines for Martha's mother as Freema plays out phoning her and trying to get her to go online. She's got to find out who had more Number One records, The Beatles or Elvis Presley?

"Gareth, is it 'I need you to do something for me?'…"

Freema's line query is confirmed as being right. By the third take, she's hitting a brilliant pace and level of frustration.

"And cut! I love it!"

Onto Area 17, another question and another door to open, but there's a hitch. Ashton arrives.

"Burn with me!"

Freema hits a control panel on the wall, Martha and Riley dive through the hatchway. This links in to some of the first scenes we recorded for the episode, with the escape pod being ejected as Ashton thinks he's as good as killed them.

Mist-guns are fired across red-gelled lights by the main doorway to the area as Gary makes his entrance, framed both as a mid-shot then low and wide to play up the menace.

David comes hurtling through on the next set-up, and never even clips the lower hatchway frame with his feet. The Doctor tries to stop Ashton sabotaging the pod's controls, but he's too late.

"Gary, turn slowly with a real burn at him."

Ashton ignores the plea and punches out the control panel.

"Just one more, Gary. And can we have a real sense of violence when you hit it?"

His arm goes right back, the fist flies and part of the panel crashes onto the floor. Maybe a touch too far?

"Hang on a sec! We haven't opened that doorway yet, have we?"

David's peering round the bottom of the hatchway leading into the Escape Pod's airlock. In the background, the entrance to Area 17's open.

"Yeah, Scannell's opened it."

"Oh, okay…"

He disappears back to his start position.

"And action!"

On cue, he throws himself across the floor as the Doctor fights the agonising pain that's battering his body. He's been possessed by the sun.

We're running out of time. We've got one take at best, and I need a close-up on David. Make-up drenches him in sweat, he falls against the wall, eyes screwed shut, near hyperventilating with concentration, spitting out the words, bellowing in agony.

"And cut! Tremendous! That was just amazing!"

The crew break into a round of applause. I don't know where he pulled that performance from after such a long day, but he played a blinder. I'm thrilled, absolutely thrilled.

25TH JANUARY 2007

Episode Seven – *Spaceship Central Corridor Area #22, #21 and 2 (in that order) have scenes completed, along with two in the Spaceship Ante Room at St Regis Paper Company, Caldicot, Monmouthshire.*

We're between takes. Still drenched in sweat and still possessed, we're picking up from where we wrapped yesterday, and David's watching intently, always keeping an eye on exactly where the camera's positioned and listening to what's being said behind it.

The Doctor's doubled up in pain on the floor, he swings round into a close-up shot, and it's that precise moment that we're trying to find the right lighting for. We're using a small hand-held spotlight, with blue gel held in place across its barn doors with clips, and aiming it directly at him from the front isn't working. We try something else. The light gets moved to his left side and positioned so it's tilting at 45 degrees towards him. It's taken six takes, but we've got the shot. Almost mechanically, David's hitting his mark time and again for us.

Gareth wants to know if we're done. He's anxiously watching the clock and knows we have to move on.

"Have we got that?"

"We'll look at them all, Guv. But I think the last two were terrific."

The camera's about 30 feet away from one of the hatchways in Area #22 of the Pentallion's main corridor. There's plenty of foreground detail in shot; a chain swinging from an overhead pulley, steam pumping out of a pressure valve on the right.

From ground level, holding the angle low and wide, we rapidly track in on David as he scrambles across the ground, and the spotlight's brought in, aiming directly at his face on cue.

"Burn with me, Martha! Burn with me!"

We do the same in a very tight close-up. After each take, David's nearly breathless because he's putting so much energy into every shot.

The next set-up's simple by comparison; Martha's reunion with the Doctor. Freema charges down the corridor and throws herself at David, and he holds her tight as she dangles against him.

"When you're ready? When you're ready, Freema?"

David's hinting, but Freema just holds on tightly and doesn't let go...

Must have been tricky to get all the panels down here to assemble, but the TARDIS is in position, lit with reds and hints of orange and yellow, and ready to record its two brief scenes for *42*.

Just David and Freema for the arrival, with Riley and Scannell there for the departure. The Doctor warns that the sun deserves attention, just like anything else, but the TARDIS door sticks as he tries to use the key.

"I couldn't open the door then!"

We need to bring the others into the scene a bit more.

"Anthony, make sure you look towards Freema's end of the TARDIS."

We swing round and take in their incredulous looks. Can they really fly in that thing? But Riley's not that concerned, he's more interested in saying goodbye to Martha. Three takes get their farewell kiss in the can, and Freema and Will play it light, with a real spark between them, and when she pulls him towards her, you really wonder why she doesn't hint to the Doctor about another passenger.

But then again, that's not really where her heart lies!

26TH JANUARY 2007

Episode Seven – *Spaceship Medicentre scenes are filmed at Unit 1, Trefforest Industrial Estate, Trefforest.*

"Don't forget the ticking clock! Time-bomb's about to go off!"

Gareth calls for quiet. The main location for the SS Pentallion's wrapped, and the Medicentre, from a practical point of view given all the set elements we need to control around it, has been built back at the Upper Boat studios.

We're about to roll.

"And action!"

Matthew's being held down on the platform that slides into a stasis chamber. It's kept its basic shape from the role it was originally built for, as the MRI Scanner in the season's first episode, *Smith and Jones*, but Ed's team have painted it red, redesigned and redressed parts of it, and added new control panels for the cast to work with.

Lerner and Ashton are desperately trying to help Korwin as the Doctor and McDonnell arrive. Out comes the sonic screwdriver set on its diagnosis level.

"Oh, bugger! Sorry!"

It's shot straight out of David's grasp, bounced across Matthew and been caught by Gary.

"It's quite hard to do all that and act! Oh, butterfingers!"

David's mortified. Reset and off we go.

"And action!"

Gary gets tongue-tied and loses his place. In on a tight close-up on Matthew, who starts screaming in pain, but suddenly he stops dead.

"Damn! What's my first line?"

Roger moves in, gently having a word with him while we reset.

"On one of the earlier takes, after you've been sedated, you fell with your head lolling to your left…"

"Does it look better?"

"I think so, yes…"

Every take, I call out emotional pointers for the cast, emphasising the urgency and pace they've got to hit… If this is going to work, it has to be frenetic; they're running for their lives for practically every second of the story.

We lens up a close-up on David, just before he runs out of the Medicentre. There's a loud crash as he reaches the door.

"Oh, I'm so sorry!"

He's knocked the boom mic flying. It was lying close to the ground and out of shot, but nothing's damaged.

The back of the stasis chamber's been built with a clear perspex panel that can break away, so we can move a camera in to focus from the back of its funnel and create a kind of telescopic view of the action as everyone peers down at Korwin. As he revives from the tranquilliser, we switch to using the camera as his POV, closing in on Lerner, demanding that she 'burns' with him.

"Remember, Vinette. Look straight into the lens. It's Korwin and he's heading straight for you!"

The bulk of Lerner's scenes are nearly done, and the last set-up for the day revolves around the Doctor examining what's left of her; nothing more than a scorched silhouette. No ash, no bones, no charred remains, nothing.

Come to think of it, that's very economical on the special effects front.

29TH JANUARY 2007

Episode Seven – *Spaceship Medicentre scenes are filmed at Unit 1, Trefforest Industrial Estate, Trefforest.*

I think there must have been about a week's notice. When the decision was made to cast Derek Jacobi in *Utopia*, his agents stressed that yes, he'd love to do it, but that he'd only be available on certain dates. He had a window that lasted for about ten days from 1st February onwards, but no sooner. This left a question hanging in the air. Do we stick with him and try and make it work? Or do we drop him? Over my dead body!

Looking at the schedule, the only way to make it work and keep him as Professor Yana was to swap the production order around, so *42* moved forward and took over *Utopia*'s original filming slot. As a result, Ed Thomas' team had barely any time to assemble the studio-based sets for the spaceship interiors.

To lighten the load, the Medicentre scenes have been staged during the last couple of days' work on the episode, so at least there was construction time while we worked around the paper mill. Even so, it's still been tight, but the results are fantastic. It's sort of scorched red, with huge green light-boxes mounted around the framework of the wall panels, and we've got people behind them moving parts of the engines in silhouette, so it looks as though we're right in the heart of the ship. Look carefully and there's always some kind of motion going on in the background, even when they're only seen for a few seconds.

The main scenes for the day revolve around Martha trying to manoeuvre the Doctor into the stasis chamber and freeze him, and a section of plating inside it has been removed so we can mount the camera to get top shots looking directly on David's face as he starts to ice up. The make-up team are using layers of crystals stuck to his face to create the effect of his body temperature plummeting, and Louise Page has used the same kind of material to distress a spare copy of his spacesuit, so it all looks pretty realistic.

I talk to Freema about the dilemma Martha's facing; there's the side of her that's medical, absolutely professional and knows she's got to save him, but there's also the side that loves the Doctor and can't bear to hurt him like this. It's tearing her in half, and he keeps having to stress that she's got to freeze him.

Working with the overhead lighting, adding white and blue to heighten the cold effect, David screams in pain for every take, giving the scene a pretty disturbing quality.

As I've said before, you build up the detail, cut fast to create urgency, keep the story running at that pace and you're halfway there. But you'd be lost if the performances didn't energise what you're trying to achieve. His Doctor's not been seen in this kind of situation before, and the performance he's giving is incredible. I couldn't be happier with it.

30TH JANUARY 2007

Episodes Seven and 11 – *Spaceship Control Wall scenes are shot for 42 and Radiation Room Scenes for Utopia at Old NEG Glass Site, Glass Avenue, Cardiff Bay.*

"Two seventy three. Take one…"
Lots of short sharp scenes, building up the sense of emergency around Martha as she tries to freeze the Doctor.

The panel at the back of the stasis chamber's been removed, David's lying inside and the camera's by his left shoulder, focused on Freema as she peers in from outside.

"Freema, can you make it '*I will* be back for you'?"

She gets the inflection spot on. We need to see her panic; she's completely at a loss with all this hi-tech medical equipment, and she desperately tries to find help with an incomprehensible manual.

"We need to be quick on this, otherwise it's going to happen every time..."

Roger's concerned about the steam being pumped into the set at the point where the camera's positioned. It's misting up the lens in seconds.

"If you could hold it away, then swing it in when the camera pulls back, that would work."

The nozzle spitting out the mist does just that, Freema races onto her mark, directly under a green spotlight. The action's no more than five seconds, but the camera's still hit. The second take works and we're moving on.

The Doctor's fighting with what little strength he has left to keep control, falls out of the stasis chamber and crawls across the floor in agony. David goes for it, slowly edging past a cylinder, which he pulls himself up against, moving into close-up at the same time, before practically falling out of shot.

"I love it! That was fantastic, David! I want that, but..."

David's eyebrows rise in mock alarm. "But?"

"When you land on the floor, use the trolley to the side to try and lift yourself up and hit the communicator panel. Then fall and do just what you did before."

He goes for it again, hitting the moves around the set I wanted, and then crawling towards us. Only he shuffles off round the wrong side of the cylinder.

"He's gone!"

Roger's the first to say anything.

"Ah, sorry."

David gets up, dusting himself down, laughing just as much as everyone else.

Riley and Scannell have reached the final door and race into the auxiliary control room as it opens. There's a metal-framed podium with control panels on its railing at the centre of the room.

Take One. Anthony hits his mark, but starts swinging around.

"Oh great! I've got my foot stuck!"

His boot comes off, jammed in a gap on the control frame's mesh floor.

Take Two. No boot malfunction this time.

"Three... Two... One... Go!"

Gareth cues them in to move to the front of the set, branching off towards control panels on either side of two large screens, so they free up the podium for Freema to make her entrance.

"Fuel dump in progress. Next Scene... Here we go!"

We've blocked the sequence so the actors play out all the short scenes we need, which will cut between them and the Doctor, in one continuous take. All three throw themselves around as the ship starts to regain control. More cues from Gareth.

"And lurch! Tilting! Hold it, hold it, hold it! Feel the strain! And levelling out, levelling out! Next scene, and action!"

Three takes and we're there, but it's not over yet for the actors. We lens up on mid-shots and close-ups individually as they get buffeted again and again.

"And cut!"

Just some close-ups on levers being thrown and dials being switched, and that's practically it for *42*. Back to *Utopia*...

Elsewhere and far deeper into the glass factory, the Radiation Room's lit, cameras are set up and we're ready to shoot. David's cleaned up, back in his Doctor's costume and he's got a familiar face with him. Captain Jack's back, and the first thing John Barrowman does is start to take his clothes off.

There's only time to establish that Jack's going in to the radiation chamber, and one take ends in hysterics as John gets jammed in the doorway, before we have to wrap for the day. The sequence can be picked up in the morning, and I've no doubt that the laughter will be as well!

31ST JANUARY 2007

Episode 11 – *Scenes between Jack, Lt Atillo and the Doctor are completed on the Radiation Room set, along with Martha's arrival as she realises what Professor Yana really is. The unit is filming at Old NEG Glass Site, Glass Avenue, Cardiff Bay.*

It's confrontation day for the Doctor and Captain Jack. Lots of home truths and plot points to plough through, with David partitioned off from John by the

Radiation Room door for a large percentage of the dialogue. Lots of bonds to be retied and common ground to be realised.

Through a tremendously tense moment, with Jack trying to make the nuclear rods work, he starts talking about his life, the fact that he's immortal, which makes the Doctor question if he likes that fact. But he avoids answering him until the Doctor reasons that he keeps coming back to help human beings because they can be fantastic. They get pushed down... but somehow they always manage to get up again.

The two of them find the human survival instinct fascinating, and ultimately it brings them back together, making them realise a friendship's still there between them. I've asked David to play this with wary caution, but for John, it's really a great character moment – he's resigned to his fate, he can see the Doctor doesn't really want to know, but he still keeps on fighting.

I'm moving in with tight close-ups, framing shots with John in the foreground and David in profile through the door's tiny window, all bathed in red from the stet radiation. I can't swing round or open this up much, because the script dictates that it should be intense, intimate, and driven by a real urgency. But what about the rest of the script? The radiation's one threat, but there's also something far more mobile to contend with.

Russell has written the Futurekind as a tribe of *Mad Max*-style nomad warriors, all leather-clad with bolts pierced through their noses, ears and faces, which are also lined with tattoos. They're humans who've devolved into cannibals, so their teeth have been ground down to look like fangs.

The idea in the script was that they're mainly seen running, chasing their prey into the ground, but there is a Chieftain, along with two or three henchmen, who rides on a quad bike armed with vicious blades and spears. So that was the original set-up, like the Merry Men gone wrong, squatting round camp fires and hiding in trees to keep watch.

So, picture this, we're well under way with pre-production and I get a phone call. It's Russell.

"Graeme, I'm really sorry to have to tell you this, but financially we really have to drop the quad bikes."

Now I'd gone down the road with this, had the main quad bike designed, sourced motorbikes to be used by outriders and even gone through initial designs with Ed Thomas, discussing how I wanted them to look, etc. There was talk of bolting chunks of armoured plating on them, adding extra lights on a metal framework around them, so you were never quite sure of the shapes heading through the darkness. There was even an idea of incorporating chunks of metal and small lights into the costumes, to make them look semi-organic, as though they were trying to simulate being part of the vehicles. But that's all gone. The cost of the stuntmen and the time it would take to stage the opening chase through woodlands, it's all too prohibitive financially. There were better areas for us to spend on with the budget.

Was I disappointed? No kidding! The original images Russell had written for Padra's human hunt were stunning. The idea of putting the camera on the ground, shooting low so you see a quad bike come flying up towards the lens or coming up the hill right into frame, then rising up and leaping into the air. I thought it would be really exciting, as opposed all the Futurekind just running. I didn't think there was a lot of danger in that.

I've fought my corner, but the decision's been made; it's not as important as other areas, where the money could be spent far more effectively. But it doesn't end there.

Fast forward a few days. The whole human hunt and the TARDIS arrival scenes are looking like three, maybe four days of night filming, and there's one unwavering fact with that kind of shoot. No matter how well you plan it, no matter how well prepared you are with rehearsals, costumes and props, it will still take you three times longer to complete anything compared to a day shoot.

We're looking at three main locations: the forest Padra's first seen running through, the quarry where the Futurekind are in full hunt mode, and the Silo 16 gates that prove to be sanctuary for both him and the TARDIS crew.

As we progressed with our recces, it quickly became evident to Phil Collinson that financially we could not afford to shoot in all three. So Phil asked me to meet up with Gareth, the first AD, and go to his office. Ed Thomas was there as well and bit by bit we talked through the whole of the night schedule. At the end, Phil just sat forward, clearly wanting to talk about the bad news he had on his mind.

"I'm really sorry, guys, but we can't afford to go to the forest and the quarry, and then onto the second quarry for the Silo. It can't happen. My suggestion is forget the forest and make it all the quarry, and switch all of the things you've planned to there."

Again, I was quite down about this, because when you have a chase in a forest, you can have people running through trees and frame them like a fence, so as you track past them in the foreground, with your actors running amongst them, it can create a frenetic pace with real energy; the tree trunks wiping past as you track, the visual detail of never knowing what's going to move past the screen. But if you're working in a big open space, there's nothing to break it up and give you an edge. I was really sad about losing this.

Fast-forward a few days. We've been shown the most fabulous quarry which has a variety of tiers, and as I walked round it with Ed it became clear that if we added some bits of derelict metal structures in certain areas, I could use a quad bike as a camera platform to create movement across this rough terrain. We could block out group shots, high shots and face shots, all at great speed, and have a kind of metal forest, with these jagged remains sticking out of the ground. Now that means I can still get the energy that I wanted.

It's a big rule to remember: forget what you could have had and make what you do have just as exciting.

Martha arrives as Jack and the Doctor complete the rocket launch procedures. She's seen that the Professor has a Time Lord's DNA Rewriter – a pocket watch, just like the Doctor's. But did he see through the perception filter? Has he realised what it is? David hits the scene at full throttle, terror clearly coursing through him as he realises what it means. We agree that, for the moment when he shouts at Martha, he should play it as if the reality of who she is and what she means to him just falls away, as the potential danger they're facing makes fear take over.

Take One.

"But did he see it!"

Freema's nearly blasted back by the force of David bellowing. Take Two's just the same. The atmosphere, well you could cut the tension he's generating on screen with a knife.

"And cut! Fabulous, I'm happy with that."

There goes the smile, a reassuring squeeze of the arm for Freema from him.

"Something's just flown into my ear."

John's defused it completely.

"It was probably an innuendo, you know how quickly you pick them up!"

Freema's so quick with that response that John's lost for a reply, but laughs outrageously at being stumped so easily.

Well, tomorrow we've got two new arrivals; Derek Jacobi and the winner of a *Blue Peter* competition. There aren't many directing jobs where you can say that's going to happen.

1st FEBRUARY 2007

Episode 11 – *Corridor #2, #3 and Rocket Silo Door scenes are completed at Old NEG Glass Site, Glass Avenue, Cardiff Bay.*

"Three one five. Take One. 'A camera' mark…"

"Set?"

That's a familiar voice!

"And action!"

Susie's back in town.

The door leading into the launch chamber of the rocket silo slides open. The camera's been positioned in front of it, wedged into a pretty cramped space so it's facing the inner side, with a row of lockers lining the wall directly behind where Roger Pearce is working. We hold on a low three-shot as the Doctor swings into view and nearly falls to his death, but gets caught just in time by Captain Jack and Martha.

This is part of the set that Ed Thomas' crew have supplemented the already grimy corridor we're working in with. The silo hatchway's been rigged up and dressed so it blends in perfectly with the rest of the corridor.

David finishes his line and sort of stares into space.

"Can somebody shut the door, please?"

Definitely Susie Liggat's voice. David breaks into a smirk as the hatchway judders past his face.

So, apart from being without my first assistant, I'm not going to have a second camera to pick up all the shots I need until late afternoon. Gareth's off working in another part of the location, handling second unit stuff for about three quarters of the day. This is why Susie's stepped into the breach.

A couple of days ago, I had to talk to Phil Collinson about how to play this, and that's when he flagged up Susie's interest in directing the scenes in the Radiation Room, working to my brief and storyboards. "Phil, that's a strong possibility," I said, "but the person who actually knows exactly how it all fits in with what I've mapped out visually is Gareth Williams. He knows the artists, he knows the set, so my suggestion is why don't we let Gareth go and do that, and let Susie cover for him?"

This was backed by two reasons: firstly, I just knew I'd enjoy working with her again, and secondly, I knew she'd drive the set and make sure we'd get through it. With Susie on board, I knew she'd go for it and make everything run like clockwork.

In principle Phil agreed with this, but only as long as Susie was happy to do that. As I understand it, Susie was a bit surprised at being asked to be first AD as she's now a producer, and could easily have handled calling the shots, but Gareth knows everything about my ideas for the story. It's all ingrained in his brain, and it just feels better to do it this way. In no way, shape or form is it any kind of reflection on her, it's just that my instinct was to ask for her to stand in for Gareth and work alongside me.

Susie will be a fabulous producer for several reasons; she has a great eye for what makes a good story, she's got such a fantastic heart, she likes people, she understands what we all do very well and she understands the day-to-day mechanics of production. She is full of good ideas that can get you out of trouble when the old clock is ticking away and your brain has seized at a most critical time. She has this care and consideration for the wellbeing of everybody, so no one is put in danger in any way. All the safety aspects of the production are overseen by Susie and she makes sure, as does Gareth, that everything is secure and as safe as possible in order for the day to become enjoyable, but she also runs the unit with a rod of iron when necessary. Any production would feel absolutely secure with her in charge in whatever capacity she was involved. She is an absolute joy to work with.

"Ready? Steady? Keep it lively everyone…"

The corridor is now lined with refugees – very World War Two, like people sheltering from the air raids on London Underground platforms. Susie's just cued in Creet.

"Don't I get a *Blue Peter* badge as well?"

Everybody ignores my joke.

We have young John Bell on set, completing his scenes and claiming his prize at the same time. More than eight thousand children jumped at the chance when *Blue Peter* announced they were going to search for someone to play a part in *Doctor Who*, and that number got whittled down to ten. Annette Badland, minus her Slitheen tendencies, Andy Pryor and the producer of *Blue Peter* worked with them directly for a day at the Globe Theatre, running scenes and seeing how they played with dialogue. From that, the last three contenders emerged, and the plan was for Russell and myself to choose the winner. Sadly, the workload of prepping for the recording block caught up with me, and Russell had to make the choice for both of us. So here we are with John, and he's smashing. Within seconds of rehearsing, I could see that he really understood what he wanted to do, and completely got who Creet was, where he was at and how he was part of the system. Now and again, I've just wanted to tweak one or two moments of his performance, and suggested he say certain lines a different way etc, but he's listened intently to me and, sure enough, he's done it.

Between set-ups with the main unit, I've got to run over to the Radiation Room set and discuss the shots I want setting up by Gareth. There's only enough time to suggest the broad strokes of what I need before I have to race back and leave him to choreograph them within that scene, light it and then shoot it.

Take One, Take Two, Take Three with Creet, the Doctor, Jack and Martha, and I'm happy. So, while another scene's being lit, I leave Susie orchestrating that, run back up the same stairs, down some corridors and find Gareth to see what he's shot. "I love it!" Or maybe he'll get, "Would you do it again, because of..." And I rattle off some notes. That's how the day's running, and it feels like I'm directing and competing in *The Crystal Maze* at the same time!

Martha's curious. She wants to know what's ticking in Creet's head, and what he thinks about going to Utopia, what he's been told it'll be like. That sort of thing. As he heads off, she fires one last question at him.

"How old are you?"

He turns round. "Old enough..."

And then he's gone. Rehearsing the moment, I've drawn him to one side.

I don't want him to be indignant, just cool and collected with her. "Just look at her and say your line, but all the time keep thinking, 'Mind your own business, bitch!'"

Brilliant! He's got it in one. David, John and Freema, well, they absolutely loved him. I think they were very impressed with how professional he's been considering I don't think he had ever spoken in front of cameras before. But he's not the only new face working on set.

You can really sense that the crew are excited about Derek Jacobi arriving today, but I can't help but wonder how it'll all go. Will he like us? Will the way we're working instantly put him on edge? Will he wonder what the hell I'm talking about? But within 30 seconds of Derek walking onto the set, all the fear and concern evaporates. He's come on with a huge smile. "How marvellous! This is so exciting. Right, so what are we doing?"

I go through the motions of explaining how the Professor is instantly clinging onto the Doctor like he's their last hope, and with David, John and Freema, we quickly put a shape to the sequence. Cue the first rehearsal, and on he rushes laughing with enthusiasm. It's full of energy, it's light and joyous, you can immediately see he's an absent-minded professor. I'm thrilled, it's taken us all by surprise.

I don't know what we thought we were going to get, but he's made him the most delightful, vivid character, who's been on this planet for what feels like an eternity and is desperate to win through. It's a brilliant entrance and everybody's genuinely sad Derek's had to go so quickly. But there's a week of working in the studio with him to look forward to.

That's a wrap for the day.

There've been a lot of laughs with Susie. She came up to me as the crew were packing up and said, quite honestly, that she really enjoyed being back on set and getting a taste of her old job again. There's been a terrific working dynamic between us, just like there was staging the Dalek-Cyberman war last year, and she's skilled enough to have come in and picked up the threads of the story, without being involved before, and run the floor magnificently.

2ND FEBRUARY 2007

Episode 11 – *Scenes in the Radiation Room are completed, along with shots of the main corridor, holding area and corridor #1 at the Old NEG Glass Site, Glass Avenue, Cardiff Bay.*

As a director, I love getting the chance to work in real locations. Problem is, when you've got fixed ceilings, you obviously you can't remove walls for certain camera positions. You've got to make do with what you can achieve within the visual boundaries on offer.

Studio-based sets? Sure, that would solve it. That's when you can plan for sections to break away so as to fit in cameras and sound equipment, or have backdrops that can be removed fast and efficiently, without causing any real delays to what you're trying to shoot.

It's extremely rare to go for a full ceiling with a studio build, mainly because it increases the complexity of hanging and positioning lights from the overhead grid. *Doctor Who* allows you to cheat a bit and only have certain aspects of it there – girders, low-hanging pipes, maybe a small section directly over the action on screen – because ultimately The Mill can step in and patch up the holes later on.

But if you're using something established, something real, it generates a sense of live geography. If you can stage a shot moving around 360 degrees, or force the perspective to show the audience that the location clearly hasn't been faked, then it adds a definite atmosphere to what's taking place in the story.

The Radiation Room is, at a guess, 60 per cent real.

It's got no natural light, but there's a kind of ambience being generated from the consoles lining the walls. Ed Thomas has added an additional bank that's now face to face with them, duplicating the style of the real dials, switches and monitors with incredible accuracy. This has supplemented the lighting effect to the extent that we're now able to heighten it and actually control it.

It's just like a scene out of *Quatermass*: a genuine, fully functioning, 1950s nuclear reactor control room. We can go low, shoot it wide, track down the aisle of the room and swing the camera round. It's created a sense of movement and a lot of versatility.

There's an industry truism that says a production design should assist the story, and not overtake the picture, and while Ed's on watch, that's never going to happen on *Doctor Who*. It's really an intricate balancing act he has to do, weighing up the pros and cons of what needs to be built in studio and what we can realise within tight time constraints on location.

If an issue's forced – say, there's an effect or prop that needs a safe, studio-controlled environment, or there's simply no other way to stage what's visually required than to create a set from scratch – then, financially, this can have an impact elsewhere. We might have to recce and use one building, and through careful set dressing and lighting make it double or even triple up as three different places. You see, that saves money, and that will allow Ed to comfortably deal with the expense of whatever he's having to accommodate at Unit 1.

Without fail, his team strive to achieve the very best they can. If there's a way to do it, then they'll find it, but there are limits. Saying that, though, if it really becomes impossible, there's the option of Russell stepping in and reworking the script to find an alternative that's more workable.

From the outset, I'll have sat down and discussed how I'd like to see the shape of Professor Yana's laboratory, or the corridors where the refugees are sheltering, all in order to get the best visual impact I can for the story. So Ed's there on my side and knows what I'd like to do. He also knows what's good for the show and what kind of money he's got available, so ideas are being refined or adjusted all the time until, eventually, several weeks into pre-production, there comes a point where we have to commit to what we've agreed. It's locked off, we've agreed what we want to see and the whole thing is absolutely sorted.

Fast-forward several days, maybe a couple of weeks. You walk into the studio, ready to shoot for the day, and there it is. Somehow his team have interpreted and evolved your ideas into something tangible, and I've never been anything less than delighted with the results.

5TH FEBRUARY 2007

Episode 11 – *Work begins on recording the scenes set in Professor Yana's laboratory at Unit 1, Trefforest Industrial Estate.*

Five days solid now on the same set: the Professor's lair, all decaying technology and a hint of World War Two underground operations centre. Hard concrete walls, overhead strip lights, damp and crumbling. Ed Thomas has even added an old hot-water boiler to make the coffee, complete with flaking white paint. It must be 30, 40 years old at least.

The space we've got to work in is big but cluttered with radar equipment and control consoles, and the slightly inverted main walls are broken up with a few brightly lit alcoves. There's a retro edge to it, like a slightly more hi-tech take on the kind of place you could imagine Oppenheimer would have worked in. It's utilitarian, but functional.

I've already thought through all the different camera positions and angles we can practically achieve, so that no matter when you see the set in the finished episode, there'll always be a different aspect about it visually that won't interfere or confuse, but still make the environment look as interesting as possible.

Derek Jacobi arrives on set, full of energy and enthusiasm. There's a palpable buzz in the air because he's here, and we're off, recording most of his scenes in story order, and I'm the first cue!

"Ping!"

Not the best sound effect, in fact I just call it out, but in an instant Derek peers round into a monitor screen and sees the first signs of the 'human hunt' on the radar.

The drive and pace is instant on the set. We move to medium close-ups; Professor Yana drinks coffee and Chantho politely refuses his offer to join him, thanks to her own, well, let's say, resources.

"Can I try something different, Derek? Just a little twinkle on the internal milk line? 'That's quite enough information, etc'…"

There's a slight hint of mild horror when he hears what she's using for nourishment on the first take, but he nails what I'm looking for instantly when we go again.

"I came in too soon," Derek corrects himself.

"And I missed a Chan!"

Chipo wasn't happy with that take either. She has to really concentrate on adding the 'Chan' prefix to every line, followed by a 'Tho' to punctuate with a full-stop. She's been in make-up since six o'clock this morning. Layers of latex and make-up piled on, and there must be a continual 'whirr' going on just in front of her ears, with the servos working the ever-moving mandibles Chantho has protruding from her jaw-line. And you know what? Never even so much as a word of complaint. The main problem about the overall look of Chantho is the fact that she's an insect, based on a kind of beetle or moth.

What I asked Millennium Effects to consider, when they were designing and then making her eventual make-up appliances, was that although it's quite shocking when you initially see her, I wanted to make sure that within seconds of hearing her performance you began to be at ease with the way she looks and actually begin to warm to her. There's a lovely, friendly, shy, awkward personality here, which you have to complement more than distract from.

Originally, the designs were very spider-like and were going to cover her face completely with prosthetics, but we needed to maintain her personal features; her mouth, her cheeks and eyes. One of them just left her mouth clear, with her eyes hidden behind multi-pupil lenses. It was just too alien and spider-like; there had to be a soft human quality that meant she was still strange, but gentle rather than just frightening, with the face merging up into the more insect aspects of the rest of her head.

Now, cue the drums. This is the first time we see Professor Yana's malaise in full flight. The distant sound of drums in his mind that's haunted him since childhood, slowly building up both in volume and pain. Derek knows what he wants to do with this scene, so I've explained to him that I'll slowly develop in with the camera so it'll start a loose mid shot, then go right into a big close-up on his face while he is hearing the drums, and then hold on that until Chantho's voice brings him back and grounds him again.

Right into the top of the set now, lensing up to take in as much of the laboratory as we can, with wiring and pipes draped across the foreground. Derek stands working with some wiring at a console. Chipo's standing to his left.

"Chipo?" Gareth runs onto the set, carefully leading her to the right a few feet. "Can I start you further back, back here, and walk into the shot with energy?"

"And once she's there, Gareth, that's when the tannoy starts."

I'm giving Gareth the cue point, because he has to read in the dialogue coming from Lt Atillo. Neil Reidman, the actor playing Atillo, is not available this day so his voice will be dubbed on at a later date.

As soon as the Professor hears that the Doctor's been found, and that he's a Doctor of 'everything', Derek explodes with energy and excitement, nearly dropping equipment and flapping with panic, eager to meet him. I can see there's a more elegant way to shoot this. The camera's lined up to move from a close-up on Yana as he hears the news and move round the console he's at in a wide arc, then following him as he charges out of the door.

Take after take, Derek's hitting the floor running, energising David, Freema and John as they arrive for the next scene with his enthusiasm. The Professor rattles off what he's trying to achieve with the rocket.

"But without a stable footprint…"

"And cut!"

"We're screwed!" Derek ad-libs a new ending to the line.

"I thought that!" David chips in. "I was going to say so myself."

Back to the lab's main doorway, which squeaks, judders and rattles every time it opens. Captain Jack's arrived with his vapour trail of testosterone and immediately hits on Chantho. They get their lines right, but the words collide head on a couple of times. Giggles, smirks, but by the next take they've got it.

Onto the scene revealing that Captain Jack's 'Doctor detector' is the Time Lord's severed hand from *The Christmas Invasion*. Shame the additional line's been cut where Jack explains that it "landed on a newsagent's roof in Dulwich. Nice people."

Last shot of the day as the Doctor asks the Professor what exactly Utopia is. Half-smiling, Derek gestures to them, beckoning them to follow him with his finger.

"And cut!"

"You know," David puts his hand on Derek's arm. "You looked really, really wicked when you just did that!"

6TH FEBRUARY 2007

Episode 11 – *Scenes in the Professor's laboratory continue filming at Unit 1, Trefforest Industrial Estate, Trefforest.*

"That is a great ass!"

John Barrowman is eyeing the way David Tennant's leaning over the console next to Derek, who's busily finding his way through a ream of dialogue laying in the plot. Freema's very conscious of the distance she's keeping from the Doctor.

"I'm trying not to touch it!"

"Touch it! Touch it!" David's being provocative right back at her, but as soon as "Action" is called, all three snap instantly back into character.

It's only a few days ago, but the evening before Captain Jack was due to turn up I said to David that I was looking forward to having him on board. I'm sure I saw a mischievous glint in his eye.

"Yes, it's going to be very interesting…"

Now, David and John both have very powerful personalites, and from my point of view as the director I wanted to see how they sparked off each other, how their relationship both as characters and actors was going to develop when we reached their scenes together.

From the moment they walked onto the set together it was an absolute joy – if they had any fears about each other, well, that was dissipated within seconds of their meeting because they were absolutely giggling their heads off all the way through, every day from that moment on. I never saw a bad look between them or the slightest hint of any atmosphere. What great performances they gave, sparking off each other and raising their game. Freema raised her performance too. What an exciting episode this is going to be.

When you're mentally putting a scene together, where there's a strong emotive point coming across in the dialogue, you might think, right, I've got to keep movement going, but keep the stillness for this key moment. The answer's actually no, not necessarily. I keep the camera moving as much as I can, even if it's only slight, so I can jump from a wide shot to a big close up around the face of whoever's saying the line. By keeping the camera moving it will make the cuts smoother and the storytelling more fluid.

The important thing is to be close on the actor for their big line. If you want their dialogue to be really taken in, that has to be shot on a wide angle, then cut hard and tight, moving in close for their lines. It's not that nobody will listen when you're doing a group shot, a single or two-shot of people walking, but the impact of what they are saying can be lost.

To maximise the force of a line, you can jump-cut to a big close-up for that moment, then it will sink in. Most of what we're lining up to shoot will do exactly that – focus on close-ups.

We're on a sequence with the Doctor and the Professor chatting as they wire up a circuit board they're facing, one on either side, with organic wiring. Trouble is, it's at a cluttered point of the set. No way to circle round it or shoot through it. Best way forward is to shoot big close-ups on a long lens, looking through the board and holding on either David or Derek.

Take One runs fine. David's peering over his glasses at the various wires hanging in front of him. Gareth's quick on the mark to check he's going to be using the same one for the next take.

"Which wire did you start with?"

"Oh, good question. Hang on a sec." David starts muttering to himself as he sorts through them. "It was that one… No, that one. Come on, Dave, get yourself sorted."

Phil Collinson wants a word. He loved the set-up for the first couple of shots, but he's worried that we'll get sick to death of it if this two-minute scene ends up full of cuts.

"Okay, Guv. I'll give you a version where they come clear of the screens, and slightly angled. We'll do close-ups, like a three-quarter profile, where you can see both eyes, nose and mouth. It won't be a full-on front shot but it'll work."

Both David and Derek, they're the kind of actors who, once they know where the camera is, they'll make it interesting. You watch David and he'll make sure the camera sees both eyes, and Derek will be just the same.

This kind of scene must always seem a bit dull for the other actors, the ones who stand in the background with no lines at this particular point. Now, I knew that Freema has experience, but I didn't know how far that went with this kind of material, so I made a mental note to say to her on the first day, "Whenever we're shooting a scene and we've been concentrating on your shots, even after that, when you know that David or someone else is talking, always be aware that I might cut away to you. You have to be giving a performance all the time, just in case I cut to you for a reaction shot."

And you know what? I forgot to say this to Freema, but I didn't have to worry in the slightest, because she never comes out of character. She gives me 120 per cent all the time. Nobody's had to tell her; she has learned fast through all of her previous jobs.

7TH FEBRUARY 2007

Episode 11 – *Scenes in the Professor's laboratory continue filming at Unit 1, Trefforest Industrial Estate, Trefforest*

8.30 am… The studio's already buzzing with activity.

Russell made a fleeting appearance yesterday; he wanted to greet Derek Jacobi and tell him personally how thrilled he is that he's here. Apparently, as soon as he answered his trailer door, Russell was a bit overcome, hugged him and then ran off leaving a rather bewildered Derek smiling benevolently behind him.

Day Three shooting around Yana's laboratory set.

John and Chipo have taken up their marks by one of the monitor banks. The crew flit around them as we run up to a take; costumes are checked, lighting and camera moves finalised and, just before the camera rolls, one of Neill Gorton's crew reaches under the back collar of Chantho's lab coat and clicks a tiny switch at the back of her head prosthetic. There's several batteries concealed inside, which make it weigh quite heavily, and a remote control unit off camera makes her mandibles start to move.

"Right, working… Busy as usual… Here we go…"

David's in shot for the B-Camera just behind them. It's a short, sharp scene as they realise the power's failing all through Silo 16.

"And cut…"

I'm not as happy with that as I could be. We need to go again.

"One more, please." Take Two. The lights dim and start to flicker as soon as "Action" is called.

Gareth's voice booms out. "No, no, no, no, no! It's action, wait three beats and then the lights start!"

John Barrowman's burying his face in some cables trying not to laugh. Too late. It's infectious, Chipo's giggling as well. As the second take ends, he turns and looks directly into camera chewing his nails in mock panic.

Gareth's grumbling. "That's the fourth time today that lighting cue's gone wrong."

John latches onto this as we move onto a wide shot, taking in Derek, Freema and David, working at a console behind them. He points and winks at the lighting desk. "You're the best. That cue was a masterpiece."

Reset and relight.

Captain Jack's been electrocuted jumpstarting the override, Martha rushes over to him but he's lying dead on the floor. Chantho, Professor Yana and the Doctor look on in horror, with a certain degree of bemusement added to the facial mix from the latter. The camera's low and wide, John's lying in front of it, feet pointing towards the TARDIS in the background. On cue, Freema's got to charge over and try giving him mouth-to-mouth resuscitation.

"Action!"

She takes off and moves to jump over Jack's legs, but she trips over a power cable leading out of the TARDIS, then nearly falls flat on her face as she stumbles over the 'corpse'.

"Oh, my God! I'm sorry, I'm so sorry!"

Freema's mortified, but reassuring voices, particularly from John, quickly find some humour in what's happened. Second take, she doesn't even hesitate when she jumps to try and help Jack and gets it spot on.

Now, I've got to build on the moment when Jack comes back to life, and John's confident he can hold his breath for long enough to make it look convincing. His singing experience has taught him how to channel his breathing and, after a couple of deep gasps, we roll camera, focused tight in and side on to him at ground level.

"Give me a cue so I can let my breath out."

He doesn't flinch, his chest's still, not even moving a fraction as Freema examines him. You don't doubt that this guy's dead. It's remarkable, brilliant concentration, and with an overhead shot looking down on him as his heart kick starts again, it'll make the moment work perfectly.

"Non? Is it space and time, or time and space?"

Freema's got lost over where exactly the Doctor travels in the middle of a line.

"Time and space…" Non knows the hardcore facts by heart now.

Martha and Chantho are facing a console, talking over com-link to Jack and the Doctor. This is a crucial scene. As she explains about the TARDIS and Time Travel, her words hit the Professor with waves of memory, as long-forgotten thoughts start to stir. Carefully rehearsing the moment, I ask Derek if he feels he should cry in this scene.

"Yes, but not much… It's more inward."

So now we're closing in slowly on Derek, moving tighter and tighter from a medium shot into a close-up, so the frame is full of nothing but his eyes. Fear, confusion, melancholy, you see it all in Derek's face, and then a tear trickles down his right cheek.

"Daleks... Vortex... Time Lords..."

I'm reading in cue words, and he reacts to each one as his memory is bombarded with things he's never seen or heard of before. He controls exactly the amount of tearfulness he wants to give.

"Excellent... That was smashing... Absolutely smashing..."

The thing about directing *Doctor Who* is that it allows you to heighten the whole drama and scale of the stories, because the very nature of the programme dictates that it's larger than life, but then it also has great moments of reality. There's a depth of reality in the relationship between the Doctor and Martha, for example... There are quiet, gentle, tender moments when they reach out to each other, but that's mixed with those bolder moments when everything becomes energised around them.

Phil's not happy about bringing the TARDIS into the Professor's laboratory. It's been planned out with a crane lowering it into shot, giving a bit of scale to the scene where the Doctor's reunited with it, and also adding impact for another of the Professor's subliminal flashback moments when he sees it. But he's quite right. It's all going to take too much time.

Lining everything up accurately, rehearsing and making it work visually, then potential retakes. You're looking at two hours at least. The rate we're going, well, that's going to cause serious problems in the schedule. Russell's been phoned, ideas chewed over and a solution has been agreed. We'll just have the TARDIS seen in a storage bay on a monitor screen, with an intercom voice saying it's been found. I can still create a moment of haunted recognition with Derek as he sees it, and we'll just move it into Yana's lair and take it as read that it's been shifted there by Lt Atillo's men.

Well, that's another studio day gone, and it's our final day with Derek tomorrow.

On our very first rehearsal, Derek came on as this absent-minded professor, and the moment he walked into rehearsals we saw him laughing. He'd though it all through and decided to make Professor Yana full of energy. It was light, boisterous, overflowing with enthusiasm and delightful; it took us all by surprise.

I honestly don't know what we thought we were going to get, but with a few simple broad strokes he'd created this most delightful, lived-in human being, and from that moment onwards Derek made the character a total joy. But that's all going to change tomorrow. I think he's looking forward to the next few scenes, because the Professor is about to realise who he really is…

8TH FEBRUARY 2007

Episode 11 – *Scenes in Professor Yana's laboratory and the adjacent corridor are filmed at Unit 1, Trefforest Industrial Estate, Trefforest. Green screen special effects sequences are also shot in the studio by the second unit for both episodes.*

There's no David or Freema today. Everything's centred around the Professor and Chantho, lots of relatively short scenes, some involving complex CGI set-ups, and all building up to the episode's finale.

Over the past few days, my main concern has been whether I've given Derek enough information on what I want to see from his character? But, like all good actors, he's done his homework and he's on set, ready with something he's carefully thought through, injecting subtle atmosphere and different levels of feeling.

Now, there's a clear division in the script; he's obviously the Professor for three quarters of the story, but then we reach a specific moment when his true character boils to the surface and erupts. No matter which way you look at it, serious acting pyrotechnics have got to be pulled out of the bag. It's got to be a precise, very distinct change from giving me this sometimes grumpy, irritable, absent-minded scientist, who's completely blinkered and willing to sacrifice his life to make the Utopia rocket's mission succeed. The audience has to see him become, well, about as malevolent as you can imagine.

At a basic level, that's all I need from Derek, as far as the Master's concerned, because the baton is passed to John Simm for the final two episodes. But what really interests me is how far can we go with this, literally exploring what level of darkness we can manifest before he regenerates. I've asked him to do two things during filming, so we can adjust the tone and find the right balance; one's to go large with the performance, and the other is to pull right back. My gut instinct is to use the latter. If you start on a theatrical high, there's going to be nowhere for John Simm to go with it, no leeway to build up a sense of menace. Also, underplaying a villain can make him unpredictable and far more interesting.

Most of the background work building up to the 'reveal', well, that's already been done. Day after day this week, I've been careful to remind Derek of the niceties of the character we want to get, no big hits, no blatant hints of what's brewing… Particularly when the Professor hears the drums.

We could have alerted the audience to the evil side that's seeping through, and allowed just a taste of what was about to happen in his performance, but Derek chose to play it gently, chained to the sound and desperate to be free of the agony it causes, like a migraine which he's had all his life. Even when it was gradual, half-remembering moments of his life as the Master, Derek did not want to give that away. Instead we both wanted it to be obvious that the Professor is in terrible trouble and you sympathise with this poor man. What is it that's wrong with him? Can he save the human refugees? What will put him right? Can the Doctor do anything?

"And action!"

We slowly close in on Derek, holding the watch up, running his fingers across the patterned surface. What *is* this? Surely it's just a broken fob-watch? It can mean anything, it's just a memento from the past… Then he looks up… Trying to reach into his memory, there's something there! What does it mean? Why isn't it clear?

Now, what Derek needs to know is where his key light is. All the other lights focused on the set are secondary to the one that will highlight him. He's got to move to and hold the position we've agreed for the shot, because that's his favoured position, highlighting the tone and atmosphere I want for him at that moment. It applies to every scene, whenever an actor hits their mark, there's a key light on them, unless I've negotiated with the lighting director for movement into shadows, or any other similar effects.

Take after take, moving on to each set-up, he's completely focused. The set is strangely free of its normal chatter between shots, everyone's watching the monitors. It's electrifying.

"And cut!"

This isn't quite right. It's nothing to do with Derek's performance, it's the camera… It's moving in too late. It's got to start earlier and drift in. I've got to sort this out with Roger, who's immediately got a solution.

"You call out when you want me to start moving in."

Derek's chuckling at this, probably thinking, "Here I am, concentrating on trying to give a very deep moment, and at the same time I'll hear 'Camera!'" But he's such a gentlemen and professional that he's probably reasoning, "If that's the only way we can get it right…" In fact, he will be in the zone, blocking everything out except that precise moment that he wants to bring to life. He won't even hear me say it!

High and wide, we rapidly sweep in towards the Professor, standing in front of the TARDIS, contemplating the watch. He knows it'll all become clear, everything is pivotal on opening it. As the lid flicks up, it cues in a golden gelled light just beneath where he's standing, which bathes him in its glow as the Master's DNA is reintegrated.

Onto a close-up, always building up options for cutting the finished sequence together. That's one take with the watch in view at the bottom of the frame, then one without, as I tell Derek to drop it down slightly.

"Can we do one more? Roger, as the light comes on Derek, can we squeeze it on the zoom…"

The subtle movement nails it. That's what I wanted to see.

This is it. A slow reveal, moving it towards the Professor, facing the TARDIS as Chantho pleads for him to say he's all right. Derek edges round and looks straight into the lens, and we move in tight on his eyes; hatred, contempt, seething with malice…

"Up to this point, you've been this wonderful, gentle and lovable professor, but once the watch is opened, it enables you to be the Master. Up until now, that's been locked away… You become the complete reverse of what you are now… So I want to see the glory and the enjoyment of the rays hitting you and, eventually, as you turn… That's got to be the defining moment where we see that he's evil."

I give him a broad sketch, just an idea to see what he can find in his performance, and I just don't know how he did it, but the look Derek produces, instantly cold and harsh... It's better than I could have hoped for. That's a showstopper moment. The evil he's conjured up within that stare is electrifying.

The reverse shot is on Chipo, and she has to show absolute terror.

"Really fearful. Here we go..."

She wants to help, she knows something's wrong, but just can't figure it out. The light from the watch is cued in.

"And he's turned!"

As I say that, she gasps and reels back slightly, petrified. You know she's not got long left as soon as he sees the clock face.

Derek moves round a console, edging closer and closer, holding up a sparking power cable, aiming its tendrils threateningly towards Chantho. It's clear he's no longer the Professor. Her dying act is to ask who he is.

"I... am... the Master..."

Take Two. Derek plunges the cable forward so it goes under the camera lens. His face suddenly drops.

"Oh, I'm so sorry! I thought I'd taken your eye out!"

It wasn't even a near-miss for Roger, but that's the first time an apology has been heard from that particular character!

What's proved interesting about Derek and the impact he's had working on this story, is that I'm always aware of his presence, even when he's not on screen. The Professor sort of resonates throughout; even when you're elsewhere with the Doctor and Martha, his style of acting is so strong you can't help but be aware of him and want him to come back.

Meanwhile, back in the space/time vortex...

John Barrowman's singing 'Xanadu' while the second unit crew line up their shot on him. A green framework has been rigged up to represent the outline of the TARDIS exterior, and mounted on a podium to give a hint of height for the camera to work around.

Captain Jack's thrown himself at the TARDIS during *Utopia*'s opening moments, and he's now clinging to the hull as it spirals through space. John's warming up his voice, because he's got to scream his head off as the camera starts to rolls, trying to make himself heard over the wind machine that's been aimed at him for each take. For close-ups, one of the panels from the TARDIS itself has been propped at an angle for him to lean against. All this will be composited against the time-tunnel effect that The Mill created for the show's opening title sequence, and matched up so the TARDIS ricochets from side to side, trying to throw him off.

All the other effects shots we've storyboarded for the refugees boarding the rocket are also under way. Side angles, close-ups and overhead shots, all showing them filing across a simple gantry. By varying the order they're moving in, and making the line-up slightly different for each take, it'll allow the shots to be multiplied using the same 20 or so extras, so on screen, when they've been composited, we'll see about a dozen walkways flanking down the side of the rocket and into the distance, with hundreds of people boarding it.

Back to the TARDIS tomorrow, and hopefully the visual highpoint of the story!

9TH FEBRUARY 2007

Episode 11 – *Scenes from the episode's finale in the Professor's laboratory and the adjacent corridor are filmed, along with some brief TARDIS scenes at Unit 1, Trefforest Industrial Estate.*

Slate 470, Scene 79 – Take One.

The Futurekind are chasing the Doctor, Martha and Jack. Their only retreat is clearly Professor Yana's laboratory. Only problem is, he's locked it!

"Loads of energy. I know it's going to happen anyway!"

And they're off. David, Freema and John crash into the exterior of the bulky green metal doorway. Mass panic, shouting and some serious 'jammed door' acting.

Because the drive of what's happening in the scene has to carry on straight into Scene 81, I've blocked the sequence so that the cast just keep acting, and the first assistant shouts out to let them know the break point when they reach it, mainly to help cue in the relevant dialogue. The problem is that no matter how valiantly he acts, John manages to open the door far too easily.

The *Doctor Who Confidential* documentary crew arrive on set and he's quick to taunt them.

"Confidential, you just missed a brilliant bit!"

Onto the reverse shots, moving the cameras into the lab set. Just before each take, you can hear David's feet pounding on the ground as he runs on the spot, building up the energy and panic he needs to find. Focus, focus, focus, two moments of realisation for the Doctor: the Master's got his TARDIS, and as we fade up an orange light inside it. Bingo! Guess who's regenerating?

The first assistant reads the feed of what will eventually become John Simm's dialogue for David to react to. Tight close-up on the Doctor, cue the wind machine behind camera as the TARDIS dematerialises right in front of him. Not that effective, David's hair is so short that there's very little movement as a result.

Now onto Chantho, dead on the ground as Martha examines her. David and Freema charge onto the set and nearly go flying as they skid across some cables.

"Oh, my lord!"

Freema's fine. Take Two.

"Action!"

Sorted. Moving on.

Derek Jacobi arrives on set. Now we see why the Doctor's so full of panic. Wounded and dying, the Master's in the doorway of the TARDIS, and he's locked himself inside before the Doctor can reach him.

The energy is high and the takes are rattling past. Scene after scene is locked, loaded and shot.

Back to the main doorway. The Doctor and Martha race past, Jack's attention goes on trying to shut it behind them as the Futurekind arrive en masse. Well, okay, six of them, but they're still hungry.

Take One. The studio work light's been left on and the floor's fully illuminated. Take Two, John breaks out of character midway.

"I'm going to have to say 'cut'."

He points to the top of the door-frame.

"It's come off its track and it's not moving at all... So sorry..."

On comes a technician to fix it, whistling cheerfully; the Futurekind amble away gossiping.

Next take, and I've noticed something's not quite right.

"Can we have some wind blowing on Jack and Martha as the TARDIS fades away?"

Quiet muttering is heard, cursing the fact that the fan's already been taken off the set.

Time for some hand-held camera. Lensed up and framed so we move between Freema and John as they fight to shut the door, the energy of the scene escalates. It becomes real. Very intense and frightening.

Although it was originally planned out for me to shoot it, as it directly involves the set for the lab, Colin Teague's now available to shoot one of the opening scenes for Episode 12 and moves in to take over directing the main leads and the Futurekind. Good luck, they've still not been fed!

The TARDIS interior almost echoes with silence after all that. Derek Jacobi goes through his final moments on screen, gripping onto the console as his life ebbs away. Without realising it, there's something almost Biblical about the framing as he stands in front of the time rotor, throws his arms open and his head back.

"The Master! Reborn!"

He roars out the words. Someone says it's like 'Shakespearean thunder'. You can see the veins on his temples, the blood pulsing round his face as he puts almighty force into projecting the words with utter triumph. Close-up on Derek's face, his eyes glinting. For safety, I also ask for a sinister, nearly whispered version of the moment as he almost looks directly into camera, spitting out the words.

The Mill will graft on the CGI effect for the regeneration, but the movement and look will practically follow the template established for *The Parting of the Ways*, when the ninth Doctor bowed out with explosions of light from his collar and jacket sleeves. The only major difference being that I've added an overhead shot as Derek throws his head back and looks up.

This is Derek's last day, and it's been incredible. What a consummate professional, and what a brilliant performance he's given. The last hour working with him on the TARDIS set, I don't think I was the only one who didn't want it to end. Time to say goodbye to a fabulous ally.

Everything felt right with casting him, everything fell into place and I couldn't have asked for anyone better. Someone said watching him by the console was like watching 'the lost Doctor Who'. How good would that have been?

12TH FEBRUARY 2007

Episode 11 – *Surface scenes on the planet Malcazero involving the 'Human Hunt' are shot at Argoed Quarry, Llansanor, near Llanharry.*

This is strange.

No matter how often you do a night shoot, there's always the same feeling that hits you for the first day. Your body-clock screams out that you shouldn't be working all night, even though we've had a couple of days to try and get in sync with the work schedule we're facing. No matter how you look at it, it's still a full working day. The sun's due to set just after 5.20 pm, and the film unit's call is ten minutes after that. By that point, the lights are starting to go up for the first scene, and about half an hour later the main cast will start to arrive back on set. There's been some rehearsal earlier, now they're in costume and ready to shoot. Breakfast's already on the go, even though it's later afternoon, and I bet you anything you like that coffee's the favoured option on the menu.

Argoed's a disused quarry. I've got no idea how long it's been like this, but there's plenty of dead, brittle vegetation and gorse bushes around that makes it look like it's been a good few years. The site's staggered in three tiers, radiating up and out from its centre, and the warning's gone out that the only real hazard is some loose rocks on the very top level. No reason for anyone to go up there, so hopefully it won't be a problem.

There's nothing but hard hats, yellow jackets and mud-caked Wellingtons moving around. You can see a continual sheet of drizzle drifting down in front of the beams from the huge hushtower lights. They're stretching right up for about eight, maybe nine metres and flood the filming area with pools of work light.

David, John and Freema are in position. They've got to charge down a steep slope and race past the camera. Abi Collins, our stunt co-ordinator, is here and busy watching everything like a hawk. She carefully walked all three of them down the route they've got to follow, showing them precisely where they can run, while it was still daylight.

I know, I know, it's not a stunt as such, but the terrain's rough and it's her responsibility to make sure that the actors are safe, wearing the right kind of footwear for what we're doing, and know exactly how to pace themselves.

Take One. They're off. David's first past the lens, face all grim determination and teeth gritted, but Captain Jack's clearly having the time of his life.

"Oh, I've missed this."

I've got a feeling that applies to both the Captain and John Barrowman.

"Further back! Get them further back! We can still see the flambards!"

Gareth's shouting at the top of his voice. Spots of flame are clearly moving around at the summit of the slope. The Futurekind are about to descend.

The shot's clear.

"That's good there! Good there! And action!"

This is framed so the Doctor grinds to a halt in the foreground as Jack catches Padra, who's the target of the 'hunt'. John's not got an armed gun as he's out of shot, so he shouts out as he fires into the air to try and intimidate the fast-approaching cannibals.

"Bang! Bang! Bang!"

As one, 15 Futurekind barrel into view in complete silence. Nobody's actually told them to scream and roar with bloodlust. Cut and reset.

Roger Pearce isn't happy.

"Gareth, there's somebody standing right in the line of our shot!"

"They're still setting up, mate."

"Ooops, sorry…"

John's mercilessly teasing David about the way he skidded to a halt in front of the camera.

"You are so going to fall over, I know it. You're just so going to fall!"

"I'm a Time Lord, past master at this kind of stuff."

Moving on to a wide shot favouring the Doctor, Martha, Jack and Padra with branches of gorse in the foreground, as John points his gun over his head again and fires. Takes One and Two, the scrub's moving. Maybe not such a good idea.

"Stop! Stop, stop, stop, stop!"

Take Four crashes as John's gun holster comes flying off, but Take Five seems to work fine.

How do you direct a cannibal? One to one with a Futurekind, all frizzy hair, teeth, scars and eye-patch… Sticks with a cow's skull mounted on top frame the background, and I just want him to rise up, sensing his prey are near.

"Remember, really evil… Terrorise everybody…"

"Grrrrrrrrrrrrrrrrr!"

"Can I have another one?"

"Yeah, sure."

"This is gonna be good. Now, do a lower growl…"

"GRRRRRRRRRRRRRRRRRRRRR!"

"Can I do that again? That's exactly what I want. I'd just take a few seconds looking round before you go for it…"

Pause. Sniff, sniff.

"Grrrrrrrr!"

"Great, keep the sniffing… Remember you can almost taste the humans… Then a deep guttural growl… Really low, really vicious…"

Pause. Sniff, sniff.

"GRRRRRRRRRRRRRRRRRRRRRRRRRRRRR!!!!!"

He's got it! On we go.

We've got to create a sense of energy and fear. The Doctor and Jack running for their lives, and we're there with them, moving right alongside them as they sprint. But how? Ideally, you need the camera mounted on a quad bike – and that's exactly what we've got. Effectively, it's a motorised dolly, with camera fixings so Roger can work from either the front or rear of the vehicle. There's a kind of basic scaffolding cage built around it, so if anything goes wrong they act as roll bars, otherwise they're brilliant for rigging equipment on.

"Action!"

David and John take off as fast as they can. Instantly, there's a problem. We're too far back and framing this too wide. Thanks to the tower lights, you can clearly see the silhouette of the buggy a few feet in front of them. We go in tighter, they're practically running alongside us, but it creates a sense of urgency. Now you're right in there with them.

There are cracks of light on the horizon. Sunrise is in half an hour. Time to sleep while everyone else gets up, then crash out as they're hitting the sack. And while they're doing that, we'll be back here making the TARDIS land.

13TH FEBRUARY 2007

Episode 11 – *More surface scenes on the planet Malcazero are completed, with the TARDIS arriving, the Doctor being reunited with Captain Jack and* *additional shots for the 'human hunt' at Argoed Quarry, Llansanor, near Llanharry.*

"Gareth?" Freema's coming out of the TARDIS. Its windows are glowing with light and it looks so out of place next to the quarry wall. "When I first go over to him and say I can't get a pulse, would you check the neck or the wrist?"

Non steps in, both as the unit's script supervisor and fount of medical knowledge. It's the neck.

"And when I come back, it says in the script I've got a stethoscope. Is there a stethoscope?"

"I don't know."

Gareth dives into the TARDIS to look, while Freema fires off another question. "And can I use it over clothes?"

Yes, there's one hanging just inside the door tucked into a medical kit holster. His voice crackles over his walkie-talkie.

"Graeme, what move has Freema got to make?"

"Put the stethoscope under his coat, Guv."

"But on top of his shirt?" She's looking over to where I'm sitting by the monitor screens.

"Yep."

If there's a word to describe yesterday, well, it's definitely wet. Today's the sequel. Wetter...

John Barrowman's lying on the ground, already lined up for where Captain Jack's crashed down, after being thrown from the hull of the TARDIS when it landed. He's currently being shielded from the rain by several umbrellas.

"Are we ready?"

Sound, camera, lighting... Everything's set. David's arm suddenly appears round the TARDIS door, smacks the phone compartment shut as it drifts open, then promptly vanishes again.

"And action!"

The Doctor and Martha stride out into the night, and she's by Jack's side as soon as she spots him. Index and middle finger press against his neck, just as Non explained. She goes to get the medical kit, while the Doctor plays it all cool and aloof.

This has got to be a gradual, difficult reunion. I've said to David and John, play it with an awkward layer of frost between you, slightly detached, slightly cautious. There's history that's got to be addressed, issues to be resolved, but not right now. Russell's structured the script so it all carefully unfurls and the tension melts bit by bit. These guys are inherently still friends, they've just got to clarify for both themselves and the audience exactly how much they're willing to show of what that means. One of the links that still holds as a bond is their mutual love for Rose, and as soon as her fate's revealed to Jack, I tell them to drop the first layer of ice. The Doctor's face lights up, Jack hugs him.

"And cut!"

"Now let's kiss!" John lunges to peck him on the cheek, causing David to laugh out loud.

As soon as each take ends, wardrobe assistants move in from the shadows and quickly wrap the actors in full-length body warmers, shield them against the rain with a sea of ever-vigilant umbrellas. Progress is slow; we've got to get close-ups favouring the Doctor, Jack, Martha… All building up emotional detail for cutting the scene together. In between takes, John's lying on the ground holding his crash position between set-ups, and belting out *Singin' in the Rain* as the puddles form around him. He's never short of a show tune and always keeps the atmosphere buzzing.

We've got to lens up high and wide right on the opposite side of the quarry. The TARDIS is on the first tier, and we play the whole reunion scene shooting it from that distance. It's ominous, dark, and gives a real sense of scale to where we've landed. I'll only use it for a few seconds, but it adds texture, always building up visual information for the viewer to take in.

"Action!"

There's a slightly abbreviated version rattled off, lots of "blah, blah, blah" from David as he cuts dialogue so we can clearly pick out the key visual moves; Martha running to Jack, the face-off with the Doctor and the eventual hug.

"And cut! Moving on…"

Major exposition time as Jack lays out his back-story, all bullet points key to revealing the wheres, whys and hows of what's happened to him. David and John have still got to play this with a prickly edge, slightly unpredictable, so we've blocked it out with a deliberate distance between the Doctor and Jack, which Martha breaks as she walks in between them.

"Nice and careful round the edge please, guys."

We're focused high and wide looking down on the Doctor, Martha and Jack as they reach the edge of a canyon and look out at the decaying remains of an enormous hive-like city, woven into the cliffs. This has got to be framed so there's enough clear space above the actors for The Mill to create a plate-shot later on.

It's risky. They're standing on the first tier, right next to a sheer drop down to the floor of the quarry, but two takes are all we need. The camera position's held and realigned so we lens up towards the ground level. We've got to be quick, you can clearly hear birds waking up in the distance and sunrise is only ten, maybe 15 minutes away. Ideally this has got to be one take, fast-paced, loads of energy and right on the mark. Rene has to hurtle through the scrub as Padra's pursued by the Futurekind. Framing is key on this, just like the last shot – there's got to be plenty of room for a plate-shot of the city in the background.

Come on, guys. Ten minutes max before the sun dilutes the darkness. Only a handful of shots and we're there.

Orange gels, low lights pointing up at the Doctor, kind of a residual glow from the city as he stares down, almost lamenting what's happened. Take One grinds to a halt as a lorry arrives nearby. I thought the quarry was out of action?

Close on the Doctor, a sense of wonder from Martha, slight unease from Jack. It's beginning to sound like an aviary with the dawn chorus!

"And cut!"

That's a wrap. We really had to chase the night before the day shift took over! Only one more day, and we're done.

14TH FEBRUARY 2007

Episode 11 – *Scenes set around the perimeter fence and gates leading into Silo #16 are shot at Wenvoe Quarry (Cemex UK Ltd), Wenvoe.*

Different quarry tonight, quite a bit closer to base, which is just as well. There's been a major build to make a practical, functioning set, and it's just for one night of filming.

Wenvoe Quarry was used last year when James Strong shot *The Satan Pit*'s underground sequences here, but we're just using the site's main entrance, which is actually a tunnel that's been bored through the rock face. Arwel Wynn Jones, who supervises the construction of set designs, has mocked it up as a passageway that theoretically leads down into Silo 16, and built a security compound around it. The perimeter has thick corrugated iron walls, broken up by a large mesh gateway, illuminated by spotlights on an adjacent watchtower. In the rain and darkness, it wouldn't look entirely out of place as part of the Iron Curtain's security surrounding the Berlin Wall.

Actually, Arwel's one of the first people I see every morning on set. He quickly checks that I'm happy with the way it's been rigged and prepared for the day's scenes, that the props are right and dressed so they're spot on, that sort of thing. When he goes, he's undoubtedly overseeing set construction and decoration for the following day, always working one step ahead of the game. The stand-by art director runs the floor from a design point of view while he's gone, but he's always available to troubleshoot if there's a problem.

Think of it like this: if Ed's the Design Colonel, then Arwel's his Sergeant Major. Everything radiates out from the head of department's power base but everyone functions as a team. It's the same with Ernie Vincze. As the director of photography, he's ultimately in charge of the canvas. As camera operator, Roger Pearce has got the paintbrushes, and Mark Hutchings, the gaffer, makes sure the paints are being dished out in the right colours via the lights. It's an intricate process and the cogs are so well oiled that it runs as smoothly as you could wish. *Doctor Who* has drawn together people from all areas of the industry and created a working system that seems to make anything possible.

"Here we go, folks. Nice and quiet please. And, action!"

Gareth's voice echoes slightly, but the cue's heard. David, John, Freema and Rene hurtle into view, charging down the dirt track leading to the gates. The camera's positioned to swing in a wide arc and hold on them, taking in the whole hoarding of the compound. We've got four guards there armed with machine-guns, and the first thing they want to do is check their teeth.

The Futurekind have all gradually filed their teeth into razor-sharp fangs. All very tribal, definitely very cannibal and user-friendly for chewing on 'h-u-u-u-mans'. The thing is, we've had to be very sparing over which ones get the dental plates to create the effect. For one convincing set, you're looking at something like £900 to £1000. Once you've taken the Chieftan into account, and the Wiry Woman who infiltrates the Silo compound, well, the budget's stretched to cover just four more of the 15-strong feral pack we'll be seeing on screen.

They've been divided up between two of the men and two of the women, and I've tried to use all of them for tight close-ups, always shooting a fraction lower than normal so when they snarl into the lens, the angle can heighten the effect slightly. If you emphasise physical and visual detail like that, it always creates an impact, just like the prosthetics for the Chieftain's facial scars. The idea there is to suggest the vestiges of a savage initiation ritual. The markings have been stylised to look like the pattern of a tyre track, hinting that he's literally had a motorbike run over his face at some point. Survive that, and you've earned the tribe's respect.

We hold the shot wide. The TARDIS crew and Padra's dentistry pass muster, they're let in and the Futurekind pace angrily around the shuttered mouth of the gate, like caged-in wolves.

Abi Collins has gone through rehearsing very specific marks the cannibals have to hit. Charges have been planted in the ground just ahead of them, so when we're lensed up and rolling they ignite on cue, and we get a strafing machine-gun effect as the guards fire a warning volley. Even minute detonators like that can hurt if you're too close.

Got to build up the energy and drive with this. Lots of short, sharp shots that can be cut together with real pace. Action sequences are always driven by speed and not words. Angles from behind the gate, further back and wide on the guards as the Futurekind close in, tight on David, Freema and John with wire mesh in the foreground. Tons of fear, pushing the adrenaline fast and hard.

Time is running out already, there's about an hour till dawn. Roger's got the next shot ready. We've hired an old French army lorry, grimy and sort of sandy-coloured, very *Wages of Fear*. Story-wise, it's been out collecting water rations. On screen, it creates a great sense of scale for the moment when we see it arrive back at base. Thankfully, there's no sweaty gelignite in the back of this one!

The dawn chorus has caught up with us. One last set-up; the Futurekind are watching from the slopes of the quarry's rock-face while the rocket takes off across the horizon. The Chieftain is tight in the foreground, with his pack flanking either side of him, gradually branching upwards on the inclines they're standing on.

"Rory, can you hold the torch down a bit?"

The bald cannibal to the far right looks up.

"That's what I'm trying to do, but I'm trying to avoid Natalie's hair."

She's right by his side, all teeth and angry bouffant frizz. Gareth's in the thick of it and tries to offer a solution.

"Put it in the other hand, boss."

That's not so good visually, so I step in.

"No, no. Hold it behind you. Up a bit and behind you."

Roger gets instructions relayed to him from the DOP, who's scrutinising what's being relayed on a monitor a short distance away.

"Ernie's asking for it to go low, so it up-lights their faces."

"Okay, down you go. Now, I want everyone to look up. Tilt your heads slightly. Lots of anger and energy..."

A voice mutters from the tribe with a heavy Welsh accent.

"Yeah, dinner's just escaped in a rocket!"

There's just time for a couple of shots silhouetting one or two of the Futurekind, baying for blood and standing on pinnacles of rock, swinging flambards down as they scream.

It's now 4.30 am. David, Freema, John... They're all long gone. Is that really it? We've cut a day off the schedule and finished the main shoot in 24 days. Just one more to go. Bit of a mix this time; part location, part studio. Colin Teague will be busy directing the final recording block for the season, and we're sliding in discreetly to pick up brief scenes for both *42* and *Utopia* in the middle of his schedule.

And somebody very different is about to step into Derek Jacobi's shoes.

20TH FEBRUARY 2007

Episodes Seven and 11 – *All TARDIS scenes with the freshly regenerated Master are shot at Unit 1, Trefforest Industrial Estate, Trefforest as the last scenes for* Utopia. *Then Francine Jones' house interior scenes are completed at 7 Cwrt-y-Vil Road, (Lower) Penart, Cardiff for the final moments of* 42.

1ST MARCH 2007

Episode 11 – *Captain Jack's frantic dash towards the TARDIS is recorded on Mermaid Quay, Cardiff.*

One last shot, and we've got John Barrowman for a couple of hours to record it in. The opening scene has been rewritten, as there's just been no time to get David and Freema to Mermaid Quay to shoot their opening dialogue. That's been restaged around the TARDIS set, but we still need footage of Captain Jack racing towards it.

We can lens up wide and have him running towards camera, but when it comes to the leap I want for Jack, as he just reaches the TARDIS and clings onto it in time. Well, John is insisting he does the stunt himself. A small trampoline has been positioned by the camera, with crash-mats on the other side, and sure enough, he does it. We get to see Jack in mid-air, and without a stunt double in sight!

AFTER THE WRAP

Everything's done and dusted, you've 'lopped off' the shoot and if you're lucky, your editor's got all the footage you need safely digitised and has already started putting scenes together. Maybe there's a cut of the episode already in place? If not, there'll certainly be major sections that have been assembled, working from your camera script and shots list to find the route of what you've visually planned, so now they're ready to start being refined. This process is the 'fine cut'.

I'll start to view all the scenes and re-cut them if necessary to get them just as I want, or maybe I'll love the way he's taken on board the vision I had for the story, seeing a way to play it slightly differently and creating something that blows me away.

Now, some editors have a routine where they'll put in every shot you completed, trying to wedge them in somewhere, so you at least see what's available and what's on offer to you. The editors I've worked with recently have a different approach, and it's a way I really like, which is as I've described... Putting in what they like and what they think works to tell the story. Now, if you remember your material, you'll spot when they've missed a shot that you thought was brilliant for a key moment, and you can swap it round. But it does offer you an alternative. You don't have to accept it, but it is a choice.

Again, it's a process of negotiation. It's ultimately my choice what's used, but the editor strongly advises against your ideas if he thinks you're going seriously wrong. You go through every scene like that, pulling it all together until the story's there and ready to watch, but chances are you'll end up with an overall running time that's too long.

If we're really lucky, there'll be maybe three to four minutes maximum to cut out, so the episode's standing at around 48 minutes. We then re-cut it closer to the time it needs to be, say about 46 minutes 30 seconds in its entirety, from the opening credits to last frame. This is when Russell, Julie and Phil will come and see it. They'll give me an overall impression of what they feel about it, alongside notes of things they think might need to be altered or improved in certain ways, and within two days we'll have re-edited it, trying to incorporate all the things they asked for.

Time for more notes. This isn't working, that scene needs to have more of this and a little less of that. The edits continue, and eventually Phil will come in, and we spend a morning just trying all the options. When that's done, we all agree to have one more viewing. If we're happy, then that's a locked picture and you move on to completing the CGI, the sound design and incidental music, plus all the colour grading and filmising to make the episode complete.

Sometimes the post-production period will be incredibly tight for time, but you also might have the luxury, specifically with a show like *Doctor Who*, when your episodes could be finished and ready for transmission about four months ahead of the game.

But this is the final stage.

Your job's done, it's finished and the DVD release is already scheduled. It's in the viewers' hands now, for 45 brief minutes after months and months of work. All that shooting, all those days, takes and close-ups, all crammed into so short a space of time. And it's theirs now. I can't do any more, my job's done.

And I've loved every single minute of it.

EPISODE FIVE: NEXT TIME...

FRIDAY 7TH AUGUST 2007

I've come full circle. Almost two years have passed since I started working with Susie Liggat as my first assistant director, and now she's the producer for the first recording block of Season Four. Agatha Christie and the Ood... One story a real mystery, the other non-stop action.

Day one, and we were off. The TARDIS arrives, there's David Tennant and Catherine Tate, and a couple of days later it was all over the press.

Now, after four weeks filming, the last shot is approaching fast and we're working until the early hours of the morning. But that's not the end of it – there are three more episodes to do for this season, and I'm thrilled. I still can't believe that, after all this time, I've got such a brilliant directing gig.

Right at the beginning of the book I wrote about *The Seeds of Doom* and working with Douglas Camfield. After I finished work on Utopia I was given two episodes of *The Sarah Jane Adventures* to direct, reuniting me with Elisabeth Sladen, the co-star of *The Seeds of Doom*. She was just the same as I remembered her, and a real joy to work with. Can it really have been 30 years?

Will I be asked back beyond all of this? I don't know, but I'll always keep climbing, trying to reach for the top and do the best I can. Hopefully there's a few mountains left in me yet!

APPENDIX

BROADCAST DETAILS

SEASON TWO

Rise of the Cybermen
Broadcast: 13th May 2006 at 1920hrs-2005hrs
Running time: 46'03"
Ratings in millions: 9.221
Audience appreciation: 86%

The Age of Steel
Broadcast: 20th May 2006 at 1900hrs-1945hrs
Running time: 45'52"
Ratings in millions: 7.635
Audience appreciation: 86%

Army of Ghosts
Broadcast: 1st July 2006 at 1900hrs-1945hrs
Running tme: 43'18"
Ratings in millions: 8.19
Audience appreciation: 85%

Doomsday
Broadcast: 8th July 2006 at 1900hrs-1945hrs
Running time: 46'23"
Ratings in millions: 8.22
Audience appreciation: 89%

SEASON THREE

42

Broadcast: 19th May 2007 at 1900hrs-1945hrs

Running Time: 45'24"

Ratings in Millions: 7.41

Audience Appreciation: 85%

Utopia

Broadcast: 16th June at 1915hrs-2000hrs

Running Time: 45'49"

Ratings in Millions: 7.84

Audience Appreciation: 87%

CAST AND CREW

2005/6 RECORDING BLOCK

Episode 5 (*Rise of the Cybermen*)

Episode 6 (*The Age of Steel*)

Episode 12 (*Army of Ghosts*)

Episode 13 (*Doomsday*)

CAST IN ORDER OF APPEARANCE AND EPISODES

The Doctor	(David Tennant) (all episodes)
Rose Tyler	(Billie Piper) (all episodes)
Jackie Tyler	(Camille Coduri) (all episodes)
Mickey Smith	(Noel Clarke) (all episodes)
Pete Tyler	(Shaun Dingwall) (5, 6 and 13)
John Lumic	(Roger Lloyd Pack) (5 and 6)
Jake Simmonds	(Andrew Hayden-Smith) (5, 6 and 13)
The President	(Don Warrington) (5)
Rita-Anne	(Mona Hammond) (5)

Mrs Moore	(Helen Griffin) (5 and 6)
Mr Crane	(Colin Spaull) (5 and 6)
Dr Kendrick	(Paul Antony-Barber) (5)
Morris	(Adam Shaw) (5)
Soldier	(Andrew Ufondo) (5)
Newsreader	(Duncan Duff) (5)
Cyber-Leader	(Paul Kasey) (All Episodes)
Cyber-Voice	(Nicholas Briggs) (All Episodes)
Dalek Voices	(Nicholas Briggs) (12 and 13)
Yvonne Hartman	(Tracy-Ann Oberman) (12 and 13)
Dr Rajesh Singh	(Raji James) (12 and 13)
Adeola	(Freema Ageyman) (12)
Gareth	(Hadley Fraser) (12)
Matt	(Oliver Mellor) (12)
Peggy Mitchell	(Barbara Windsor) (12)
Indian Newsreader	(Hajaz Akram) (12)
French Newsreader	(Anthony Debaeck) (12)
Japanese Newsreader	(Takako Akashi) (12)
Weatherman	(Paul Fields) (12)
Police Commissioner	(David Warwick) (12)
Eileen	(Rachel Webster) (12)
Japanese Girl	(Kyoko Morita) (12)
Housewife	(Maddi Cryer) (12)
Himself	(Derek Acorah) (12)
Himself	(Alistair Appleton) (12)
Herself	(Trisha Goddard) (12)
Dalek Operators	(Barnaby Edwards, Nicholas Pegg, Stuart Crossman, Anthony Spargo, Dan Barratt and David Hankinson) (12 and 13)
The Bride	(Catherine Tate) (13)

With thanks to Marc Platt

Daleks originally created by Terry Nation

Cybermen originally created by Gerry Davis and Kit Pedler

CREW (ALL EPISODES UNLESS STATED)

1st Assistant Director	Clare Nicholson (5 and 6)
	Susie Liggat (12 and 13)
2nd Assistant Director	Steffan Morris
3rd Assistant Director	Lynsey Muir
Location Managers	Lowri Thomas
	Gareth Skelding
Unit Manager	Rhys Griffiths
Prod Co-ordinator	Jess van Niekerk
Prod/Script Secretary	Claire Roberts
Production Runner	Victoria Wheel (5 and 6)
	Tim Hodges (12)
	Sarah Davies (13)
A/Prod Accountants	Debi Griffiths
	Kath Blackman
	Bonnie Clissold (5, 6 and 13)
Continuity	Non Eleri Hughes
Script Editor	Helen Raynor
Camera Operator	Roger Pearce
Focus Puller	Terry Bartlett
Grip	John Robinson
Boom Operators	Jeff Welch
	Bryn Thomas (5 and 6)
Gaffer	Mark Hutchings
Best Boy	Peter Chester
Electricians	Chris Davies
	Clive Johnson
	Stephen Slocombe (12 and 13)
Choreographer	Ailsa Berk
Stunt Co-Ordinator	Abbi Collins
Stunt Performers	James O'Dee (all)
	Derek Lea (6)
	Shelly Benison (6)
	Paul Kennington (12 and 13)

Supervising Art Director	Stephen Nicholas
Art Dept Prod Manager	Jonathan Marquand Allison
Stanbye Art Director	Nick Burnell (5 and 6)
	Arwyl Wynn Jones (12 and 13)
A/Sup Art Director	James North
Design Assistants	Matthew Savage (5, 6 and 13)
	Rob Dicks (5 and 6)
	Peter McKinstry
	Al Roberts
Standby Props	Phil Shellard
	Trystan Howell
Standby Carpenter	Silas Williams (6)
Standby Scenic Artist	Louise Bohling
Set Decorator	Julian Luxton
Property Master	Adrian Anscombe
Production Buyer	Catherine Samuel
Props Chargehand	Paul Aitken (5and6)
	Phil Lyons (12 and 13)
Assistant Prop Master	Paul Aitken (12 and 13)
Props Storeman	Stuart Wooddisse
Forward Dresser	Matthew North
Storyboard Artist	Shaun Williams
Practical Electrician	Albert James
Art Department Driver	Patrick Deacy
Specialist Prop Maker	Mark Cordory
Prop Maker	Penny Howarth
Construction manager	Matthew Hywel-Davies
Construction Chargehand	Allen Jones
Graphics	BBC Wales Graphics
Costume Supervisor	Marnie Ormiston
Costume Assistants	Lyndsey Bonnaccorsi
	Barbara Harrington
Make-Up Artists	Anwen Davies
	Steve Smith

	Moira Thomson
Prosthetics Supervisor	Rob Mayor
Prosthetic Technicians	Martin Rezard
	Jo Glover
Special Effects Co-Ordinator	Ben Ashmore
Special Effects Supervisors	Mike Crowley
	Paul Kelly
Special Effects Technicians	Danny Hargreaves
	Richard Magrin
On-Line Editor	Matthew Clarke
Colourist	Mick Vincent
Visual Effects Co-Ordinator	Kim Phelan
Casting Associate	Andy Brierly
Assistant Editor	Ceres Doyle
Post Production Supervisors	Chris Blatchford
	Samantha Hall
Post-Production Co-ordinator	Marie Brown
Dubbing Mixer	Tim Ricketts
Sound Editors	Paul McFadden
	Doug Sinclair
Sound FX Editor	Paul Jeffries
Finance Manager	Richard Pugsley
Original Theme Music	Ron Grainer
Casting Director	Andy Pryor CDG
Production Accountant	Endaf Emyr Williams
Sound Recordist	Simon Fraser
Costume Designer	Louise Page
Make-Up Designer	Sheelagh Wells
Music	Murray Gold
Visual Effects	The Mill
Visual Effects Producer	Will Cohen
Visual Effects Supervisor	Dave Houghton
Special Effects	Any Effects

Prosthetics	Neill Gorton and Millennium Effects
Editor	Dave Cresswell
Production Designer	Ed Thomas
Director of Photography	Ernie Vincze BSC
Production Manager	Tracie Simpson
Producer	Phil Collinson
Executive Producers	Russell T Davies and Julie Gardner

2006/2007 RECORDING BLOCK

Episode Seven (*42*)
Episode Eleven (*Utopia*)

CAST IN ORDER OF APPEARANCE AND EPISODES

The Doctor	(David Tennant) (both episodes)
Martha Jones	(Freema Ageyman) (both episodes)
Francine Jones	(Adjoa Andoh) (7)
Kath McDonnell	(Michelle Collins) (7)
Riley Vashtee	(William Ash) (7)
Orin Scannell	(Anthony Flanagan) (7)
Hal Korwin	(Matthew Chambers) (7)
Dev Ashton	(Gary Powell) (7)
Abi Lerner	(Vinette Robinson) (7)
Erina Lessak	(Rebecca Oldfield) (7)
Sinister Woman	(Elize Du Toit) (7)
Captain Jack Harkness	(John Barrowman) (11)
Professor Yana/The Master	(Derek Jacobi) (11)
Padra	(Rene Zagger) (11)
Chantho	(Chipo Chung) (11)
Lt Atillo	(Neil Reidman) (11)
Kistane	(Deborah McClaren) (11)
Creet	(John Bell) (11)

Futurekind Chieftan   (Paul Marc Davies) (11)

Wiry Woman   (Abigail Canton) (11)

The Master   (John Simm) (11)

CREW (BOTH EPISODES)

1st Assistant Director	Gareth Williams
2nd Assistant Director	Steffan Morris
3rd Assistant Director	Sarah Davies
Location Manager	Gareth Skelding
Unit Manager	Rhys Griffiths
Prod Co-Ordinator	Jess van Niekerk
Prod/Script Secretary	Kevin Myers
Production Assistant	Debi Griffiths
Floor Runners	Lowri Denman
	Heddi Jay Taylor
Contracts Assistant	Bethan Britton
Continuity	Non Eleri Hughes
Script Editor	Simon Winstone
Camera Operator	Roger Pearce
Focus Puller	Steve Rees
Grip	Jeff Welch
Gaffer	Mark Hutchings
Best Boy	Peter Chester
Stunt Co-Ordinator	Abbi Collins
Wires	Kevin Welch
Chief Supervising Art Director	Stephen Nicholas
Art Department Production Manager	Jonathan Marquand Allison
Art Department Co-Ordinator	Matthew North
Chief Props Master	Adrian Anscombe
Supervising Art Director	Arwel Wyn Jones
Associate Designer	James North
Set Decorator	Julian Luxton
Standby Art Director	Lee Gammon

Design Assistants	Ian Bunting
	Al Roberts
	Peter McKinstry
Storyboard Artist	Shaun Williams
Standby Props	Phil Shellard
	Nick Murray
Standby Carpenter	Paul Jones
Standby Painter	Ellen Woods
Standby Rigger	Phil Lyons
Props Buyer	Ben Morris
Props Chargehand	Gareth Jeanne
Practical Electrician	Albert James
Construction Manager	Matthew Hywel-Davies
Graphics	BBC Wales Graphics
Assistant Costume Designer	Marnie Ormiston
Costume Supervisor	Lyndsey Bonnaccorsi
Make-Up Artists	Pam Mullins
	John Munro
	Steve Smith
Casting Associates	Andy Brierley
	Kirsty Robertson
VFX Editor	Ceres Doyle
Assistant Editor	Tim Hodges
Post-Production Supervisors	Samantha Hall
	Chris Blatchford
Post-Production Co-ordinator	Marie Brown
On-Line Editor	Matthew Clarke
Colourist	Mick Vincent
3D Artists	Nicolas Hernandez
	Jean-Claude Degaura
	Nick Webber
	Andy Guest
	Serena Cacciato
	Will Pryor

2D Artists	Bruce Magroune
	Sara Bennett
	Russell Horth
	Bryan Bartlett
	Joseph Courtis
	Tim Barter
	Adam Rowland
Visual FX Co-Ordinators	Rebecca Johnson
	Jenna Powell
On-Set VFX Co-ordinator	Barney Curnow
Dubbing Mixer	Tim Ricketts
Sound Editor	Doug Sinclair
Sound FX Editor	Paul Jeffries
Finance Manager	Chris Rogers
Original Theme Music	Ron Grainer
Casting Director	Andy Pryor CDG
Production Executive	Julie Scott
Production Accountant	Endaf Emyr Williams
Sound Recordist	Ron Bailey
Costume Designer	Louise Page
Make-Up Designer	Barbara Southcott
Music	Murray Gold
Visual Effects	The Mill
Visual Effects Producer	Will Cohen and Marie Jones
Visual Effects Supervisor	Dave Houghton
Special Effects	Any Effects
Editor	Will Oswald
Production Designer	Ed Thomas
Director of Photography	Ernie Vincze BSC
Production Manager	Patrick Schweitzer
Producer	Phil Collinson
Executive Producers	Russell T Davies and Julie Gardner

INDEX

PICTURE CREDITS